Praise for *The Conscience Code*

"Every organization talks about values. But how can we uphold those values when bosses and peers are behaving badly? *The Conscience Code* delivers the answer. This powerful and practical book brings the science of persuasion to the problem of doing the right thing—showing leaders at every level how to stand up for their deepest beliefs."

—Daniel H. Pink, Author of *WHEN*, *DRIVE*, and *TO SELL IS HUMAN*

"Leading in the twenty-first century without a conscience is like trying to fly a plane without wings. *The Conscience Code* shows you how to turn your beliefs into action and take flight."

—Yancey Strickler, Cofounder and Former CEO of Kickstarter, Founder of the Bento Society, and Author of *This Could Be Our Future*

"A must-read in today's turbulent times. Indeed, the high road is the only road. Richard Shell will help you get there and stay there."

—Douglas R. Conant, Founder of ConantLeadership, *New York Times* and *Wall Street Journal* Bestselling Author, Former Chairman of Avon Products, and Former President and CEO of Campbell Soup Company

"Shell demonstrates that good ethics is not only good business but is also the foundation for personal and professional success. His real-world examples and research-based observations make this book a keeper for every leader."

—F. William McNabb, Former Chairman and CEO of Vanguard

"Engaging, clear, and practical—*The Conscience Code* is an outstanding guide to leading and living responsibly."

—Joseph L. Badaracco, John Shad Professor of Business Ethics at Harvard Business School

"Jam-packed with real-world examples of values conflicts at work, Richard Shell's book offers practical career guidance for every 'person of conscience' who wants to take action—effectively—on their values. This book is an inspirational, pragmatic handbook for living a fulfilled, values-driven life."

—Mary C. Gentile, PhD, Author of *Giving Voice To Values: How To Speak Your Mind When You Know What's Right*, University of Virginia Darden School of Business

"Ethisphere's research has shown that a value-based approach to business significantly outperforms the competition. Richard Shell's *The Conscience Code* provides the roadmap every employee can follow to become a committed champion for that all-important mission. It should be required reading for every global firm seeking to empower its workforce to be a force for good."

—Tim Erblich, CEO of Ethisphere Institute and Former President of NYSE Governance Services

"*The Conscience Code* offers important advice to leaders facing decisions that challenge their core beliefs. Doing the right thing isn't always easy. Richard Shell's examples show us that staying true to one's values leads to genuine, long-term success."

—Adam H. Schechter, Chairman and CEO of LabCorp

"Think business ethics are purely academic? Richard Shell's new book *The Conscience Code* puts this longstanding myth to rest! Reflecting on decades of teaching and consulting, Shell details just how critical moral issues are to successful corporate leadership, organizational culture, business strategy, and negotiation. *The Conscience Code* is a must-read for all those committed to aligning business with integrity, responsibility, and accountability."

—Larry Zicklin, Former Managing Partner and Chairman of Neuberger Berman

THE CONSCIENCE
CODE

LEAD WITH YOUR VALUES
ADVANCE YOUR CAREER

G. RICHARD SHELL

HarperCollins
LEADERSHIP

AN IMPRINT OF HARPERCOLLINS

NEW YORK

For my late friend and mentor,

Dr. Simon Auster

Published by HarperCollins Leadership, an imprint of HarperCollins Focus LLC.

Any internet addresses, phone numbers, or company or product information printed in this book are offered as a resource and are not intended in any way to be or to imply an endorsement by HarperCollins Leadership, nor does HarperCollins Leadership vouch for the existence, content, or services of these sites, phone numbers, companies, or products beyond the life of this book.

ISBN 978-1-4002-2114-1 (eBook)
ISBN 978-1-4002-2113-4 (PBK)

Library of Congress Control Number: 2021934397

Printed in the United States of America
21 22 23 LSC 10 9 8 7 6 5 4 3 2 1

CONTENTS

INTRODUCTION
THE CONSCIENCE CODE

"Start where you are, use what you have, do what you can."
—Arthur Ashe, tennis champion and social justice activist

I wrote this book to help you deal more effectively with an increasingly urgent problem in professional life: standing up for core values such as honesty, personal dignity, fairness, and justice when the pressure is on to look the other way.

The consequences of getting these decisions wrong can be significant. When a boss or peer pushes you to engage in (or go along with) conduct you know to be unethical or illegal, a misstep can ruin your career—especially in a world where social media opens the doors into every office. And standing by while others engage in sexual harassment or office bullying empowers the wrong people to do the wrong thing, destroying morale and productivity. Finally, your day-to-day tolerance for those who cut ethical corners sets the standard for the "normal" way to get things done. Remaining silent while a boss lies to a client may be only a small step, but it's a step down the wrong road. You are letting yourself be led by your fears instead of choosing to lead with your conscience.

How did I come to be concerned enough about this problem to write this book? From a course I created at the Wharton School. As a senior member of the Wharton faculty and chair of its Legal Studies and Business Ethics Department, I led the most recent school-wide initiative to redesign our MBA program. Part of that effort involved combining two short courses, one on business law and the other on business ethics, into a single, longer, required course called "Responsibility in Business." Believing I had a duty to lead by example, I volunteered to teach this new MBA class the first time it was offered. Little did I know when I stepped into this classroom how much my students would end up teaching *me* about the day-to-day ethical challenges that ordinary employees face inside the pressure cooker we call "the modern workplace."

Here are just a few of the more alarming stories my students shared in this class:

- A young, gay **management consultant** was propositioned for sex by a client while working on a project in the Middle East. He politely declined, then reported the incident to his project leader (a partner at his firm) and asked for feedback about how he had handled it. His boss responded that he had made the wrong choice and requested that he go back and "make the client happy" to increase the chances for follow-up consulting business. The young consultant answered with an outraged "No"—and received a poor performance appraisal when the project was over.
- A sales employee at a **high-tech startup** was pressured to create a list of fake clients, complete with orders from these "customers," so the firm's ambitious founder could reference it in pitches for venture funding.
- A **private equity** analyst watched as her boss blatantly misrepresented the value of several companies in the firm's portfolio. The firm was raising a new round of investment capital, and the partner did not want to disclose the true state of these poor-performing assets to prospective investors. A week after the new funds were raised, the partner downgraded the value of these companies.
- A **bond trader** joined his peers in routinely lying to customers about the assets backing the debt he was selling. He thought his moral compass would always point him in the right direction, but he found it hard to follow his conscience "when everyone around you is breaking the rules." Several senior colleagues on his trading floor were eventually indicted for securities fraud.

Stories like these opened a world of dubious business practices I had only read about. During office hours, I found myself talking with students about the challenges they had faced and their desires to meet the next ones with more courage and confidence. These conversations inspired me to offer help and redoubled my commitment to teaching the "Responsibility" course. I came to realize I was getting a unique, highly informed window into the world of modern business life for today's employees. Because many of these students had no interest in returning to their former employers, they were more than willing to tell the unvarnished truth about what they had experienced.

I now understand that my students' stories are part of a much larger pattern. A recent report published in the *Harvard Business Review* revealed that roughly 25 percent of employees report pressure by bosses to behave unethically (or illegally). Based on what my students tell me year after year, I believe this number significantly underestimates the situation. For one thing, it does not include the pressures exerted by corrupt business cultures such as the one the bond trader described above. Many professionals in fast-paced tech and finance industries stop thinking of dubious practices as improper because "everybody does it."

Just as concerning, workers are fearful about reporting misconduct they observe in others. According to the Ethics Resource Center, over 40 percent of US workers witness unethical and/or illegal conduct on the job in a given year. Other studies have shown that most of this goes unreported and, even when flagged, ends up on the desk of a supervisor who lacks the backbone or motivation to do anything about it. Well-run corporate compliance programs and healthy corporate cultures can reduce this problem significantly, but these are hard to sustain across large enterprises over long periods of time. And too many companies give only lip service to both.

In short, my students are not outliers. They are telling it like it is. But that does not mean they are happy about the situation. They keenly feel the loss of self-respect that comes when they violate their own standards of conduct or stand by as others commit crimes. As their teacher, I try to reinforce how much more satisfied they will feel about themselves and their work if they commit to upholding a very short list of core values.

All my writing and teaching has emphasized in different ways what Adam Smith, the moral philosopher credited with being the founding father of competitive market capitalism, called the profound "tranquility" that comes from living an honest life. In this book, I advocate for Smith's point of view. Authentic, lasting success in any profession demands adherence to the highest standards of integrity. When you bring your sense of right and wrong to work, you can enjoy tranquility in that most private of all domains: your conscience.

And while this sounds easy to do when we discuss it in the classroom, I constantly remind my students how hard this can be when the heat is on to make deadlines, please bosses, and fulfill client demands. You must prepare now to meet the challenges to come. To echo the subtitle of this book, I want to help you "lead with your values"—a commitment that I think will also "advance your career."

I have dedicated this book to my friend and mentor, the late Dr. Simon Auster. He was a medical school professor who specialized in patient counseling and mental health. He was a man of impeccable integrity who took me in when I was the age that most of my MBA students are now. He helped me regain my self-confidence when I had very nearly given up on myself. Simon frequently said that, "Everyone does the best they can with what they've got." He had an enormous amount of wisdom, so his best was quite remarkable. In this book, I've tried to give you the best I've got by drawing on my students' reports as well as years of research on workplace misconduct, character, values, and whistleblowing.

My goal: to provide you with a "Conscience Code"—a set of ten rules to follow as you navigate toward true success in your career.

Full disclosure: without hearing my students' candid accounts of life on the front lines of business, I could never have understood the breadth of the ethical challenges ordinary professionals face in their day-to-day work. This book is infused with the detailed, moment-to-moment dramas they have shared and the insights these stories have inspired. But when it comes to recounting their stories in this book, I have thoroughly fictionalized their narratives and quotes to protect their privacy and the privacy of their employers. So consider my students' examples as "inspired by" what they have told me in confidence rather than as word-for-word accounts. The sole exceptions to this disclaimer are "Sarah's" story in the first chapter and "Benjamin's" story in the last one. Both of these accounts are factually accurate and presented with permission. But, at my students' request, they do not use real names.

A final point. Although I am chair of the Wharton School's department that teaches business ethics, I am an academic outsider to the ethics field. My professional training is in law. I have thus followed my legal training in providing extensive references at the end of the book if you wish to find the source for a point I make in the text. But I have left the details of philosophical and moral analysis to other, more qualified scholars. I thus offer you a practical, down-to-earth guide for confronting ethical challenges at work so you will look back on how you handled them with pride rather than regret.

The pages ahead are filled with moving, sometimes astonishing real-world stories of people facing both ordinary and extraordinary pressures to compromise their values. You will meet business executives, nonprofit leaders, nurses, police officers, soldiers, and lawyers. Some of the examples come from headline-grabbing corporate scandals and some from terrifying moments in history. Many others are everyday examples drawn from the personal and professional lives of my students. You'll learn about some who failed to stand up for their values and later regretted it, and others who successfully pushed back.

All of these examples—even the ones that Hollywood made into "whistleblower" movies—involve ordinary professionals trying to get on with the business of life. I have assembled them to help you better understand your own character, values, fears, and personal aspirations. If a given issue is not a problem for you, move on. When it comes to learning about the important things in life, one of my favorite mantras is also one of the simplest: "Take what works and leave the rest behind."

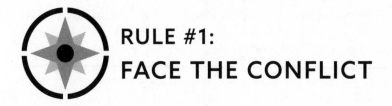

RULE #1:
FACE THE CONFLICT

"The world is a dangerous place. Not because of those who do evil but because of those who look on and do nothing."
—Albert Einstein

This book began with a story.

The students in my "Responsibility in Business" course at the Wharton School had an assignment: come prepared to share a value-based personal conflict they or someone close to them had faced at some point in their lives. As class got underway, a student named "Sarah" (not her real name) raised her hand.

Sarah was a lawyer prior to entering business school. She had been working in the general counsel's office of a small California company when she was offered a higher-paying associate position in a prestigious Los Angeles law firm. It was, she told the class, her dream job —exactly what she had hoped to achieve with her law degree.

A few weeks after starting, she was approached by a senior partner who asked her to do some research on the Foreign Corrupt Practices Act (FCPA), the major US anti-corruption law. The partner explained that the CEO of a Chinese company (and a prospective new client) wanted the law firm to hire his son for a summer position. The partner was eager to accommodate— landing this client would be very lucrative for her and the firm. But she needed Sarah to investigate if this action would be legal under the FCPA. Oddly, the partner insisted that nothing about this assignment be put in writing. Sarah was not to consult with anyone else at the firm.

Sarah did a thorough job on the research, then met with the partner to explain that, contrary to expectations, there appeared to be substantial legal risk if the partner hired the client's son. A recent corporate scandal had rocked the financial world when federal regulators fined a major US bank for hiring the sons and daughters of Chinese government officials to smooth the way for future business deals. Although the partner's case did not involve a government official or a full-time job, Sarah reported that the same FCPA ban on hiring could very well apply. The CEO's firm had close ties with the Chinese government, and the son would be a law firm employee, even if only on a temporary basis.

After Sarah reported her findings, the partner told her in no uncertain terms that her job was to "find some way to make this work." She ordered Sarah to go back and reexamine the cases. Sarah did so, even reaching out (in a roundabout way) to another lawyer known to be her firm's most experienced expert on the FCPA. But nothing she learned changed her conclusion. She told the partner that her analysis stood: hiring the son could well be illegal. This prompted a furious response from the partner. Her voice rising, she warned Sarah she had "one more chance" to get the right answer. When Sarah attempted to explain her position, the partner shouted her down. People walking nearby could hear the ruckus and stopped to see what was going on. It now began to dawn on Sarah why she and not the firm's FCPA expert had been picked for this troublesome assignment: Sarah was a new hire, and the partner felt she could be bullied into compliance. Worse, Sarah feared she was being set up to take the blame if the issue blew up.

Sarah finished her story this way: "I was literally shaking when I left her office. I was so upset that I decided to take a walk outside to clear my head. It was lunchtime anyway, so I grabbed my purse and headed out. By the time I finished my second lap around the block, I knew what I had to do. I just kept on walking and never went back. That was the last time I set foot in the place. If this was what the big-time practice of law was about, I wanted nothing to do with it. I figured I might as well go to business school and start over. So here I am."

The class buzzed when Sarah finished. I suspect some of them had harbored fantasies in past jobs of doing exactly what Sarah did, but they had never heard from anyone who had actually done it. I capped off the moment by complimenting her for standing up to her bullying boss, but I noted that a future in big business might be just as ethically challenging as she had found "big law" to be. Other hands went up, and other stories were shared (some of which you will hear in this book).

After class, I reflected on Sarah's situation. She was young and smart; she had options. She might have channeled her outrage into a formal complaint against the partner's behavior, but she probably saw her chances of success as low. She had only been at the firm a few weeks and would be confronting a senior partner who would doubtless deny her allegations. I understood why she headed for the exits.

I have heard enough stories like Sarah's to make me a sober realist about the professional environments many of our young people experience. I even have a name for MBA students like Sarah: I call them "ethics refugees." Unable to stomach what they are asked to do or how they are being treated, they elect to reset their careers by going to graduate school.

From where I stand, I see the best of the current generation demanding more from their working life than money. They want work that means something. But even more fundamentally, they expect their employers to uphold basic values of fairness, honesty, and integrity. I drew a clear moral from Sarah's sad tale: many employers are falling far short of these standards.

During my years as a business school professor, I have listened to more than my share of pious speeches by business leaders who say that creating a principled culture is Job #1. But unless people step up to demand accountability when bosses or peers violate basic ethical norms, including norms of common decency, talented people will flee when they can and, when they cannot, give far less than their best. Standing up for yourself and your values—following your conscience regardless of your place in the organization—affirms your true character and empowers others to speak. Your voice says to others, "I am ready to make a difference." It is an expression of faith that others will do the same thing in moments that matter.

Don't you hope, when lives are on the line, that you and your family can depend on hospital workers willing to stand up to powerful physicians who put their personal convenience over patient safety? And don't you want to be on the same team as the honest professionals who call out political corruption, corporate fraud, and sexual misconduct?

I had heard many stories about my students' ethical challenges at work, but the drama of Sarah's story combined with her impulsive decision to walk off the job was the tipping point that led to this book. She had all the right ethical instincts but seemed to be missing the tools to hold her boss accountable. In addition, for every employee who has the opportunity to walk away from the type of abusive, unethical behavior Sarah endured, there are hundreds who face the same pressures but feel powerless to push back because their choices are more limited.

I decided to map out a set of research-based rules—a Conscience Code—to help them (and you) stand and fight. Indeed, that is why I have identified the first rule of this code as "Face the Conflict." When you turn toward the problem instead of away from it, you challenge yourself to become part of the solution.

DUTY, CHARACTER, RESPONSIBILITY:
IT'S PERSONAL

As you will see throughout the book, this subject is personal for me. I was raised in a Marine Corps family. Duty, character, and responsibility were part of the fabric of our lives.

My father was a decorated World War II veteran and career military officer. By the time I was old enough to be aware of my surroundings, he was the commanding general at the Marine Corps Recruit Depot in Parris Island, South Carolina. Parris Island is one of the two training facilities (the other is in San Diego, California) where raw recruits are brought in and exposed to one of the most rigorous military training regimes in the world, departing three months later (assuming they don't drop out) as United States Marines. This training uses immersive methods to help recruits acquire habits of character, teamwork, and responsibility. Doing the right thing the right way under the most extreme pressures imaginable is what "honor" means in this environment.

When he retired from the Marines, my father became the superintendent (i.e., president) of the Virginia Military Institute, the college he had attended as a student. Watching him in both his military and educational careers, I came to understand what duty meant to him: being devoted to his family, taking care of the people he worked with, and serving as a leader for the communities we lived in. He never raised his voice, choosing to lead by his steady example. And my stay-at-home mom, though a foot shorter than he was, stood as his equal partner in every sense. Coming from this family tradition, I have always taken my duties seriously. Part of my personal mission is to influence those I teach and lead to do the same.

This book is an integral part of that effort. I wrote it to prepare you for two of the most difficult challenges you will face in your professional career. First, to do the right thing when bosses or peers want you to do something you know to be wrong. And second, to speak up effectively when you become aware of wrongdoing by others.

Every time you successfully meet one of these two challenges, you inspire others to do the same. You are part of the solution, adding one more brick to the foundations of a society you want to be part of.

IT'S ABOUT MORE THAN "WHISTLEBLOWING"

When you hear stories about ordinary people who stand up against bad bosses or corrupt organizations, one word generally comes to mind: "whistleblowers." For example, Frank Serpico is justly famous for his role as a whistleblower rooting out corruption in the New York Police Department (and for being played by Al Pacino in the hit movie *Serpico*). Serpico suffered brutal retaliation for his honesty, nearly dying when his fellow officers refused to call for medical help during a shootout in 1971. The list of famous whistleblowers, and the award-winning films based on their stories, goes on from there.

The "whistleblower" label is an appropriate term for describing those who expose large-scale wrongdoing at great personal and professional risk. But it can mislead you into thinking that everyday acts of character and courage—such as speaking up against sexual harassment or insisting on honesty with clients and investors—do not really "count." In addition, as one of the great whistleblowers of the 20th century, Dr. Jeffrey Wigand, noted, the label carries a negative connotation: whistleblowers are sometimes seen as "snitches"—people who break faith with loyal colleagues by calling out their bad behavior. Wigand, who was famous for exposing the tobacco industry's decades-long conspiracy to suppress research linking smoking to cancer, preferred a broader term for those who stand up for their values: "people of conscience."

As this book's title suggests, I hope you will embrace Wigand's phrase. Most of us will never meet a "whistleblower," but we all know people of conscience we admire as role models. And even if you are never pressed into service to call out high-stakes wrongdoing, you will add huge value to your organization and stand taller in your own eyes as well as the eyes of those who love you by speaking up on behalf of core values that are being ignored. Indeed, these everyday moments are what stop organizational corruption from taking hold, maintaining the honest corporate cultures that make whistleblowing unnecessary. The "person of conscience" label also captures the importance of standing up for *yourself* as well as your values. That means speaking out when you experience discrimination and other forms of disrespect.

I'd like to encourage you to adopt this label as a part of your personal identity. People of conscience are those who take actions in everyday professional life that protect and promote the human good. They consistently speak up on behalf of professional standards and personal principles that are important to us all—ranging from scientific and accounting standards to honest dealing and fair play. If you are someday called to be a whistleblower, this book will help you think it through. In the meantime, whenever you face a tough ethical decision, I suggest you focus on your identity as a "person of conscience" who can tell right from wrong.

The phrase "person of conscience" also has personal significance to me. Although, as I noted above, I was brought up in the Marine Corps, I took a very different road in my early twenties. I was in college during the Vietnam War era and faced a choice between military service to fight a war I believed was morally wrong, and finding a way to resist. I resolved this dilemma by becoming a "conscientious objector"—a legal term for a person of conscience who objects to military service on principled grounds. Conscientious objectors serve their country by doing non-military forms of national service, and mine was to work in the most impoverished sections of Washington, D.C., helping relocate poor families who lived in condemned housing. Needless to say, my decision to protest the war caused a split in my family, but my father and I ultimately reconciled our divergent views about war through our mutual respect and love for each other. We understood our duties differently in two very different eras of American history. But at the end of the day, I was my father's son. I answered my call to duty, just as he had answered his.

In addition to conscience, I favor words such as "values" and "character" as touchstones for ethical conduct rather than technical, philosophical terms. As I see it, you do not need to be a philosopher or theologian to know that you should be honest with your investors, fair to your customers, and unwilling to tolerate workplace sexual harassment or racism. There may be circumstances when you will need an ethics consultant's expert advice on a moral dilemma involving life and death or corporate social duties to the world's poor. But I think most of the value conflicts you will face at work will ultimately boil down to your personal character and your identity as a person of conscience.

YOUR CONSCIENCE CODE: THE ROAD AHEAD

The book is structured around a research-based process that provides the context for the ten rules of the Conscience Code. This process carries you forward from your initial perception that a value is at risk to the strategic planning needed to take effective action.

This values-to-action process has four stages:

- Recognize that a value is at risk,
- Own the problem,
- Analyze your decision, and
- Design your action plan.

These four stages (which you can easily remember by thinking of them as the ROAD to value-based action) give you a simple, actionable framework for orienting yourself when you are confronted by a conflict and find yourself on an emotional roller coaster.

Below, I provide a brief summary of the journey ahead. It begins with identifying your values and understanding the forces that will tempt you to compromise them. From there, the Conscience Code gives you the rules for taking responsibility, thinking through your decision, and setting a smart strategy for solving the problem.

Recognize That a Value Is at Risk
(Conscience Code Rules #1, #2, and #3)

This chapter has launched the book with Rule #1 of the Conscience Code: "Face the Conflict." Leaning into the situation instead of turning away from it is your first step toward successfully resolving a workplace dispute over values. As tempting as it might be to shrug off a team leader's sexist comment, your boss's bullying, or the falsified data that just went out to a client, you have a duty—to both your own conscience and to the victims of these behaviors—to face up to what is happening in front of you.

The next chapter, Rule #2 ("Commit to Your Values"), asks you to connect what you see happening in front of you with the principles that matter most. Which core values are worth fighting for? I'll survey what research tells us about the values that most frequently spark workplace conflicts and examine the barriers that can make values hard to recognize in professional settings. Values are the unique products of experience, family, and culture, and three moral emotions—anger, guilt, and shame—play surprising roles in helping you identify which values are at risk in a given situation.

Rule #3 ("Know Your Enemy") completes the work of recognizing values by revealing the pressures that can push you to ignore what your conscience is telling you. Animals sense earthquakes and tsunamis coming long before humans do. They are tuned to subtle changes in their environment that signal danger. To stand up for your values, you need to acquire similar instincts regarding the situational influences that can swamp your better judgment.

The whistleblower who helped bring to light the massive Enron corporate accounting scandal in 2001, Sherron Watkins, once said that you need only three things to create an ethical crisis: pressure, opportunity, and a face-saving rationalization. This chapter introduces you to the "pressure" factor by helping you understand the powerful social forces that can aim you in the wrong direction. We will use two vivid stories from World War II to illustrate how situational pressures can overwhelm even the best of intentions.

Own the Problem
(Conscience Code Rules #4, #5, and #6)

The next three chapters tackle what I think is the most demanding aspect of the Conscience Code: owning the problem by assuming personal responsibility for resolving it. Even after recognizing that a value is in danger, people find reasons to leave these disputes alone. These range from rationalizations, such as "everybody does it" and "just this once," to a personal distaste for conflict and a lack of confidence that you can win the fight. These chapters thus call on you to gather your inner resources to meet these obstacles: Rule #4 ("Summon Your Character"); Rule #5 ("Channel Your Personality Strengths"); and Rule #6 ("Leverage the Power of Two"). We will see that the last of these three factors plays a surprisingly important role in ethical conflicts for a very good reason: having an ally at your side when you face a dispute over values bolsters your confidence that you are, in fact, "doing the right thing" and can prevail. A detailed case study of the two heroes who helped to expose wrongdoing at medical device company Theranos, Inc. will bring these points home.

Analyze Your Decision
(Conscience Code Rule #7)

Rule #7 ("Ask Four Questions") requires you to carefully consider your duties at the decision stage of the values-to-action process. You have recognized that a value is at stake and accepted ownership of the problem. Now it is time to deliberate about costs, benefits, and precedents. Rule #7 calls on you to ask four key questions. These questions concern the potential *consequences* of deciding one way or another, the conflicting *loyalties* you may feel, the effect of this decision on your *personal moral identity* (can you live with yourself after deciding one way or the other?), and the application of *general moral principles* (such as "keep your promises") to the situation. This four-question checklist is useful in every ethical conflict, but it is especially important when you face those toughest of all cases, the ones where someone will pay a price no matter which decision you make.

Design Your Action Plan
(Conscience Code Rules #8, #9, and #10)

With your decision made, the final three chapters summarize the options for strategic action. The first is to talk it through with the person who has the power to make a decision. Rule #8 ("Engage the Decision Maker") thus calls on you to master the dialogue tools you need to manage these difficult conversations effectively.

When dialogue is not enough to solve the problem, you will need to skillfully navigate the maze of organizational politics—and/or outside regulatory systems—to find an appropriate outcome. Rule #9 ("Hold Them Accountable") examines your options for escalating an issue effectively within—and beyond—your organization. These include elevating an issue to higher levels of authority, reporting misconduct to appropriate tribunals, using political pressure to motivate change, and, that most dramatic of all moves—whistleblowing. This chapter concludes with a vivid, real-world case study of an effective "campaign" that used all four of these options to deliver a stunning result.

Rule #10 ("Choose to Lead") concludes this section (and the book) with a call for you to become a leader who consistently stands for positive, value-based work environments. If you take up this challenge, you and everyone around you will benefit. Career success in any line of work depends on taking responsibility for three things: doing things right (duty-of-care values), doing the right thing (ethical values), and being the right kind of person (character values). Every time you object to cutting corners and making ethical compromises, you are a force for good within your organization. You become more than a colleague or peer. People look to you as someone committed to creating the kind of positive workplace culture everyone needs to thrive. Morale, productivity, and trust all rise when people are held accountable to fair, honest standards. Thus, although stepping into workplace conflicts always feels risky and sometimes results in what people temporarily view as career setbacks, choosing to lead with your values will, when done right, allow you to both sleep well at night and do well at work.

THE ROLE OF VALUES IN LONG-TERM CAREER SUCCESS

Following your conscience is a good thing in and of itself. Your values are *who you are at your best*. Remaining true to yourself is reason enough to embrace the challenges of ethical conflict. But I have subtitled this book with a link between honorable behavior and professional success: "Lead with Your Values. Advance Your Career." So I owe you an explanation of how these two aspects of working life fit together.

You will be reading stories in the following pages that feature people who succeeded in making a difference by speaking up for their values. But make no mistake: the system can come down hard on those who dare to stand up to it. Your fears and anxieties are real. Public whistleblowers suffer from the stresses of taking on the rich and powerful. And corrupt bosses as well as office bullies will fight back when you threaten to reveal their misconduct.

Against this reality, I offer three reasons why I have written a book to inspire you to step up to these challenges even when it may be risky to do so. First, as I noted above, I care about your ultimate success as a professional, not just your status within a particular organization at a particular time. In researching this book, I came across the story of a lawyer named Matthew Farmer who left his law firm for another, lower-paying job because he refused to be complicit in his firm's practice of overcharging clients by lying to them about the number of hours the firm had spent on their cases. He vigorously protested this bill-padding behavior to senior members of the firm, but they refused to own up to it. So Farmer quit and reported his former partners to the appropriate legal authorities. This led to an investigation and professional penalties for the people responsible.

Quitting a job may seem like an odd way to "advance a career," but ask yourself: What would Matthew Farmer's professional life have looked like if he had stayed? At some point, the habit of compromising his most important values to sustain his standing within this firm would have led him to become a person he no longer respected. Whatever security he would have purchased with this surrender of his principles would have come at a steep emotional cost: disengagement, perhaps even depression. When you stop respecting yourself and the work you do, no amount of reassurance from people who love you can cure it. Only you can—and that usually means you have to take action to regain your self-respect. So, the way I see it, Farmer "advanced his career" by quitting. He found a way to continue doing work he loved but with people who shared his values instead of trampling on them.

Second, my decades of work in executive education and coaching have taught me something important: even when they are reasonably happy with the places where they work, successful people frequently change jobs as they advance through a career. Careers tend to be marathons across many organizations, not sprints within a single one. Your professional skills in areas such as leadership, negotiation, and communication are capabilities you carry in a backpack. You bring them along as you move from place to place and use them to seek higher and better uses for your talents. I believe your willingness to stand up for positive workplace values deserves a place of honor in your backpack. You will create more value for everyone around you—and become a more trusted leader—if you acquire the habit of calling out serious ethical concerns when you see them and working to resolve them to the best of your ability. This habit will also help you hone essential professional skills, including conflict management, political savvy, and persuasive dialogue.

Third, the worst-case scenario in a workplace conflict over values is that you might be fired. Unless you work for the mob, nobody is going to shoot you. Keep that in mind. Throughout the book, I will offer examples of people who worked successfully to minimize this risk by forming alliances instead of working alone, by understanding the politics of their organizations and the vulnerabilities of their bosses, and by whispering their concerns to the right people rather than shouting them from the rooftops. This book is about following your Conscience Code *skillfully*, not just vocally. That means doing the right thing while protecting yourself as much as possible. But if, in the end, you suffer the worst-case scenario and end up out of a job, I will refer you back to the first point I made above. To be a person of conscience at work, you need to accept some risk that the corrupt people will win and you will (temporarily) lose.

Whether you are willing to accept that risk is ultimately for you to decide.

WHAT BECAME OF SARAH?

Sarah's story of walking out on her law firm job launched this book, so before I published it I checked back with her to see how she was doing. In an unexpected way, her decision to quit advanced both her career and deepened her maturity as a person of conscience.

Our class had marked more than just the beginning of her MBA experience. It also turned out to be the occasion for her to recommit to workplace values. Surprisingly, after recruiting for some high-flying business jobs, she decided she could make the best use of her business degree by returning to law practice. She found a firm with a different set of values from the one she had walked out of. I quote from her report (with her permission) below.

"The partners," she told me, "are sane and decent people; there are no screamers, and no one has ever, ever asked me to do anything shady." The firm is paying her well because it sees her business training as extremely helpful in serving their entrepreneurial and venture capital clients. "The work is hard, but it is the best job I have ever had," she said.

Then came another surprise. "By the way," she wrote, "your note caught me at an awkward but interesting moment. I am recovering from being roughed up last night at a peaceful protest against police brutality. It was the first time I have ever been tear gassed, and I don't recommend it. When the police moved toward us, I found myself on the front lines and scrambled to get out of the way, turning from the police with my hands in the air. That's when I got hit in the back with a tear gas canister. Two people ran out from a nearby store and dragged me off the street, pouring milk and water on my head to try and get rid of the gas. I spent last night in the emergency room. They ran some tests and everything seems to be OK now, though I have a cracked rib and a purple bruise the size of Texas on my back. The irony is not lost on me that I was injured by police at a peaceful protest against police brutality."

Sarah's update was one of the most striking I have ever received from a former MBA student. A commitment to core values need not lead you to engage in street protests, but Sarah's report somehow fit with what I knew about her. Her impatience with bad behavior by people in authority had been apparent from the first day I met her in class. She was now finding ways to express that impatience on a larger social stage.

Sarah's story was also a reminder that values are as important in personal and community life as they are at the office. You need not be a social activist to be a person of conscience, but concerns for honesty, accountability, and fairness are not clothes you put on (or take off) when you go to work. Rather, values are beliefs about how people should treat one another in every aspect of their lives.

To sum up: this book will help you gain genuine, long-term success in your professional career. The Conscience Code distills decades of research from ethics, psychology, persuasion, and office politics to crystalize ten rules for effective action on behalf of your values—no matter where you happen to stand in your organization. Mastering the four steps of the values-to-action process protects the dignity of the work you do, promotes your self-respect, and provides opportunities for you to grow as a leader. Unlike status-based bosses, people who lead with their values measure success by how they conduct themselves when the pressures to behave badly are highest, when the deadline or quarterly goal is tempting everyone else to take a shortcut. They are the people who stand for "getting it done *right*"—not just getting it done. You belong in the ranks of such leaders.

A MOMENT FOR PERSONAL REFLECTION

At the end of every chapter, I will give you a chance to reflect on how the insights and examples I've provided might apply to your own personal experience. For this first chapter, I invite you to think for a moment about Sarah's story and her decision to walk away from the conflict with her boss.

Have you ever stayed in a job too long, putting up with bad behavior or ethically dubious colleagues to avoid the uncertainty of seeking a better alternative? How did you begin to feel about yourself and your work the longer you stayed? Looking back, could you have done a better job of asserting your values to help create a more positive workplace? At the very least, could you have spoken up so other people knew where you stood?

If you finally found your way to a more suitable situation, what was it about this new environment that made you feel better about yourself?

Finally, if, unlike Sarah, you elevated the conflict with your boss to a higher level, what happened? What inner strengths did you call on to give yourself the confidence to take action? And what lessons did you learn about how to do a better job solving this sort of problem next time?

NEXT UP: THE VALUES WORTH FIGHTING FOR

The next chapter introduces Rule #2 of the Conscience Code: "Commit to Your Values." A commitment is a statement about the price you are willing to pay to keep a promise. Commitments to values are promises you make to yourself about the principles you consider most important in your life. In general, your moral emotions will signal when your values are being challenged and help motivate you to protect them. In the next chapter, you'll see how otherwise troubling emotions such as anger, guilt, and shame can play positive roles when you face a conflict over values.

RULE #2: COMMIT TO YOUR VALUES

> "[I]t's easier to hold your principles 100 percent
> of the time than it is to hold them 98 percent of the time."
> —Clayton Christensen, *How Will You Measure Your Life?*

Employees at Google recently organized a global protest against what they saw as the firm's lax attitude about sexual harassment and misconduct. Google had awarded a $90 million severance package to a male executive after the firm's own investigation found "credible" evidence that he had coerced a female employee into having sex on a business trip. One of the protest organizers, Claire Stapleton, noted that employees were upset by the firm's "flimsy" justification after word leaked out about this payout. "[W]e had the iron hot," she told reporters. Stoked by their outrage, tens of thousands of Googlers walked out of their offices on cue, gaining widespread media attention and setting the wheels in motion for a major review of sexual harassment policies at the firm. The firm eventually agreed to strengthen its rules against workplace romances, provide direct oversight by its board for sexual harassment complaints, and allow victims to speak out about their complaints more candidly even after receiving a legal settlement award.

Soon after these events at Google, a similar employee-organized walkout took place at the online retailer Wayfair. In this case, workers were angered when they learned that their company was supplying furnishings for migrant facilities detaining unaccompanied immigrant children at the US-Mexican border. They wanted the firm to stop associating itself with what they saw as human rights violations. It was a small contract that had already been completed, so their demands were simple: don't do it again and donate the money the firm earned from the contract to a group working to reunite migrant children with their families. They made their point. Wayfair agreed to be more thoughtful in the future and donated the profits from the deal to the American Red Cross.

Compare these two examples of employees rallying around shared values of dignity and social justice to a more common and intimate story of workplace misconduct. One of my students, "Gina," told her classmates about this incident in my Responsibility class. It shows why standing up for your values, when you stand alone, can be hard.

GINA'S STORY

"Gina" was one of the quieter students in my class, so when she raised her hand to share her story, people leaned in to listen. She told us that these events had happened at her prior job, and that she had never told the story to anyone before. She shared it now because the class was prompting her to rethink some of her personal decisions at her prior jobs. She had decided that a first step was to own this situation, one in which she felt she had let herself down.

She worked as an analyst for a well-known marketing firm in London, and the incident she told us about concerned a late-night celebration at an expensive restaurant marking the completion of a major project.

Gina was the most junior member on this team, and as the party was breaking up at around 3 a.m., her boss ("Adrian") approached her. Gina told us that she had adopted a rule in college never to have more than one drink when everyone around her was likely to get drunk. Recognizing that Gina was the only member of the team who was sober, Adrian asked her for a favor. He said he faced a long trip back to the suburbs that night. Could she see to it that their client—the chief marketing officer from a global automobile company—got back safely to his hotel? She agreed.

The client could barely walk, so Gina ended up accompanying him in a cab to his hotel and escorting him onto the elevator. When he was unable to make the key swipe work to operate the elevator, she took his keycard and did it for him, deciding she had better make sure he got to the right room. A few seconds after the elevator door closed, however, everything changed. The client came to life, pinning her against the wall and trying to kiss her. Shocked by this sudden, aggressive move, she wrenched herself out of his grasp and was about to push the emergency button when they arrived at his floor. The elevator doors opened, he made an ugly, sexist comment and then exited.

She took a taxi home to her apartment, where she spent what remained of the night reliving what had just happened. Gradually, as the sun rose, the adrenaline in her system ebbed, leaving her exhausted.

She arrived at work the next morning with no sleep but a lot of anxiety about what to do regarding this incident. This man was an important client for her firm. And nothing like this had ever happened to her. After a few minutes, Adrian stopped by her desk.

"Did the client get back to the hotel OK?" he asked.

"Sure," Gina replied, trying to figure out how she could tell Adrian about what happened.

Then Adrian looked at her curiously and asked, "Are you OK, too?"

There was something about the way Adrian asked his question that caught her off guard. Was he checking to see if something had happened? She managed to nod her head and say that she was tired but fine. Adrian then made what she described as an "unforgettable comment."

"I'm glad you're OK," he said quietly. "Just between us, he asked me specifically if you could take him back to the hotel. He's a key client, so I thought you would be OK with it." And then he walked away.

She never reported either the assault or her conversation with Adrian to anyone. Instead, she waited a few weeks and then asked to be transferred to another office in Brussels. After that, she did her best to forget about the whole incident, chastising herself whenever she thought about it for being "so stupid."

But she saw things differently that day in class. "I'm making a commitment today to never let anyone get away with something like that again," she concluded. Her voice was tense with unexpressed anger. A number of women in the class immediately stepped in to voice their support.

Gina realized that her reluctance to report wrongdoing at work was a habit she needed to break. On a personal level, she was still paying a price in unresolved emotions. But just as important, she sensed that her choice might well have had consequences for other people. What about the next young female employee or intern in that office? Would Adrian offer them up to another client (or maybe even the same one)? What had happened in the hotel was a crime, not just harassment. Gina was ready to channel her anger into a commitment to become a more effective, assertive professional.

The first step in resolving any conflict over values is to turn toward—rather than away from—that conflict. It is one thing to have values and another to find the courage and skill to fight for them.

Values are abstractions—ideas such as compassion, fairness, and respect. But when mixed with the right emotions, they will spark you into action. The most potent of these emotions are anger, guilt, and shame. While we normally think of these as "negative" feelings, they need not be negative in conflicts over values. The employees at Google and Wayfair acted because they got angry. Gina failed to act because she let uncertainty and anxiety bury her outrage. She blamed herself instead of the people who had wronged her. But anger can boil when fueled by memory, and Gina will be drawing on her newly embraced outrage for the rest of her professional life.

Rule #2 of the Conscience Code calls on you to commit to your values so you will be better prepared than Gina was to speak up for them. The chapter is organized as follows. First, I will define more completely what values are and identify five key areas that trigger most value-related conflicts at work. Next, I will revisit the four-step process by which people typically move from perceiving that a value is at risk to taking action to protect it. A compelling, real-world story will help illustrate both of these two points. With our definition of values and the process for acting on them firmly established, we will take a deeper dive into the three moral emotions mentioned above—anger, guilt, and shame—that provide the energy powering many value-based actions.

DEFINING VALUES: FIVE THEMES

Values are the principles, standards, and commitments that form the foundations for how you think people ought to live and, by extension, how institutions ought to work. An almost infinite number of values inform our personal, civic, and professional lives, but research suggests that five values spark most of the conflicts we are treating in this book. To make them easy to remember, I've summarized these with the word "CRAFT," which stands for:

- Compassion,
- Respect,
- Accountability,
- Fairness, and
- Truth.

Each of these five values is surrounded by a cluster of associated principles. For example, compassion points to concerns such as the public's safety and protecting the innocent from suffering; respect gives rise to a desire that everyone be treated with equal dignity; accountability implies being fully responsible for one's actions; fairness gives birth to moral outrage at evidence of injustice; and a commitment to truth demands honesty and transparency.

These five values tend to trigger significant conflict because they often reflect *core beliefs*—not mere opinions or attitudes—about how the world ought to work. Social psychologist Milton Rokeach offered a useful metaphor for visualizing such beliefs. He saw them in architectural terms. As a builder uses strong structural supports to hold up a house, so we use our core values to create a stable worldview. Values are the weight-bearing walls in our moral homes. They answer the question "What is the best way to live a worthy, self-respecting, socially responsible life?"

Values, then, are beliefs about how to live. But which ones will end up—for you—being the ones worth fighting for? My thesis: you will often discover the answer to this question by observing how you respond emotionally in real-world conflicts. As you grow and mature in a profession, you will gain confidence in your judgment about which values matter and how best to stand up for them when they are challenged. The following true story will help you understand how this discovery process takes place.

As you read it, notice the role that emotions play in the way the hero—a rookie state trooper—responds to what happens. He discovers his values by becoming aware of his feelings about what has happened. In addition, I hope you will discern the underlying pattern playing out in this narrative. It is the story of an aggressive boss within an ethically challenged culture trying to indoctrinate a new employee into "the way it works." My students have taught me that the same process can be common in the world of finance—only for a lot more money.

STEP OUT OF THE CAR

You can sometimes trace important values to your youth. This was certainly the case for Justin Hopson, who began dreaming of a career as a police officer in grade school. His father was a federal law enforcement agent, and Hopson resolved early on to follow in his footsteps.

His decision took him in his early twenties to the New Jersey State Police Academy where, following six months of rigorous training, he graduated as a state trooper. All was well until, eleven days after joining the force and on his first night duty shift, he and his training officer, Trooper Patrick Cole, arrested a young woman for drunk driving. It was an event that would shape the rest of Hopson's career.

The incident happened near the end of the shift. Trooper Cole was at the wheel of their cruiser when they spotted a car at an intersection with an expired registration. They could clearly see that a young man was driving with a woman sitting next to him. It was less clear who was in the back seat, but a blonde woman appeared to duck out of sight as the car passed the cruiser. Cole gave chase and finally caught up with the car as it was sitting, lights out, in a parking area just off the road near some woods. When the cruiser pulled in behind the car to make the stop, Hopson was surprised to see that the situation in the vehicle had changed. The blonde woman was now in the driver's seat sitting next to the other woman he had seen before. The young man was nowhere in sight. It later turned out he had been driving on a suspended license and had persuaded the blonde woman—his cousin—to take his place behind the wheel while he fled the scene.

The troopers approached the car, and Cole took the lead by presenting himself on the driver's side. He asked the blonde woman sitting there (Hopson later called her "Krista") to produce her license and registration, then to "step out of the car." She was clearly intoxicated and Cole, eager to have something to show for the evening's work, put her through a rudimentary sobriety test.

What happened next sparked everything that was to follow. Cole announced that he was arresting Krista for driving under the influence, even though both Cole and Hopson knew she had not been driving. The scene escalated from there. Krista, protesting her innocence (but refusing to say who the boy was or where he had gone), bolted away from Cole when he tried to handcuff her. This led to a chase into the woods, where Krista was finally caught and subdued.

With Krista screaming at Cole, Hopson found himself frozen in place. He later wrote, "The whole scene had become surreal. . . . At what point was I supposed to speak up? I was completely unprepared." After calling for a tow truck to impound the car, they returned to the state police barracks to book Krista.

It was on that return trip that Hopson let the reality of what had just happened sink in. He was a rookie cop who had participated in a false arrest for drunk driving on his first night shift. Sure, it was only a minor traffic stop involving an unruly teenager, but it violated everything he had been taught—and respected—about policing. Going along, he later wrote in his book *Breaking the Blue Wall,* meant "that the dream career I'd pursued for most of my life was nothing but an illusion." He vowed to do whatever it took to make sure Krista was not punished for a crime she had not committed.

Hopson made two decisions in the coming days. First, he refused to write up an arrest report declaring that Krista was the driver, forcing Cole to write and sign the report himself. Second, and most importantly, he contradicted Cole's report when asked about it by the prosecutor at Krista's preliminary hearing. The charge was dropped. Hopson writes, "It wasn't news to me that some law enforcement officers cut corners with the law. But I would not be stiff-armed into becoming one of those officers."

When word of Hopson's actions got back to the police barracks, he began to be subjected to persistent hazing, harassment, and confrontation by Cole's friends on the force. Hopson was a stubborn man, so this only strengthened his resolve to stay the course. He began keeping careful records of what was happening. Hopson's full story has too many twists and turns to relate here, but, after months of putting up with locker room bullying (and with the strong support of his father), he filed his first formal complaint. Eventually his efforts triggered widespread media coverage and a state investigation. When the investigation got bogged down in the bureaucracy, he took his last shot. Alleging that the police harassment he had experienced was a violation of his constitutional rights, he filed a private federal lawsuit against the state for damages.

Early on, he considered dropping the whole thing by transferring to another barracks and trying to make a fresh start. But his stand quickly brought similar cases to his attention. One case in particular inspired him to persevere. At roughly the same time Trooper Cole and his friends began harassing Hopson, a trooper in another part of the state named John Oliver filed a complaint against his training officer for using racial profiling to make arrests on the interstate highways. The peer pressure on Oliver for calling out this behavior was even more intense than Hopson endured. While Oliver was on leave for depression, he took his own life.

Hopson attended Oliver's funeral, met with his grieving father, and promised him that he would carry on his son's fight. The investigations, disciplinary proceedings, suspensions, and in-depth reports by journalists that followed made good on this promise, exposing the rogue police culture that Hopson, Oliver, and others like them had tried to curtail.

Hopson's career was cut short long before he could declare a complete "victory." He sustained injuries in an on-duty car accident that made continuing as a trooper impossible. But he had put the bullies in state trooper barracks throughout New Jersey on notice that they would be held accountable. Making a clean break after his retirement, Hopson moved to Charleston, South Carolina, where he became a successful private investigator and police reform advocate, efforts seeded by a $400,000 settlement he received from his federal lawsuit.

Hopson may not have gotten rid of all the bad cops in the New Jersey State Police. But, as he took up his new career, he had reason to respect what he had done. Married now with two daughters, he could tell his children that he had followed his Conscience Code, stood up for values he believed in, and done his best to "protect and serve."

To summarize, let's quickly review Hopson's story to see how it maps on to the five values I listed above. All five played a role, but I have listed them in the order of their overall importance in his narrative.

Fairness and Justice. This was the central conflict between Hopson and Cole. For Cole, justice was about doing whatever it took to put away "bad guys," and Krista qualified as one based on her disrespectful behavior toward him. For Hopson, justice meant following the rule of law, and Krista was arrested for a crime she did not commit. His campaign against police misconduct was ultimately about fairness and justice for all ordinary citizens abused by rogue cops.

Truth. Signing a false police report would violate most people's personal and professional standards. It is also well outside the norms of police force integrity. Cole's request that Hopson lie was a watershed moment in this narrative.

Respect. Locker room harassment by bullies offends personal dignity, whether it is in a high school or a police barracks. This violation prompted Hopson to double down on his integrity. He now had two reasons to stand his ground.

Accountability. Cole demanded that Hopson be accountable to him as his rookie trainee. Hopson felt responsibility to his oath to protect and serve, not to his boss. This disagreement provoked the feud that broke out between the two men.

Compassion. This value eventually formed the foundation of Hopson's motivation to see the conflict through to a conclusion rather than to simply walk away. The price John Oliver paid for his colleagues' hazing demonstrates the suffering of harassment victims when they feel utterly defeated. Hopson's promise to Oliver's father that his son would not have died in vain was a solemn commitment.

FROM VALUES TO ACTION:
A REVIEW OF THE FOUR STEPS

Hopson's story not only highlights the values that provoke workplace conflict, it also provides an opportunity to highlight the four-step, values-to-action ROAD process I introduced in the last chapter. Recall that the four steps involve 1) *recognizing* that a value is at risk, 2) *owning* the situation and taking personal responsibility for it, 3) *analyzing* your decision, and 4) *designing* your action plan. This model will help you locate where you are in the conflict process so you can map out your next moves more intentionally.

Stage 1: Recognize That a Value Is at Risk

In order to effectively defend your values, you must be able to recognize situations where they are at risk. This can be harder than it sounds. Here are two common reasons people overlook (or disregard) values that are being trampled right in front of them.

Inexperience in the Professional Setting. Justin Hopson's initial feeling about the false arrest was confusion: "The whole scene had become surreal . . . I was totally unprepared." The full awareness of what had happened dawned on him only later, during the ride back to the station. His problem: the uncertainty that can accompany inexperience. Hopson needed time to measure what he had seen against his professional values.

"*Distraction.*" You can easily be distracted from your values by outside pressures imposed on you. In a famous experiment conducted at Princeton University, a group of theological students training to become pastors were asked to write and deliver a sermon about a Bible story—the Good Samaritan—dealing with the duty of people to come to the aid of strangers in distress. On the day they were to deliver the sermon, they were put on a tight deadline and delayed so they would be running late. Meanwhile, the experimenters placed a shabbily dressed person, apparently in some distress, lying in an alleyway on the route the students would follow. The students had to walk right by him to get to the door. Some students were in such a rush that they did not consciously register the man's presence. Others saw the man but ignored the human suffering in front of them in their haste to comply with the deadline—the text of their sermons notwithstanding. Such is the power of outside pressures to distort our moral priorities.

You can also be distracted by competitive dynamics embedded in your situation. I was once teaching negotiation for a group of experienced executives from a major global finance firm. As an ethics challenge, I gave the group a negotiation exercise between a banker and a client over a fee. The case asked them to settle a dispute about how much the bank was owed for helping the client sell her business. A conflict-of-interest trap was tucked away in the facts. The client was now the head of acquisitions at a startup and had control over hiring new financial advisors. So one obvious compromise was to exchange a discount on the fee for the bank getting new business with the startup. The problem with this concept? The client would be gaining a personal, private benefit (the fee discount) by giving away something that belonged to her new company: the startup's business opportunities. This trade-off would be perfectly legal—but only if the client first cleared it with the startup's board of directors.

Some of the participants immediately recognized this trap and explicitly addressed the conflict of interest in their negotiation solution. But most—even in this experienced group of finance professionals—got so wrapped up in the competitive bargaining over the fee that they completely overlooked the ethical issue. In our debrief of the case, one senior executive who missed the conflict of interest became emotionally agitated, ashamed that he had failed to recognize a common legal problem that came up often in his business. He went through most of the stages of grief—denial, anger, etc.—before he ruefully acknowledged his mistake. His professional self-confidence was shaken, but he learned an important lesson. Ethical issues can literally disappear when there are competitive distractions.

Psychologists have a fancy name for failing to consciously register relevant items that are directly in front of you: "Inattentional Blindness." A simple example: when you are paying attention to a cell phone call while driving, it is all-too-easy to miss the stopped car right in front of you. Chris Chabris's and Daniel Simmons's *The Invisible Gorilla: How Our Intuitions Deceive Us* provides an excellent introduction to the research on this phenomenon and others like it. The examples above suggest that ethical values easily "disappear" when your attention is on more urgent priorities.

Stage 2: Own the Problem

Stage 2 can be the toughest of the four steps because it requires you to take personal responsibility for the value; you cannot walk away. You are committed. Hopson took ownership of his rule-of-law value only after he returned to the station. He saw his earlier inaction at the scene as unprofessional and resolved to do whatever was needed to protect Krista from the false drunk driving charge.

This is the stage where many people lose their way. Consider an everyday example that many disabled people will find all too familiar. Someone is in a hurry to pick up an item at the pharmacy or grocery store and discovers that the only remaining parking space is labeled "Handicapped Parking Only." They look furtively around and then park in the spot, denying it to a disabled person who is, at just that moment, driving into the lot. The parking poacher is probably a good person, but they gave way to a common temptation: minimizing a legitimate value when it is inconvenient to keep it. Below, I provide some simple prompts that can help you remember to take ownership of your values when you are tempted to minimize them.

Make It a Rule. One way to avoid violating a norm is to have a rule, such as "Never park in the handicapped spot." If you are a fitness buff, you probably have rules for many routine things in your life—run before breakfast, never eat dessert, save your favorite TV show or podcast for the treadmill. A rule reduces your ownership decision into a simple test of character. Can you keep a promise you make to yourself?

Take this now-famous example from Harvard Business School professor Clay Christensen's notable book, *How Will You Measure Your Life?* During Christensen's years as a graduate student at Oxford University in England, he played as the starting center for Oxford's collegiate basketball team. With his help, the team made it into the "final four" of that country's national college basketball tournament—a big deal for the team.

Then a problem arose. The all-important semifinal game was scheduled for a Sunday afternoon—which directly conflicted with a vow Christensen had taken as a youth to set aside Sundays for religious devotions. He told his coach about his spiritual commitment but got little sympathy. The coach emphasized that Christensen had also made a commitment to his team. The pressure increased when the team's backup center was injured in practice before the big game.

After "praying on it," Christensen decided he could not play. His youthful vow was for life, not just until it became inconvenient. As he later explained, by staying true to his rule when a basketball game was the only thing on the line (which his team went on to win anyway), he strengthened his will to keep it when much greater temptations arose. His pithy summation, which leads this chapter: "[I]t is easier to hold your principles 100 percent of the time than to hold them 98 percent of the time."

Visualize the Victims. In the next chapter, we will examine the classic social psychology experiments by Professor Stanley Milgram that demonstrated the power of authority to prompt people to violate their own values—including the value to protect innocent life. I'll go into the details later, but for now I want to mention that one of the behaviors observed in "disobedient" participants (the ones who resisted authority) was their tendency to break the rules imposed on them, speak directly to the potential victims, and ask if they needed help. Authority can be like the "spell" cast on people, and imagining who might pay the price if you fail to push back on those in charge can help you break that spell.

Think back to the story about Gina at the beginning of the chapter. Might she have found the courage to report both the client's assault on her and Adrian's casual disregard for her safety if she had vividly imagined the next victims of their behavior? When you feel the temptation to minimize a value rather than own it, ask yourself, "Who might suffer if

I fail to act?" Pause for a moment and think about the potential victims of allowing the values violation to persist.

A student once reported to me that she was happy in her marketing job with a credit card company until the day she spent listening in on sales calls to low- and middle-income customers. In call after call, she heard high-pressure sales tactics being used to persuade already indebted people to accept higher credit card limits. Why would the firm do this? So these customers would charge more items, take on more debt—and eventually pay more interest. She had, of course, always been aware that consumers paying high rates of interest on credit card balances funded her salary. But she had never directly confronted the predatory tactics that pushed the most vulnerable consumers deeper and deeper into debt, making it impossible for them ever to escape these traps.

Reforming the credit card business was more than she was willing to take on at that stage of her career. But she could no longer stomach working in the field. She quit and moved into health care, an industry that appealed more to her values. Directly confronting the victims her industry abused forced her to take ownership of her professional life.

Remember the Frog in the Pot. You have probably heard the mythical story about the frog in the pot. If you place a frog in a pot of boiling hot water, the story goes, it will immediately jump out to save its life. But if you put it in a pan of nice, cool water and then turn the heat up gradually, the frog can't tell when it is getting dangerous, and it may stay in the water until it is too late to save itself. Scholars sometimes call this phenomenon "ethical fading," and you probably know it as the "slippery slope" problem. Once you take a small step down the wrong ethical path, the next step looks a little less "wrong"—until you end up in a very bad place.

Pharmaceutical executive Dinesh Thakur, who led a years-long campaign to correct dangerous manufacturing processes at Indian generic drug maker Ranbaxy, once put it this way: "Decisions [to commit fraud] are built on years of working to push the ethical envelope little by little each time." What begins as a minor ethical lapse evolves into a major case of wrongdoing.

Nick Leeson was a young merchant banker who managed to conceal some $1.3 billion in trading losses before being caught, tried, and convicted of criminal bank fraud. His journey started with trying to hide a single embarrassing error in a trading account. That small cover-up then led to another, larger one—ultimately resulting in a massive trail of forged documents that catapulted Leeson's employer, Barings, into bankruptcy and landed Leeson himself in a Singapore prison.

Don't Become Addicted to Cheating. Getting away with unethical behavior sometimes leads to dependence on it. You lose confidence in your ability to win honestly. Long before Justin Hopson arrived in his New Jersey police barracks, Trooper Cole and his friends had become used to boosting their arrest records by cutting legal corners. One of the most notorious professional baseball scandals of modern times also evolved this way. It concerned the Houston Astros, the Major League Baseball team that won the 2017 World Series, and featured the use of an Excel-based application called "Codebreaker." The app was designed by an intern in 2016 as an experiment to analyze (and steal) pitching signs given by opposing teams. Such sign stealing is a legal cat-and-mouse game in baseball when limited to what players on the field can see.

But Astros personnel developed it into a systematic cheating program using illegal camera feeds during games, allowing the team to accurately tip off its batters to the type of pitch (curve, fastball, slider, etc.) they were about to face from an opposing pitcher—a huge advantage for their hitters. The Astros gradually became so dependent on this crutch that the team could not stop using it. And the peer pressure on the team to keep it a secret was overwhelming. When one of the players with a guilty conscience leaked the story a few years later, baseball fans young and old saw it for what it was—cheating. The scandal forever tainted a championship season and cost the team leaders their jobs. Had even one member of the Astros organization pushed back on this system and threatened to go public if the team persisted in using it, the team would not have become dependent on it as a crutch. Perhaps they might have won the championship legitimately. But now they will never know.

Stage 3: Analyze Your Decision

OK—you own the problem. But how should you analyze what your duties are in the situation? Hopson did not face an especially complex moral issue in this regard. He had a rogue boss who was violating the rule of law. His decision to protest the false arrest was forced on him when Cole demanded he sign a statement that Krista had been driving the car.

When you face the toughest moral conflicts—ones that involve choosing among options that may leave you unsatisfied no matter which path you take—this decision stage can require considerably more work. For that reason, we will devote an entire chapter to it (Rule #7, "Ask Four Questions") later in the book.

Stage 4: Design Your Action Plan

Actions flow from decisions, so Stages 3 and 4 are closely connected. After the employees at Google and Wayfair decided they had to do something about the social issues that concerned them, they still faced the problem of what to do. Their public demonstrations captured the attention of the world, prompting their firms to respond.

Hopson refused to lie about the arrest. That, in turn, led him to contradict Cole's report at Krista's preliminary hearing. The conflict escalated from there.

Action plans often require careful strategic thought—especially in complex organizations plagued by internal politics. In Rule #8 ("Engage the Decision Maker") and Rule #9 ("Hold Them Accountable"), I will build on frameworks I have developed in earlier books to help you think more fully about this final step. Rule #10 extends your action plan from a single event to planning your career as a value-based leader.

DISCOVERING THE VALUES WORTH FIGHTING FOR: THE ROLE OF MORAL EMOTIONS

With a definition of values and the values-to-action process to build on, we are ready to take a deeper dive into the ways you will discover which of your values are, in a given situation, worth the fight. My thesis: reason gives you the tools to think through a decision in a conflict, but your emotions will be the barometers that most accurately predict your actions.

Three emotions in particular play key roles in ethical conflicts: anger, guilt, and shame. These emotions come up in many contexts that have little to do with the values conflicts. You can be angry at your boss for rescheduling your vacation, guilty about forgetting your mother's birthday, and ashamed of your midnight raids on the refrigerator. But these feelings can also serve as powerful motivators to act on your values. Below, we'll look at each one in turn and examine how they can encourage you to stand up for what you believe in.

Anger: Don't Lose Your Temper—Use It

The *New York Times* columnist Roxane Gay summed up the role of anger in ethical decision making at work this way: "When your employer does something that violates your ethical code . . . you have to ask yourself if you are going to do nothing—or get angry." The employees at Google and Wayfair, as well as Trooper Hopson, all took action because they got angry.

Here is another vivid example—one that led to a very public resignation based on the values of fairness and dignity. Tim Bray was a vice president at Amazon in its cloud-computing division, Amazon Web Services (AWS). As the COVID-19 pandemic took hold throughout the world in early 2020, Amazon found itself with surging demand from customers reluctant to go out and shop in brick-and-mortar stores. This, in turn, put enormous stress on Amazon's warehouses as they struggled to fill customer orders on a timely basis. Before long, reports emerged that warehouse workers were falling ill with the virus, triggering urgent demands for Amazon to supply them with the personal protective gear needed to keep them safe.

The French government, acting on complaints from powerful union leaders, ordered Amazon to close its facilities to install proper worker protections. Amazon responded by saying its safety protocols were more than adequate, and it announced that it would simply suspend warehouse operations in the country until the government dropped its demands. Meanwhile, in the United States, where Amazon had successfully resisted unionization, small groups of workers began organizing protests to gain public attention.

Bray, one of only a handful of senior Amazon tech leaders to be given the title "Distinguished Engineer," watched this drama unfolding from his comparatively safe job at AWS. But the firm's sluggish response to the crisis troubled him. Did he stand with the company or the warehouse workers? If he was concerned about the workers, what could he do about it?

The final straw came when some fellow Amazon employees—several of whom he had worked with on an environmental initiative—were fired for organizing an online video conference about the safety crisis. Many saw this as a warning shot against employee whistleblowing. "They fired me to make others scared," one of the terminated employees said. Bray decided he could no longer stand by and do nothing.

Bray considered himself a loyal employee who did not think it was appropriate to "go rogue." He escalated the workers' cause through corporate review procedures uniquely available to people of his status, pushing for reinstatement using every tool the firm allowed. But Amazon took no action.

"[R]emaining an Amazon VP," he later wrote, "would have meant, in effect, signing off on actions I despised. So I resigned. The victims weren't abstract entities but real people; here are some of their names: Courtney Bowden, Gerald Bryson, Maren Costa, Emily Cunningham, Bashir Mohammed, and Chris Smalls." He concluded by saying, simply, "I'm sad, but I'm breathing more freely." Perhaps it was a coincidence, but in the wake of Bray's resignation, Amazon began taking more aggressive steps to protect its warehouse workers.

One problem with anger as a motivation is that it tends to be short-lived. As one commentator has put it, "Anger is the white sugar of activism. It's a good rush but it doesn't provide nourishment." Yet this is not always the case. One of the most acclaimed corporate reformers of the twentieth century, Dr. Jeffrey Wigand, provides a classic example of how anger can be channeled into long-term motivation.

Wigand, a biochemist, joined Brown & Williamson Tobacco Corporation as vice president of research and development to lead its team of scientists in developing a "safer" cigarette. He genuinely believed that this might be possible with enough effort and investment. He quickly became disillusioned as he settled into the job, however. For tobacco executives, the project he was leading was more of a public relations tactic than a good-faith scientific initiative. The executives knew that they were selling an addictive product that caused long-term health problems. Every aspect of the business, including empirical research on a safe cigarette, was subordinated to the goal of protecting that franchise. Wigand's disillusionment turned into outrage. "I was motivated by . . . righteous indignation for corporate executives who had a total disregard for human life," he later wrote.

He began by lobbying his bosses to double their investment in research to create a safer product. But this effort got nowhere. He also used every opportunity to point them to data about the public health dangers of tobacco. This got them annoyed. They decided to kill the messenger;

Wigand was fired five years into his job. After he was safely out of the way, the firm canceled his project, realizing that it was a misguided public relations move. By spending money to produce a "safe" cigarette, they were, in effect, admitting that their existing products were "unsafe."

Wigand now knew what he was up against. His former access to the inner workings of the industry gave him unique credibility as a reformer. And so began an eighteen-year journey that ended in the complete collapse of the tobacco industry's big lie about the health effects of smoking and the creation of a multibillion-dollar fund for victims. Wigand played a key role in this movement every step of the way, working closely with the Food and Drug Administration to classify nicotine as an addictive substance and providing crucial congressional testimony on important, anti-tobacco legislation. His initial indignation cooled into a lifelong crusade that saved countless lives.

To summarize: anger is a wake-up call, warning you that your values are facing a full-on threat. When you feel this emotion, it calls the question: something is wrong—what are you going to do about it?

Guilt: Let Your Conscience Be Your Guide

Guilt and shame reside just around the corner from anger. Whereas anger is an expression of outrage when *someone else* violates our core values, we bring guilt and shame on ourselves. Guilt is an essential building block of conscience. A sign of guilt is the desire to repair what you regret having done, to "make it right." Shame, by contrast, is the painful feeling of being harshly judged by others for your conduct. A sign of shame is the impulse to make excuses for, hide, or cover up whatever might be embarrassing to you. The pain of guilt and shame can be such that merely *anticipating* it motivates many people to act on their values.

To be clear, the same act can prompt both emotions. If you are an otherwise diligent student who, in a moment of desperation, cheats on a final exam in college and is caught, you will likely feel both guilty for letting yourself and your family down and ashamed at the humiliation of being caught. But these two emotions run on different tracks and are worth considering separately.

Let's look at guilt first. At critical moments in many conflicts over values, we face a choice between the safe path of following orders and the risky one of taking responsibility for doing what we think is right. The tipping factor in these decisions is often the degree of guilt we think we will feel if our inaction leads to a bad outcome.

Take, for example, a story from the life of Dr. Jeff Thompson, a pediatrician and onetime CEO of Wisconsin-based Gundersen Health System. As a young intern only a few months out of medical school, he faced a decision that decisively shaped his identity as a leader. He was a junior member of an operating-room team tasked with inserting a breathing tube into the trachea of a nine-month-old baby who was struggling to breathe. The senior attending physician tried three times to insert the tube, failing on each attempt. Frustrated, the attending doctor told the team he needed a break and would return in half an hour—then he left the room.

With the baby's skin turning blue from lack of oxygen, the nurses remaining with Thompson begged him to insert the tube to save the baby's life. It violated all the hospital's rules for an intern to take over this procedure, but Thompson had experience intubating babies, the nurses knew it, and they were confident he would succeed.

Thompson found himself at a fork in the road leading to his future. Down one path lay the profound remorse he would feel if he played it safe, waited for the attending physician to return, and the baby died. Down the other lay reprimands for acting without authority and potential sanctions by the hospital. He later wrote, "I didn't have time to ponder the long-term ramifications of doing one thing over another. The baby was dying, and I had to make a choice immediately." He chose to insert the tube, and the baby lived. The attending physician was "enraged" when he returned to find what had happened. He did everything he could to sabotage Thompson's career. But Thompson was backed by the rest of the medical staff. It was the first of many times in Thompson's life that he chose, as he later put it, to "lead with values."

We often experience guilt in the context of relationships—personal as well as professional. When we wrong someone, perhaps by overreacting to something that does not go our way or failing to step up for extra duty when others have already gone above and beyond, guilt provides the motivation to set the relationship back in order. Restoring goodwill often requires three things: a sincere apology that accepts blame, a promise to do better next time, and an offer to "make it right" by a generous gesture. But even when you follow up on all these remedial steps, you may still wish you had not done whatever you now regret. And other people may still remember it. That's why "anticipatory guilt" is such an effective spur to avoid violating values in the first place.

No one has expressed the power of anticipated guilt to motivate ethical action more eloquently than philosopher Hannah Arendt. In her book *Responsibility and Judgment*, Arendt discusses the moral dilemma German civilians faced as citizens living in the values-turned-upside-down world Hitler created prior to World War II. The test of how they responded, she says, came down to whether "they would still be able to live in peace with themselves after having committed certain deeds." The crisis came for many when they were drafted by the regime to actively participate in atrocities. Arendt notes that some chose to die rather than participate—but not because of abstract principles. "[T]hey refused to murder," she writes, "not so much because they still held fast to the command 'Thou shalt not kill,' but because they were unwilling to live with a murderer—themselves."

In the less-fraught world of workplace misconduct, the same motivations Arendt describes come up over and over. People who refuse to go along with misbehaving peers, bosses, or firms often describe their decisions in identity-based terms: "I had no choice," they are often quoted as saying. "I could not have lived with myself if I had stood by and done nothing."

Are You Guilt Prone?

Psychologists have discovered that some people are "guilt prone"—they tend to feel more acutely the remorse that comes when they violate even minor social norms. They more often second-guess their actions and go to greater lengths to stay true to their ethical codes so they avoid feeling guilt. An assessment for this trait asks how likely you would be to keep the extra change you receive by mistake at a store, how badly you feel about telling a "white lie" to a colleague who invites you to a social event you do not want to attend, and whether you would confess to spilling a drink on someone's rug at a crowded party. Research shows that guilt-prone people are ethical workers. They are less likely to cheat on expense accounts, cover up work mistakes, or lie on their time sheets.

A marketing professor I know ("Jill") told me that when she was a graduate student she had been offered the chance to be added to a list of five coauthors on an academic article a well-meaning relative was finishing up. She was interviewing for jobs and having this citation on her resume would have helped her stand out in the job market. In addition, the norms in her field were pretty loose about coauthorships, and not much effort would have been required to create the appearance that she had done some work on the piece. Nevertheless, Jill declined. She knew herself well enough to realize she would feel guilty getting credit for anything she had not done. In short, she was guilt prone.

Being guilt prone can create extra trouble for people, but it also enhances their reputations for honesty and fair dealing. One of my MBA students ("Andy") once told me a story about his struggle with guilt over a calculation error he made in an investment report for a private equity client. The client was using Andy's report as part of a decision to invest hundreds of millions of dollars in a high-tech business. While the decision was under consideration, Andy discovered that he had made a $30 million mistake in the financial model he used. He was the only analyst on the case, and his error amounted to less than 5 percent of the valuation, but he felt terrible and immediately told his boss. To his surprise, the boss said to forget it—the mistake would not be noticed, and revealing it could hurt the team's credibility. The boss assured Andy the deal would go through regardless; no harm would be done.

But Andy had been raised in a strongly religious family and knew that leaving the matter where it stood would bring a heavy burden of guilt he did not wish to carry. He told me his brain turned into a giant "what-if" machine, churning out arguments and testing how they might change the boss's mind. He eventually went back and told the boss he respected his desire not to make waves, but he wondered what the boss would expect if he himself were the investor. Would he want his professional advisor to correct such a mistake? And suppose it were later discovered? Wouldn't apologizing now be safer and easier than trying to apologize for it later?

The boss changed his mind and let Andy report the error.

Andy ended his story by saying he had gotten some negative feedback from the client for making the mistake. But the client also appreciated his honesty. Moreover, as the boss had predicted, the deal closed as expected.

Shame: The Pain of Humiliation

As the examples above suggest, unresolved guilt can feel like a burden. The shame of being caught for misconduct, by contrast, often feels sharper. According to a report in *Scientific American*, shame is the "uncomfortable sensation we feel in the pit of our stomach when it seems we have no safe haven from the judging gaze of others. We feel small and bad about ourselves and wish we could vanish." The report notes that chronic shame (more often than guilt) is associated with severe anxiety disorders and depression. Avoiding potential shame is thus, like avoiding guilt, a powerful motive that drives ethical behavior.

It is no accident that we sometimes speak about "dying of shame" when we feel embarrassment about some event in our lives. Psychologists have discovered that people, especially men, are more likely to attempt suicide when faced with potential revelations about sexual misconduct, alcoholism, professional disgrace, or allegations of abuse.

Sometimes the physical effects of shame are severe enough to cause death, without requiring self-harm. For example, another of my MBA students ("Kartika") was working as the head of finance for her family business in Indonesia when she discovered that her father's closest partner and oldest friend had been stealing from the firm for years. This partner was ill at the time, but Kartika knew she had to confront him to demand that he return the money. He denied everything, forcing her to call a partnership meeting (including associated family members) to present the documented record of his corruption to all the stakeholders. He still denied it all. But his health took a sharp turn for the worse immediately after this, and he died within three months. His family ultimately made restitution. Kartika believed that the shame of these revelations literally killed him.

Shame—because it prompts the impulse to cover up rather than make amends—can be a very unhealthy emotion. But shamelessness is worse. In a healthy organization, professionals believe in the enterprise's core values, feel guilty when they are violated, and try to earn back the trust they lose when this happens. When corruption takes hold of a group, the core values are still displayed for public consumption, but the behavior these values are supposed to inspire goes out the window. The leaders' job: take shortcuts, break the rules, serve themselves, and cover up what is really going on. If word leaks out anyway? Deny, deny, deny.

That raises a final danger. When you are confronting bosses who fear the shame that will come if you successfully expose them as wrongdoers, take special care. They will usually respond with adamant denial. Worse still, they may lash out, trying to ruin your reputation and career. That is why, in Rule #9 ("Hold Them Accountable"), I will touch on strategies for protecting yourself from toxic bosses in especially risky situations.

A MOMENT FOR PERSONAL REFLECTION

Consider a time when you have faced an important challenge to your values. Perhaps you felt strongly about an issue related to social justice or climate change and were moved to act. Perhaps it was an issue at work when you or someone you knew was treated unfairly. What did it take to get you moving? What role did emotions such as resentment or anger play? Was it the nagging sense that you might feel guilt or shame if you did nothing? Perhaps it was the prospect of feeling good about working for the greater good or helping people in need.

Values often spring to the forefront when we read an especially vivid story in the media or hear about a specific case of injustice or discrimination from a friend. For example, people often feel moved to donate to a worthy cause when they hear appeals that depict the suffering of specific individuals. Can you list some of the "triggers" that kick you into action? We often respond to problems that are closer to us in physical space, that affect people we love, or that someone we respect has taught us to care about. When it comes to conflicts over values at work, these "triggers" are worth remembering to help galvanize your motivation to do the right thing, even when it is risky to step up.

NEXT UP: WHY GOOD PEOPLE
IGNORE THEIR OWN VALUES

Values can easily get lost in the rush of everyday life. But they are especially hard to see when we face external pressures to ignore them. In *The Art of War*, Sun Tzu teaches that if you know your enemy and know yourself, "you will not be imperiled in one hundred battles." Rule #3 of the Conscience Code thus demands that you learn to recognize the enemies of your values—the forces of social conformity, misguided authority, and systemic corruption that will tempt you to go along when you know it is wrong to do so.

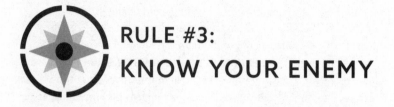

RULE #3:
KNOW YOUR ENEMY

> "Good and evil both increase at compound interest. That is why the little decisions you make every day are of such infinite importance."
>
> —C. S. Lewis, *Mere Christianity*

As the stories you have read so far suggest, conflicts over values are often unpleasant. Because this is so, many people make a convenient assumption about them. "I am basically a good person," they say, "so I will do the right thing when duty calls. Meanwhile, I'll get on with the urgent problems I am getting paid to solve."

When you hear yourself saying this, you are already halfway down the wrong road.

Why? Because you are leaving yourself unprepared. The forces you will face when your values are tested—forces that trigger temptation, fear, uncertainty, and lack of confidence—are powerful. You must give these forces names and learn to respect them if you are to have any chance to stand your ground when the pressure is on.

Moreover, you will be tested when you least expect it, and your actions, no matter where you stand in the organization, will define who you are for years to come. Simple phrases such as "everybody does it," "just this once," and "it's not my responsibility" will tempt you to put your moral alarm bells on mute. By the time you wake up, you may already be doing things you regret with no clear path to lead you home.

Consider this little-known episode from one of the biggest business scandals of the last generation—the multibillion-dollar accounting fraud at WorldCom, Inc. that bankrupted a global telecommunications firm and eventually wiped out thirty thousand jobs. I'll tell the whole story of this massive fraud near the end of the book when we discuss Rule #9 ("Hold Them Accountable"). For now, I want you to appreciate the scandal's humble beginnings in the lives of two ordinary employees who were unprepared for an ethical crisis that would change their lives.

WE NEED TO BRING THE PLANES IN SAFELY

The story centers on two midlevel employees in WorldCom's accounting department, Betty Vinson and Troy Normand. They were experienced members of the team that compiled and input financial results and had worked at WorldCom for years. One day, just before WorldCom was due to announce its quarterly financial results, they were called to a meeting with the controller, David Myers.

Myers told them that the chief financial officer, Scott Sullivan, had grave concerns about the accuracy of the accounting team's work. Their data had revealed a cost overrun amounting to several hundred million dollars compared to the previous quarter. Sullivan was certain the team's analysis was dead wrong. Moreover, this number, if publicly announced, was sure to drive down the firm's already wobbly stock price, triggering severe, firm-wide consequences. Something had to be done—and done fast—to fix the situation.

Vinson and Normand protested. They reminded Myers that they had gone over the numbers multiple times and their work had been checked by their director, Buddy Yates. Myers himself had approved their report. All true, responded Myers, but Sullivan was one of the smartest finance guys at the company—maybe at any company in America—and if he was convinced that there was an error, there probably was. The solution? Myers and Sullivan needed them to go into the books and alter a few entries so that the expenses would appropriately align with Wall Street's expectations. He assured them that it was just for this one quarter. It would buy them time to find the error and correct it before the next reporting deadline.

Vinson and Normand were uncomfortable enough to ask for a direct meeting with Sullivan to hear his concerns. That was arranged, and Sullivan gave them his commitment that the company faced an emergency situation and that the accounting adjustment would not be repeated. Sullivan said that WorldCom was like a great aircraft carrier far out at sea with planes in the air and bad weather fast approaching. The ship needed its crew to do whatever was necessary to bring the planes in safely.

The two agreed to help out. It was, after all, just for this one quarter. But on the same day the adjusted results hit the press, each was troubled enough to write a letter of resignation. As the weeks passed without any noticeable fallout from the false report, however, their resignation letters stayed in their desks. The deception continued, undetected. Day by day, quarter by quarter, Vinson and Normand became key members of the "team" running the vast accounting conspiracy. The roof fell in a year and a half later when an internal auditor at WorldCom stumbled onto some of the fake entries. In the months that followed, the VP of auditing, Cynthia Cooper, led a small team on a quest that uncovered the full scope of the complex cover-up. You will hear more about Cooper, a true person of conscience, in upcoming chapters.

Criminal indictments ensued. After a trial, the firm's CEO, Bernie Ebbers, was found guilty of masterminding the scheme and sentenced to twenty-five years in prison. CFO Scott Sullivan testified against Ebbers, receiving a five-year sentence. Controller David Myers, accounting director Buddy Yates, and bookkeeper Betty Vinson also went to prison. Troy Normand, the most junior member of the team, escaped with a suspended jail term and a lengthy period of supervised probation.

When she sentenced Vinson to her prison term, Judge Barbara Jones remarked that, "Had Ms. Vinson refused to do what she was asked, it's possible this conspiracy would have been nipped in the bud." Her colleague Troy Normand later said that he was pulled in two directions: between his certain knowledge that what he was doing was wrong and his immediate fear for his family's financial security if he refused to go along. Fear had won.

The ancient Greeks had two different ways of thinking about time. The first was chronological time, the relentless tick, tick, tick of the second hand on a clock. The second was something quite different: *meaningful* time. These are the defining moments when, like it or not, "the universe" calls on you to act in character-defining ways. These are the moments you will recall when you tell your life story to your children.

And they are the ones that, looking back, you will most regret if you get them wrong.

When Vinson and Normand met with Sullivan and he asked for their help with his accounting fraud, they entered the slow-motion vortex of meaningful time. Their decision was about to define who they were—and would be—for years to come. Could they have met this challenge better had they been better prepared? I think so.

They were aware that what they were doing was wrong. Why else write resignation letters? But they were not ready to stand up for themselves and their values. At that meeting with Sullivan, they deferred to both his authority and a flawed analogy of an aircraft carrier needing a dedicated team to bring its planes back on deck in a race against time. Had they arrived at the meeting with their minds fixed on their commitment to being "people of conscience" as well as employees, they might have better weighed Sullivan's CFO authority against the authority of their personal and professional codes. Seen in this light, his aircraft carrier metaphor would have made no sense. "It's not about bringing in planes," they might have responded. "You are asking us to lie about the seaworthiness of a ship that may be sinking." Then they should have handed him their resignation letters, with a threat to go to the local papers if he continued down his fraudulent path.

GOOD PEOPLE

As I mentioned in the first chapter, Sherron Watkins, the internal auditor who helped expose the massive fraud at energy company Enron, once said that wrongdoing requires only three conditions to take root and thrive:

- pressure,
- opportunity, and
- a face-saving rationalization.

Note: Being a "bad person" is not on her list. A University of Texas tennis coach, Michael Center, was once convicted of fraud for taking a $60,000 bribe (and a $40,000 donation to the UT tennis program) in return for designating a high school senior who had never played competitive tennis in his life as a tennis star worthy of special admission as an athlete. "I believe you are a good man," US District Court Judge Richard Stearns said at Center's sentencing hearing. Then he ordered him to forfeit the $60,000, pay a $20,000 fine, and spend six months in jail and a year under court-supervised release. Center collapsed into his chair, sobbing as the court adjourned.

He had needed the money (pressure); he had been offered what he considered a foolproof scheme for getting the money by a serial fraudster named Rick Singer who was the mastermind of the so-called "Varsity Blues" college-admission scandal (opportunity); and he comforted himself with the thought that his tennis program was also a winner because it was receiving a donation (a face-saving rationalization).

It is no accident that every major world religion depicts the internal struggle between doing right versus doing wrong as an everyday problem. This chapter's lead quote by C.S. Lewis suggests that you test yourself every day in the "little decisions" you make, decisions like admitting your mistakes, treating the people who serve you in retail stores with the respect they deserve, showing compassion to a coworker under stress, and objecting when someone makes a sexist or racist "joke."

Virtue is not a one-and-done affair; good angels and lesser angels perch on our shoulders. The lesser ones are quick to speak, and they can be quite persuasive. The good ones are often quieter, but they can be persistent—keeping you up at night when you do not listen to them. Threading through the battles are the moral emotions—anger, guilt, and shame—that we examined in the last chapter, as well as another one—fear—that we will learn more about in Rule #4 ("Summon Your Character").

Think of it this way: athletes get ready to compete by practicing their sport and soldiers prepare for battle with war-game rehearsals. In the same way people of conscience must mentally prepare to speak up for themselves and their values *before* they face a conflict like the one Vinson and Normand encountered.

This chapter will introduce you to five powerful situational forces that are your "enemies" in this daily battle between good judgment and bad. Your character and reputation depend on understanding these forces and learning how to overcome them.

Let's start by comparing two real-world stories from World War II. They show just how thin the line can be between actions we would deem to be truly evil and those we celebrate as exceptionally heroic. Imagine you or someone you love being thrust into these situations and ask yourself what choices you would make. These are admittedly extreme, high-stakes cases. But they make a crucial point about the power of the situation to bring out both the worst and best of the human spirit. Well-meaning, ordinary people are at the center of both stories.

ORDINARY MEN

In *Ordinary Men: Reserve Battalion 101 and the Final Solution in Poland*, historian Christopher Browning writes of a unit of five hundred men called Reserve Police Battalion 101 and their role in the massacre of Polish Jews during World War II. These men, many in their forties and too old to be drafted into Hitler's army, were former truck drivers, teachers, pharmacists, construction workers, and dock hands, not Nazi SS enthusiasts. All were from areas in and around Hamburg, an area that had been sympathetic to political parties opposing Hitler prior to the war.

In July 1942, the unit was ordered to a Jewish ghetto area south of Lublin, Poland, in a town called Józefów. Their commander, Major Wilhelm Trapp, had orders to round up several hundred Jewish men of working age in Józefów to send to work camps. Battalion 101 was then to execute the remainder of the population: some 1,500 elderly men, women, and children.

Trapp had grave misgivings about this mission and did not reveal what it was until the orders were about to be carried out. Before the massacre, he gave a speech stating that the killing of women and children was justified because Allied bombers were killing innocent women and children in Germany. He then gave the men an unusual option: they could step away from the duty before the action commenced if they wished and would not be punished for doing so.

Twelve out of the five hundred opted out. The rest went on to commit an atrocity that took seventeen hours to complete. Later interviews with the men suggest that roughly one hundred became so sickened by their work that they could not carry on and gathered in the town's market area while others completed the massacre. Trapp himself did not actively participate, and was heard to say "such jobs don't suit me, but orders are orders." That evening, one of his men witnessed him weeping.

Browning's book goes on to detail the grizzly role Battalion 101 played in the Holocaust. As the war continued, both Trapp and his men became increasingly desensitized, eventually contributing to the deaths of over 83,000 Jews. As the *New York Times* book reviewer Walter Reich noted in his essay on Browning's book, one puts down the work with a profound, disturbing respect for the situational pressures that can transform "ordinary" people into war criminals. These pressures, replicated every day in organizational life, are as easy to describe as they are familiar: repeated, authoritative, direct orders to commit wrongful acts, the impulse to "go along" when everyone around you is following these orders, and the fear that a refusal will be punished or will irreparably harm one's career.

Major Trapp stayed true to his word and did not discipline those who opted out of the killing. But when interviewed long after the war, nearly all the men who participated had convinced themselves that they had no meaningful choice. Reich concludes his review by saying that Browning's work left him with the "lurking fear of self-recognition" regarding human weakness in the face of strong, malevolent situational forces.

FROM SINNER TO SAINT: REFRAMING THE SITUATION TO PROMOTE VALUE-AFFIRMING CHOICES

It is appropriate to condemn the actions of Major Trapp and his men. But it is also important to understand the powerful array of forces they faced, all conspiring to transform them into moral monsters. What sort of person does it take to survive such a test and do the right thing? Perhaps someone who, surprisingly, is not dramatically different from some of the men who failed the test in Józefów. Indeed, such a moral reversal may require only a broad-minded sympathy for human suffering and a direct request for assistance. So, before you despair about the overwhelming nature of situational forces when malevolently applied, take heart. They can also be forces for extraordinary good, bringing out the best in people and prompting them to act in the most self-sacrificing ways.

Compare Browning's analysis in *Ordinary Men* with another, altogether different, window into what "ordinary" people felt pressured to do during World War II. Samuel and Pearl Oliner's *The Altruistic Personality: Rescuers of Jews in Nazi Europe* explores these cases. The husband and wife team (both professors of sociology—Samuel was himself a Polish-born Holocaust survivor) ask a very different question from the one Browning asks. They want to know why ordinary people would risk their lives and the lives of their families to save Jews who were complete strangers. To answer this, the Oliners conducted structured interviews with seven hundred Europeans from the World War II era, some of whom rescued Jews from the Nazis and others who were situated to have done so but did not.

Their conclusion puts to rest the notion that the rescuers were an exceptional set of moral superheroes. Rescuers and non-rescuers alike came from the same array of social classes, work occupations, religious affiliations, and geographical locations. Both faced similar levels of risk in harboring Jews from the Nazis. Some rescuers already knew the people they assisted, but many did not.

The variables that differentiated the rescuers from the non-rescuers? First, over two-thirds of the rescuers reported that they were *directly asked* for help by Jewish families. Few of the non-rescuers were approached in this way. The rescuers were thus approached with the assumption that they were people of conscience, making the duties of this identity immediately salient. Rescuers saw people in desperate straits; they were asked directly for assistance; they had a means to help; and they, quite literally, could not say "No" without feeling diminished by their decision.

Consider rescuer Miep Gies, an Austrian-born bookkeeper living in Amsterdam who spent several years helping to hide two Jewish families, one of whom included Anne Frank (author of the famous diaries that Gies preserved when the families were finally discovered and deported near the end of the war). Gies later voiced the inner dialogue many rescuers must have experienced. When asked why she agreed to put her own life at risk for the Franks, she answered, "These people were in need. And I could help them. You don't say 'no' to that, do you? . . . I thought it was quite normal. I thought it was nothing special." Social psychology confirms this tendency of people to assist strangers in obvious need when the stranger asks them specifically and directly for help.

Second, the Oliners found that rescuers were more likely as children to have interacted with a broader array of ethnically diverse neighbors (including Jews), and absorbed from their upbringing a view that moral duties can apply with the same urgency to "outsiders" as they do to members of one's own family, cultural group, or nation. In other words, without knowing it, the rescuers had been taught to see themselves as people of conscience in a particularly broad way.

The Oliners identified this factor as the possession of an "extensive" rather than "constricted" moral imagination. Thus, when asked to help strangers facing the threat of genocide, rescuers framed their choice in moral, not just practical, terms. The moral quality of the decision meant they had to consider the profound, identity-touching guilt that might haunt them if they failed to step up. Again, Miep Gies expressed this well: "My decision to help . . . was because I saw no alternative. I could foresee many sleepless nights and an unhappy life if I refused. And that was not the kind of failure I wanted for myself. Permanent remorse about failing to do your human duty, in my opinion, can be worse than losing your life." This sentiment echoes the modern psychological research discussed in the last chapter, which has found that people who are especially prone to feel guilt when they act against their conscience are more likely to behave honestly and ethically.

When you put the stories of Police Battalion 101 and the rescuers side by side, they provide sobering reminders that the actions of saints and sinners may not be separated by the wide gap we usually associate between people we label "good" and those we label "evil." The random pharmacist drafted into service for Reserve Police Battalion 101 was, in ordinary life, a dispenser of remedies to relieve pain. Perhaps he was a "pleaser"—someone who was always trying to be agreeable to everyone around him. The order to kill civilians in Józefów would have thrown him into a personal crisis, but he may not have had the strength of character to resist. And once he had started down that path, even though he was sickened and disgusted by his actions, his desire to please his commanders gradually transformed him into a hardened mass murderer.

Bookkeeper Miep Gies, who but for an accident of birth might easily have been friends with that pharmacist, faced different pressures that pointed in a different direction. She encountered a specific request for help from innocent people who faced almost certain death if she refused. Turning them down would leave her facing a lifetime of emotional guilt. Once Gies and her group took their first steps to hide the Jewish families, the pressure was on to continue the work. Everyone's safety, including her own, depended on staying the course.

Make no mistake: Major Trapp and his men committed unspeakable war crimes while Miep Gies and the rescuers are justly numbered among the moral heroes of World War II. But it takes nothing away from the nobility of the rescuers' actions to realize that a German pharmacist raised by broad-minded parents in Hamburg might have become a rescuer if only he had confronted the situation Vienna-born Miep Gies faced instead of being drafted into Police Battalion 101.

SITUATIONAL FORCES THAT CAN OVERRIDE YOUR VALUES: PAIRS

With these two examples in mind, let's take a deeper dive into the situational forces that prompted such different responses from Major Trapp and Miep Gies. Five otherwise functional (and often benign) human desires, all of which arise from our basic wiring as social animals, can cause us to experience the kind of "pressure" we saw illustrated above. I call these the PAIRS Pressures—this stands for Peers, Authority, Incentives, Role, and System. Social psychologists have demonstrated how these forces can affect your perceptions and motivations, triggering actions that can sometimes seem almost involuntary—and that can prompt good people to perform bad acts. Below, I briefly review these five forces. In future chapters, we will investigate some of the conditions that social science has shown make it easier to resist them.

1. Peer Pressure: To Get Along, Go Along

One spring evening I was heading down the main walk through the center of the University of Pennsylvania campus when I saw a striking sight. Emerging over the crest of a pedestrian bridge ahead of me and heading straight in my direction were over a hundred undergraduate women, all dressed in black dresses or black skirts with black tops. They swirled past me abuzz in conversation. I later asked one of my students about this. "It was the first night of sorority rush," she replied. "They were all on their way to the house parties."

"Do you have to wear a black outfit to be considered?" I asked. "No," she said. "But everybody wants to fit in, and black is the current style."

Social scientists call this phenomenon "social conformity," and you often find it when people work together on teams. A team working toward a shared goal will establish shared norms of behavior, which then become standard operating procedures. These SOPs can be ethical, unethical, or a mix of both—depending, as the WorldCom example shows, on the values of the team's leaders.

The men of Police Battalion 101 were part of a quasi-military unit in which peer pressure would have been quite strong. Military training emphasizes teamwork against the background of norms supporting military missions. This explains why Major Trapp presented the choice of "opting out" of the massacre duty. The twelve men who stepped away were the outliers, calling attention to themselves. Indeed, Browning himself concluded from his interviews and other evidence that the military norm "Don't break ranks" was probably the main reason that 488 men participated in this war crime.

Might things have turned out differently if Trapp had framed the choice differently, first by calling attention to the unit's identity as "police" rather than an army group and then by asking for a show of hands from those who wished to *volunteer* in the killing of women and children? We will never know. But that would have given more situational protection to the men who wanted to act as people of conscience.

The science on social conformity has been with us for decades. Professor Solomon Asch conducted a series of classic experiments in the middle of the twentieth century demonstrating that bizarre behaviors can sometimes emerge in group settings when peer pressure is applied. Asch induced college students to report that two lines of unequal length were, in fact, equal. He placed a subject in a room with a group of seven people (all of whom were his confederates). The task: identify which one of three different lines on one piece of paper was the same length as a single line on another paper.

In Asch's control group setting, subjects matched the lines working by themselves with nobody else in the room. They got the right answer 99 percent of the time. In the experimental condition, the seven confederates in the group named their choices out loud, one at a time, and the lone subject of the study was always the last one to speak. There were multiple rounds of this task, and in two-thirds of them all seven of the confederates were instructed to confidently name the same, *incorrect* line as the right match. Faced with a group consensus converging on the wrong answer, only 25 percent of the subjects held out for the correct answer through all the rounds. Meanwhile, roughly 36 percent of all subjects' responses deferred to the inaccurate group consensus, and 75 percent of subjects went along with the group at least once. An outlier set of 5 percent of socially conforming subjects followed the "fake" consensus *every single time.*

The subjects had a variety of explanations when later asked why they had gone along with the group, many of which were rationalizations more than reasons. Some said they became confused by the task; a few reported that they actually came to believe the different lines were the same length; many admitted that, like soldiers who do not wish to "break ranks," they wanted their responses to blend in with everyone else's. They conformed to avoid the awkwardness of social isolation and embarrassment.

It thus seems clear that peer pressure affected the men of Police Battalion 101. Did it affect rescuers such as Miep Gies? On the one hand, they were standing against massive social pressures unleashed by the Nazis against the Jewish people. But I wonder if, within the smaller social circles of those who committed to months and even years of sheltering a Jewish family, they might have felt social pressure to make sacrifices and face risks. If so, the peer pressure they experienced acted to support, not subvert, their desire to do the right thing.

2. Authority: Obey the People in Charge

As a child raised in a Marine Corps family whose formative years were spent on military bases and the campus of a military college, nothing is more natural to me than obedience to authority. But as I discovered when I faced the prospect of fighting in the Vietnam War—and Betty Vinson and Troy Normand found out at WorldCom—authorities sometimes give orders that abuse your trust, demanding obedience to further corrupt, self-serving goals of their own. When that happens, how hard is it to say "No"? Harder than you might think.

Asch's most notable student, Stanley Milgram, conducted a set of now-famous power-of-authority studies at Yale in the 1960s and '70s. He ran nineteen experiments involving nearly one thousand people (none of whom were students), demonstrating that ordinary citizens from New Haven and Bridgeport, Connecticut, could be pressured into delivering what appeared to be lethal levels of electric shocks to human "victims." I won't belabor the details of the experimental setup, which are well known and easy to research on your own. Suffice it to say that, to gain his compliance effect, Milgram dressed up his situation to resemble a laboratory setting with authoritative "scientists" in white coats and a room that appeared to be a well-ordered space with realistic electronic equipment. His subjects were told they were involved in a Yale-sponsored project to test punishment-based ways of learning. They played a role called "Teacher."

When actors who were paid to play a "Learner" failed to give the right answer on a quiz, the subject playing the "Teacher" role activated a fake "shock box" device (so famous it now resides in a museum in Ohio), which appeared to give an electric jolt as punishment. At each wrong answer, the Teacher had to increase the shock level—from an initial (trivial) 15 volts all the way to 450 volts. Levels at 300 volts and higher were clearly labeled as severe. The 450-volt level was marked with a menacing "XXX." If Teachers hesitated to give the next level of shock out of concern for the well-being of the Learner (who was scripted to moan, shout, and eventually scream in pain before lapsing into silence), the fake scientists ordered them to keep going in firm, simple, uncompromising language. In one experiment, all 40 subjects delivered electric shocks of at least 300 volts, and 26 went all the way to the XXX level of 450. A few delivered this lethal jolt as many as three times in a row before the experimenters ended the session.

Milgram and others replicated these findings in a variety of cultural settings, leading him to a grim conclusion. "Ordinary people," he wrote, "simply doing their jobs, and without any particular hostility on their part, can become agents in a terrible destructive process. Moreover, even when the destructive effects of their work become patently clear, and they are asked to carry out actions incompatible with fundamental standards of morality, relatively few people have the resources needed to resist authority."

The story of Police Battalion 101 strongly supports Milgram's claim. Trapp not only invoked authority by giving a direct order that came from the highest levels of the German command, he also presented a reason for the order, allowing himself and his men to rationalize their behavior as tit-for-tat for Allied bombing raids. Buttressing this invocation of authority were the men's fears related to personal and family security.

Disobedience, the men later testified, carried a risk to their future careers, placing themselves and their families in jeopardy.

In the case of the Milgram studies, the subjects did not face penalties for breaking off the experiment. But, like Police Battalion 101, they were provided with a "story" explaining why obedience was necessary. Their work, the white-coated men said, was important to the advancement of science.

One behavior that was observed in subjects who, in spite of being told that "science" required them to keep increasing the shocks, broke off the experiment before reaching the lethal levels. They "spoke to the victims," asking if they needed help, in violation of the experiment's rules. Later on, we'll see that another group of subjects dropped out when they observed others in the experimental setup objecting to what was going on. In short, authority is a powerful force, but there are things you can do—as the twelve members of Police Battalion 101 did—to resist it.

3. Incentives: The Pressure to Meet Goals, Deadlines, and Expectations

I teach my Responsibility course several times every year, and each time I do, there are fresh examples of firms triggering massive employee misconduct by tying compensation to overly aggressive sales targets—without sufficient accountability. Survey research consistently shows that unethical conduct frequently follows when top managers, supervisors, and coworkers are striving to meet performance goals under deadline and competitive pressures. My Wharton colleague Maurice Schweitzer led the research team that produced the first laboratory evidence documenting this problem. He found that the closer people get to achieving a specific, challenging goal under deadline pressure, the more often they misreport the data measuring their success. The problem disappeared when his subjects were simply told to "do their best," without being given a concrete goal on the experimental tasks he gave them.

Bernie Ebbers and Scott Sullivan launched the WorldCom accounting fraud in a misguided effort to meet Wall Street expectations regarding the firm's quarterly earnings. The stock price was already under pressure in the overall market meltdown that followed the collapse of the "dot com" bubble. As Sullivan saw it, missing WorldCom's earnings target would mean a lot of bad things happening to a lot of good people. His own compensation was tied to the stock price. Meanwhile, Bernie Ebbers had borrowed hundreds of millions of dollars using WorldCom stock as collateral. If the stock tanked, Ebbers's debts would come due, ruining (and disgracing) him. WorldCom's own debt obligations were also tied to its ever-rising stock price. If the stock fell far enough, the firm could fail, leaving shareholders with nothing and resulting in layoffs that would hurt the small Mississippi city where many of the employees lived.

Sometimes the pressure to meet goals can lead to tragic, even deadly results. Not long ago, US Secretary of Veterans Affairs Eric Shinseki was forced to resign when dozens of patients died while waiting for care from Veterans Administration hospitals. The problem? The agency had been given an unrealistic goal to shorten hospital admission wait times to no more than fourteen days. Faced with receiving poor performance evaluations for failing to meet the goal, administrators erased hundreds of names from the wait list, retaining only those who were treated within the fourteen-day window. Veterans died because they were no longer in the system and, when they attempted to get back in the queue, they were put at the back of the line.

4. Role Expectations: Doing Your Duty

Sociologists use the term "role theory" to capture the idea that people often enact behaviors they think are expected of them in certain well-established social roles. If you are a young person without much leadership experience, you may think that being a "leader" means giving orders. Why? Because that is what you expect "leaders" to do. The more experience you have, the less you care about others' expectations and the more you do whatever the group you are leading needs from you. But your role still defines you to some extent.

The Milgram experiments showed how far people will go when they are following orders, but I think they also demonstrated that our social roles matter. The subjects were labeled "Teacher" and given specific instructions on what this role entailed—delivering electric shocks to Learners who missed questions. Thus, to get his project off the ground, Milgram needed to have his subjects buy into a social role that came with distinctly odd expectations. The force of authority came into play when it became glaringly apparent to the subjects that the role was actually "Punisher"—not Teacher.

The men of Police Battalion 101 faced a similar "role switch." Before the morning of the massacre, they were members of a police unit. The unit's mission, backed by honorable moral norms, was to maintain public order and protect citizens from criminals. The Nazis switched this up, replacing the "policeman" role with a state-sanctioned "executioner" identity. The urgency of the situation—the orders had to be carried out that very day—gave the men little time to consider what higher duties might conflict with this switch. But at least twelve men had the presence of mind to object, holding firm to the policing role and refusing to participate in the massacre.

A high school classmate of Milgram's, Stanford professor Philip Zimbardo, famously set out to study the power of social labels to induce "bad behavior" in an otherwise normal group of people. In a real-life version of William Golding's *Lord of the Flies*, Zimbardo set up a "prison" in the basement of a Stanford building in 1971 and arbitrarily assigned twelve student volunteers to play roles as "guards" while an equal number had to be "prisoners." The guards were given the trappings of their social role, including guard uniforms, sunglasses, and wooden batons symbolizing their power. This experiment, now known as the Stanford Prison Experiment, is chronicled in Zimbardo's book *The Lucifer Effect*. Zimbardo himself played the self-assigned role of "superintendent" overseeing the guards and took notes as his "employees" became increasingly aggressive in their treatment of fellow students.

In recent years, this experiment has been strongly criticized because audiotapes suggest that student guards were coached into acting tougher than they might otherwise have done. And one of the student prisoners has reported that he used the experiment as an opportunity to go slightly haywire to relieve the boredom of an academic summer session, not because he was a "prisoner." These revelations indicate that Zimbardo, unlike Milgram, was a sloppy social scientist. But they do not, at least in my mind, negate the main finding: that many of the students became swept up in their make-believe prison world, behaving in ways they would never have acted in their ordinary lives.

I find Zimbardo's experiment plausible because I have witnessed the same phenomenon countless times in my work as a negotiation trainer. If you tell people they are negotiators for "Warring States," you will get aggressive, deceitful behavior and many rounds of spiraling conflict. If you take the exact same negotiation payoff structure but label the exercise as "Winning Hearts and Minds," many of the people playing the negotiator roles will work hard to establish trust so they can find win-win outcomes.

Another bit of evidence—the way the experiment ended—also suggests to me that the Stanford Prison Experiment, however flawed, touched a core of behavioral truth. A psychology PhD student named Christina Maslach came into the setup from outside to conduct interviews and quickly sensed that the behavior she was observing from the guards violated basic moral norms. At her urging, Zimbardo stopped the experiment on ethical grounds on the sixth day of what was supposed to be a two-week experience.

Maslach's experience suggests that your social role can be a source of ethical protection rather than danger. It may enable you to persuasively reference professional and moral standards others have lost sight of and that support doing the right thing. Maslach was not given a formal "prison" role to play in the Stanford Prison Experiment but instead brought her ethical standards as a professional social scientist. That social role provided a very different lens for evaluating what was going on.

5. Systemic Pressure: The Power of Social Structures

When you add all four of the above pressures into a single mix, and then add widespread cultural beliefs about "the way things are done," you arrive at our fifth force: "The System." If you are crossing a border in a poor, developing country and a customs officer demands a bribe to let you enter, you are probably confronting a "system" problem, not just a single instance of situational pressure by officials abusing their role. Corruption may be a way of life for the entire immigration authority. Either you pay the bribe and get on with your journey or you try to talk your way out of it. But the border crossing kiosk may not be the best forum for waging your own private war on systemic corruption.

Widely shared cultural norms that undercut basic morality and fairness present some of the most difficult challenges for people of conscience. Such system-wide corruption can include everything from cultural acceptance of racism and sexism to Wall Street norms that condone insider trading and corporate cultures that encourage ripping off customers or investors. When "everybody does it," otherwise immoral and unethical behaviors become normalized. To overcome a corrupt system, you may need to form alliances with people who have exceptional levels of commitment and moral courage. And the process is likely to look more like a sustained, multi-step political campaign than a one-on-one dialogue or confrontation. Taking on a system means "speaking truth to power."

I have used Zimbardo's experiment to illustrate the power of identity-anchoring social roles. But Zimbardo considered it a demonstration of the indirect-but-pervasive power of the larger systems that allocate control in a social order. As he saw it, Milgram's experiments showed the direct influence of authority over individuals, while Zimbardo had illustrated how social concepts such as a "prison" set the norms everyone is obliged to stay within. In other words, social roles gain their legitimacy from the social structures that contain them.

The prison setup imported a wide-ranging set of expectations about the dominance of the "guard" role in a "prison system." So it must have seemed to the men of Police Battalion 101. In the Germany of World War II, racial hatred against Jews had been perversely woven into the fabric of the nation's culture, releasing the men from standard, moral beliefs about the sanctity of innocent human life. Genocide was no longer a crime. Jews were no longer people. Standing behind these norms was a Nazi power structure that was firm, unified, and brutally coercive. Against such a force, even the twelve men who refused to participate in the massacre were helpless. By their continued service in the unit, they were complicit with this system.

Finally, it is worth noting that, like authority and peer pressure, social systems can be constructed to work toward the good. One of the great leadership challenges for people of conscience is creating ethical work environments in which "doing the right thing" is the norm, not the exception. We will touch on this issue in the final chapter.

A MOMENT OF REFLECTION

As we wrap up this chapter, you may find it useful to reflect on your own past experiences in the face of pressures from peers, authorities, incentives, role expectations, and larger social structures. My guess is that you have encountered them all and, depending on the situation, pushed back against some and yielded to others. Nobody is morally strong enough to stand up for themselves and their values all the time against all opposing forces.

Try to remember a time when you felt the pressure of peers or bosses to compromise your standards or values—but found a way to effectively assert yourself. What were some of the factors that led to your success? The strength of your beliefs? A creative solution that solved the problem a better way? An ally who stood with you? The credibility of your social role in standing for these values?

How about an example of when you yielded to some of these pressures and later regretted it? My students have reported many such examples. They have ranged from accommodating peers who asked for help cheating on exams to padding expense accounts and lying about the number of billable hours they worked because it seemed "everyone was doing it."

One particularly moving story came from a woman who, as a young adult, was close friends with a young gay man who was a member of her family's church. When church leaders discovered that her friend was gay, they forced him out of the congregation. Torn between her loyalty to her friend and her commitment to her family, which endorsed the church's action, she did nothing to help him. Years later and with more independence regarding both her family and faith, she deeply regretted her failure to act on his behalf. She told me that she drew on this episode from her past for motivation to proactively support gay causes. She also learned a powerful lesson about balancing the potential consequences of speaking up for her values versus the lifetime of remorse that can follow if you remain silent.

NEXT UP: THE ROLE OF CHARACTER IN OWNING YOUR VALUES

With an appreciation for your values and the pressures you face to compromise them, it is now time to turn your attention to how you can assume responsibility for the ethical problem in front of you. As I have mentioned several times, I think this stage of the values-to-action process is the toughest one because it can be so easy, in the face of pressure, to talk yourself into looking the other way. The Conscience Code therefore provides three rules to help you mobilize the confidence you need to step up. The next chapter, Rule #4 ("Summon Your Character"), begins this investigation where all great philosophers and religions do: with your personal integrity. What habits of behavior do you consider nonnegotiable in the way you live your life? How can you practice these habits so they stand by you when your values are tested?

RULE #4: SUMMON YOUR CHARACTER

"Heroes don't fall from the sky.
They're just ordinary people who stepped forward."
—Web comment on the death of Dr. Li Wenliang,
Chinese physician who first warned of the dangers
of COVID-19

Y ou now have a clearer appreciation of the difficulties that await you
when you are called to stand up for your values. But there is good
news: to meet these challenges, you have three powerful allies that will, if
you summon them, bolster your confidence and help you succeed. These
include your character (Rule #4), personality strengths (Rule #5), and
trusted partners who share your values (Rule #6).

We start with Rule #4: Summon Your Character. Character has many
facets, from generosity to loyalty, but the one you will call on most often
to overcome the forces we met in the last chapter is courage. Courage is
your willingness to step forward on behalf of your values even though
you are experiencing anxiety about the consequences of doing so.

You may see courage as a rare trait, something only heroes exhibit.
But we will see that it is often less daunting than that. Aristotle taught
us that courage is the "golden mean" between cowardly timidity on the
one hand and reckless disregard for your safety on the other. Acting
courageously requires no more (or less) than this: sound, practical judgment about risk. People who behave courageously don't overthink it. They
weigh the possible consequences of taking action, remind themselves of
their duties, and confront how they will feel about themselves if they

retreat. An essential step: reminding yourself that your core values are worth fighting for.

The chapter proceeds as follows. First, we will examine what character is and where it comes from. A vivid, real-world example of character-in-action will help frame these questions. Next, we'll look more closely at the key emotional obstacles you may confront when deciding to step forward: fear and its more subtle sibling, anxiety. That will bring us to a deeper examination of courage. The chapter concludes with an investigation of the great enemy of character—rationalization.

It is easier to recognize good character than to describe it. To begin, therefore, I'd like you to consider the following story from the life of a twenty-seven-year-old man working as a part-time security guard. He confronted what can best be described as a once-in-a-lifetime "moral emergency," but he got through it by drawing on the same inner resources we tap into every time we choose to do the right thing instead of the safe thing: our commitment to our values and the courage to stand for something larger than ourselves.

"I GOT YOU, BUDDY"

It was a Friday morning at Parkrose High School near Portland, Oregon, when the calls started coming in to Keanon Lowe, the school's football coach who also served as one of its three security guards. Students were reporting an active shooter at the school. An eighteen-year-old boy named Angel Granados-Diaz had been seen with a shotgun wrapped under a garment bag. He was upset and talking about suicide. Lowe sprinted to the hallway where Granados-Diaz had last been seen and entered the classroom where the call had come from. To his surprise, Granados-Diaz came into the classroom just behind him, pulling out his shotgun as he entered the room. Screaming students scrambled to exit by the other door.

As Lowe turned to face him, the boy turned the gun toward himself, reaching for the trigger. But before he could get off a shot, Lowe lunged forward, wrapping him in his arms. With one hand, Lowe wrestled the gun out of the boy's hands and backed both of them out of the classroom and into the adjacent hallway. Another school staffer in the hall took the weapon Lowe handed to him.

Then, instead of pinning Granados-Diaz to the floor and securing him until law enforcement could arrive, Lowe embraced the boy the way a loving father might, letting him sob on his shoulder. "Nobody cares about me!" Granados-Diaz was crying. Lowe spoke softly into his ear, "I care about you . . . I got you, buddy," he said. As he later explained, "I just wanted to let him know I was there for him . . . [that] I was there for a reason and that this . . . life [is] worth living."

Lowe was the former captain of the nationally ranked 2014 University of Oregon football team. So he knew a thing or two about powering through his fears to tackle an opposing player who did not want to be stopped. He later told his former Oregon coach, Chip Kelly, that "it was kind of like you taught us on kickoff, coach. It may not be pretty, but we've just got to make sure we get him to the ground." Lowe's football experience thus played a role in his decision to run toward rather than away from this danger. But where did his instinct to show compassion instead of hostility to Granados-Diaz come from?

Bruce Alexander, a law enforcement expert with wide-ranging experience in crisis situations, later praised Lowe in an interview with the *New York Times*. "I think it says a lot about his character," Alexander commented. Typically, he went on, people either freeze or flee when they confront a life-threatening crisis. Lowe not only neutralized the danger in this case, but also brought exceptional humanity to his embrace of the troubled boy.

As Lowe explained in an interview with the cable sports channel ESPN, "It wasn't in me to beat him or hold him down or hurt him, even though it was seconds after this crazy thing happened. . . . I felt how scared he was; I felt it all."

Summing up the entire episode, Lowe put it this way: "When confronted with the test the universe presented me with, I didn't see any other choice but to act. Thank God, I passed."

WHAT IS CHARACTER?

Bruce Alexander thought that Lowe exhibited "character." But what exactly does that word mean? Philosophers and psychologists have debated this question for centuries, but I'd like to keep it simple: character describes people's tendency to prioritize the social good over their own self-interest. At one extreme, there are people of notably bad character who exploit others whenever possible. Psychologists have identified what they call the "Dark Triad" of personality traits that characterize these selfish (perhaps truly evil) people: narcissism (a pathological need for approval and self-aggrandizement), Machiavellianism (a propensity for cold, calculating social manipulation), and psychopathology (apparently normal people who ruthlessly exploit others because they are incapable of empathy, guilt, and shame). When you have bosses or coworkers with these traits, run for cover. They will betray every trust others put in them and then set you up to take the blame for their actions.

Good character of the type Lowe exhibited lies at the other end of the spectrum. It consists of three facets. First, you must have *moral impulses* that prompt you to behave well (in a prosocial way) in the face of temptations and pressures to behave badly. Psychopaths lack such impulses. Second, you need to have enough *awareness* to know that these moral values are relevant in the situation you face. This means recognizing that there may be conflict between what you are feeling pressed to do and what your values demand. Finally, you must bring sufficient *self-discipline* to "take ownership" of the situation and act on your values when it is costly or inconvenient to do so. When you have a discerning level of moral awareness and a lot of self-discipline, you are said to have "strong character."

In talking about character, it is easy to get lost in the philosophical weeds of whether humans have free will (if not, then holding people responsible for moral choices is a problem) and long-standing psychological debates over whether "personality" or "situation" dominates as the cause of human action (if behavior consists entirely of robot-like responses to situational stimuli, then self-discipline loses its place as an aspect of character). After years of head-spinning efforts to sort out these and related controversies, I find myself somewhere in the middle of the warring camps. I hope you will join me on this middle ground for the rest of this book.

We will be assuming that you can freely choose to behave well or badly, at least some of the time. So character matters. But as we saw in the last chapter, even people of generally "good" character can be prompted to do some very bad things if enough situational pressures are applied. Your actions, then, are the product of an interaction between circumstance and choice.

Two important insights can help you tip the balance more often in favor of actions that reflect good character. First, you can harness situational forces to your advantage by living (as much as possible) in positive moral environments—such as a loving family and an ethical workplace. Working to help create such environments for yourself and others can be an important part of a well-lived life—a point emphasized by Rule #10 ("Choose to Lead"). Second, good behavior requires less effort (and therefore becomes more automatic) when you establish it through daily practice as a habit. Every parent trying to teach their children to say "please" and "thank you" is showing commitment to this insight—which applies to virtues such as honesty and accountability just as much as to common courtesy. Most religions provide inspiration and reinforcement for such habits. The ancient Greeks also understood character this way. Will Durant's pithy summary of Aristotle says it best: "You are what you repeatedly do. Excellence [of character] is therefore not an act, but a habit."

We will also assume that character is affected by certain morally significant, stable personality traits—patterns of behavior that have a genetic component. The Dark Triad marks out the negative side. But there is a positive side, too. You probably know people who are naturally accommodating and cooperative. This trait can give rise to virtuous acts of generosity.

Thus, when it comes to personality, it can be useful to distinguish between two types of morally relevant traits: those baked into your genetic inheritance and those that require more intention to establish as character habits. For example, practicing the virtue of compassion requires you to sense that someone else is suffering. People endowed with a genetic gift for empathy can sense such suffering on an individual level without much effort, giving them many opportunities to practice this virtue. People lower in empathy who nevertheless aspire to behave compassionately may need to work harder at it. They might try to improve their empathy through training and practice. For example, I once taught in an FBI hostage negotiation program that trained nononsense law enforcement officers to be empathetic listeners. I suspect that this training helped some of them to be more effective fathers, mothers, and spouses, not just crisis negotiators.

In their book, *Character Strengths and Virtues*, positive psychologists Christopher Peterson and Martin Seligman provide a list of twenty-four character-related personality traits and an assessment to help you measure which ones come most naturally to you. Their list includes such items as a passion for justice/fairness, honesty, diligence, social intelligence, optimism, leadership, bravery, discretion, self-control, and citizenship. You can assess yourself on all twenty-four of these traits by taking the VIA Character Strengths Survey (VIA stands for "Virtues in Action") on the VIA Institute on Character's website.

I have taken this assessment many times as part of my teaching work, and I consistently score very high in diligence and optimism but much lower in citizenship. This insight helped me understand why I needed to acquire a deliberate habit for voting (which I neglected when I was in my twenties) but require no special prompts to submit my grades on time or look at the bright side when I suffer a setback.

Other psychologists have devised an Honesty-Humility personality scale that is tailored to measure traits related to ethical conduct, such as transparency, respect for rules, humility, and modesty. That assessment, which is part of a larger, comprehensive model of personality, can be found by searching online for the "Hexaco Personality Inventory." I score high on transparency and respect for rules but, to be transparent about it, need to work harder when it comes to humility and modesty. You can also investigate this scale in more detail in Kibeom Lee's and Michael C. Ashton's book, *The H Factor of Personality: Why Some People Are Manipulative, Self-Entitled, Materialistic, and Exploitative—and Why It Matters for Everyone.*

The traits you actually exhibit in your behavior are the product of several intermingled factors: your situational environment (treated in the last chapter), the positive social habits you have acquired through training and practice (explored in this chapter), and your baseline personality (investigated in the next chapter: Rule #5, "Channel Your Personality Strengths").

WHERE DO CHARACTER HABITS COME FROM?

Both the psychological and the philosophical/religious views of character share a common belief: whatever genetic character traits you were born with, good character habits are best nurtured through daily practice. The family you were raised in—or, lacking strong parental role models, the relatives, teachers, coaches, pastors, and others who substituted for them—were the proving grounds for creating these habits. Depending on your personality, some of these were easier for you to learn than others.

Every semester I ask my students to reflect on the people and experiences that have shaped their characters in positive ways. I invite you to do the same. Such reflections help you redouble your commitment to the lessons you learned early in your life and prepare you for bigger challenges that lie ahead. Consider, for example, this story an MBA student ("Bill") told our class about a lasting character lesson his father taught him.

When Bill was ten years old, he entered a two-day "soapbox derby." These are races kids compete in while sitting in small, wheeled carts they have built themselves (in a former era, these boxes were crates for delivering soap). The racers are placed at the top of a hill and zoom down using only the power of gravity. The winners are those with the fastest times. Given that the competition extended over two days in Bill's case, there were strict rules that forbade repairing or tampering with the racers between Day 1 and Day 2.

Bill finished near the top of his group after the first day and was excited by the prospect of coming in first place overall on Day 2. On his way home with his dad, he said he had heard some kids talking about fixing their racers overnight and wondered out loud if it would be OK if he lubricated his wheels a little bit. His father answered without ever taking his eyes off the road. "You could do that," he said. "But then you would never know if you could have won without breaking the rules." Bill said he thought about it and decided not to touch the racer. He ended up in third place the next day and was disappointed to lose. But he never forgot the choice his father had given him—a lifelong character lesson about winning fair and square.

Character education does not stop just because you grow up. As the son of a Marine Corps general, I not only learned the usual character lessons about honesty and reliability at home, but I watched every day as rigorous military training instilled character habits in the recruits who aspired to become professional soldiers. These habits included self-discipline, team loyalty, and, to quote a famous American military motto: duty, honor, country. Military training provides an especially intense environment for acquiring character habits, and many report that these habits last a lifetime. As you reflect on your own character, consider the classrooms, sports, summer jobs, early work experiences, and even personal traumas that have instilled the character habits you now draw on.

CHARACTER AT HOME VS. CHARACTER AT WORK

As I suggested above, there is a dispute between those who see all behavior as situationally driven and those who, like me, view character as an inner aspect of yourself that you can, with self-discipline, bring with you from one situation to another. One way to test who is right in this debate is to ask whether someone's character is stable between their personal and professional lives.

Keanon Lowe's story provides encouragement that a character-based approach to your personal life can indeed carry over to how you behave at work. So let's dig a little deeper into it.

First, Lowe's actions exhibited habits acquired both at home and in sports. Chip Kelly, Lowe's former Oregon football coach (and later a coach for the Philadelphia Eagles and San Francisco 49ers in the National Football League), later commented that, "Keanon's preparation for what happened has been engrained in him for a long, long time." Raised in a modest neighborhood a few miles from Parkrose High School, Lowe was taking responsibility as "the man of the house" by the age of nine, helping his then-single mother to care for his younger brother. He was taking his duties seriously from an early age.

He also started playing football in high school, acquiring habits of teamwork, leadership, and self-discipline. Part of his football training required him to become comfortable with physical danger. He had never captured an active shooter before that day at Parkrose High School, but he had tackled hundreds of football players, many much bigger than he was, trying to run over him at top speed. When Lowe spoke to Chip Kelly after the Parkrose High School incident, Lowe used football terminology to describe the habits that had kicked in during the emergency. As I noted earlier, Lowe told Kelly that the events of that morning had felt like he was trying to make a tackle during the kickoff of a football game.

Second, Lowe's decision to work at Parkrose High School was part of a larger, values-oriented approach to life that was grounded in character. Parkrose was not just a "job." He was there for a reason. After college, Lowe followed Coach Kelly to the National Football League as an offensive analyst, working first for the Philadelphia Eagles and then for the San Francisco 49ers. But Kelly's pro coaching career was short-lived, and when Kelly was fired from the 49ers, Lowe was cut loose.

Then came a tragic, life-altering event: Lowe's best friend from both his high school and college years, Taylor Martinek, was found dead of a drug overdose. Lowe had known Martinek was sinking into addiction but had been too busy with his glamorous NFL career to pay attention. Now, with his friend gone forever, he blamed himself for failing to provide the support that might have saved his life. Lowe returned to his hometown on a mission, motivated by remorse over what he considered a major character failure. He was determined to find ways he could play a positive role in young people's lives.

He started as a volunteer for his former high school football team, work that combined the sport he loved with his new sense of purpose. Next, he landed a paid coaching job at Parkrose High School. The school was locally famous for its dismal football team, which had a twenty-three-game losing streak. Nobody wanted to coach it. But the twenty-seven-year-old Lowe was thrilled to get the chance. He agreed to become one of the school's three security guards as part of the deal.

Thus, lurking in the back of Lowe's mind every single day was his personal commitment to never again let someone down as he had let down his best friend. One of the first calls he made after the incident was to a close high school friend who had also known Taylor Martinek. "Taylor was with me," he told his friend as he described why he had embraced Granados-Diaz with such compassion. "He was right there the whole time."

It was an accident that Lowe was on security detail the day the active-shooter alarm went off at Parkrose High School, but he was ready for the moment because he had been focused on his character for years before that day. His values were front and center in both his private and his professional life. Fate gave him a test of whether, under pressure, he would act on those values when his job demanded it.

Lowe's example gives us hope that building good character habits at home can set the stage for doing the right thing at the office. But his story also shows that consistency of character takes intentional effort. And it seems that the higher you go in terms of status and power, the easier it may be to stop making this effort, leaving your character at home when you go to work. Business and political history are full of stories about corrupt leaders who appear to have led exemplary personal lives. CEO/ felons such as Enron's Ken Lay and WorldCom's Bernie Ebbers were beloved by their children and regularly taught Sunday school classes at church. Yet they led massive frauds at the office. Maintaining your character, then, is an ongoing project that requires you to bring your "best self" from your personal life to your duties at work.

Unfaithful at Home, Crooked at Work

What about the other way? Suppose you found out that a financial advisor you had hired to help you invest for retirement had been repeatedly arrested for shoplifting—i.e., that they had manifestly demonstrated bad character in their personal life. Would you believe them when they said these were just "personal matters" that would not affect their professional behavior toward your account? I doubt it. A massive new research study published in the prestigious *Proceedings of the National Academy of Sciences* confirms your instinct. Bad behavior at home does, in fact, predict bad behavior at work.

In 2015, hackers revealed the personal identities of millions of users of a website called Ashley Madison, an online dating service for married people seeking to have "discreet encounters." Its corporate slogan: "Life is short. Have an affair."

Seeing a golden opportunity to test whether misconduct in personal life might be linked to bad behavior in the professional realm, a team of social scientists used this treasure trove of data to find Ashley Madison users who had also been sanctioned for workplace misconduct. Their search came up with 960 Chicago police officers with proven professional infractions against the public; 1,319 financial advisors who had cheated clients; 613 white-collar criminals sanctioned for insider trading and fraud; and 149 CEOs, CFOs, and other C-suite executives leading firms that had misstated their financials or engaged in other corporate wrongdoing. They then created randomized control groups of similarly situated professionals in each employment area—people who did not use Ashley Madison but who had profiles as close as possible to the study's target group of felons in age, marital status, qualifications, years of experience, location, and so on.

Their statistical tests showed that Ashley Madison users were much more likely than average professionals to have workplace misconduct records. Specifically, C-suite executives, financial advisors, and police officers who used Ashley Madison were two times more likely than their peers to have been caught breaking the rules at work. Securities traders who used Ashley Madison were *three times* more likely to be convicted of insider trading and fraud.

Summing up, the researchers concluded that "personal and professional lives are connected" in ways that make it easy for bad character habits to travel from home to office.

FIVE SIMPLE TRUTHS ABOUT CHARACTER

Capping off this investigation of character, I want to offer five simple "truths" that may help you call on this inner resource when you feel workplace pressures are pushing you to compromise your values.

You Will Make Mistakes. Your actions result from a complex mix of situational pressures, learned character habits, and genes. Because everyone has their character tested every day, you should expect to fall short of your aspirations some of the time. Keanon Lowe let his best friend down. One of my all-time historical heroes, American founding father and scientific genius Benjamin Franklin, wrote in his autobiography that as a young man he had stolen money from a friend, broken a promise to his half brother to assist with his printing business, and abandoned his fiancée for over a year while he was in London (she married someone else in his absence). He felt deep remorse over all of these lapses and did his best to make up for them. Perhaps as a result of his early failings, character meant a lot to him. His writings on its importance for a truly successful life, as well as his advice on how to use a daily diary to practice good character habits, are as justly famous as his experiments on electricity. When you fall short, resolve to do better next time—as Keanon Lowe did when he turned his character lapse into his motivation for serving others.

It's Not about You. Good character is about focusing on others—people, causes, and duties that are larger than yourself. Keanon Lowe did this both in disarming Granados-Diaz (helping his community) and in consoling him (showing compassion for his suffering). Poor character is the opposite. You let yourself down when you favor yourself at others' expense.

Self-Discipline Is Essential. You need self-discipline to overcome self-protective impulses and selfish desires. The greater your self-discipline in the face of pressures to relax your standards of conduct, the stronger your character. Self-discipline is a muscle. It gets stronger with use and rapidly loses its effectiveness when you let it lapse.

Habits Help. When good character practices become habits, you don't need as much self-discipline. This applies to telling the truth, being generous, exercising patience, and, most importantly, choosing to lead by standing up for yourself and your values.

Social Environments and Networks Matter. If you want to stay healthy, don't swim in a polluted pond. Your character is influenced by the behavior of those around you, so pay attention to the values of the people you work (or hang out) with. Entrepreneur and author Jim Rohn once put it this way: "You are the average of the five people you spend most of your time with." Lesson: always stay in touch with friends who are, like you, people of conscience. You'll need their support when your values are on the line.

CHARACTER, FEAR, AND COURAGE

As you saw above, self-discipline is an important anchor for your character. When it comes to speaking up for your values, the self-discipline you need will likely relate to one of your strongest and most uncomfortable emotions: fear. If you push back against your peers or bosses, will they react angrily? Could your relationships, job, or career be at risk?

In this section, I want to help you understand a bit more about the fear and anxiety you will inevitably face in crisis moments. That, in turn, will bring us to that daunting word we often use when people behave well in the face of fear: courage.

Working through Fear and Anxiety

In his book *The Emotional Brain: The Mysterious Underpinnings of Emotional Life*, New York University neuroscientist Joseph LeDoux explains that fear is one of evolution's most important emotions—one we share with virtually every sensate form of life. It is evolution's way of sensing threats in our environment so we can get out of harm's way as quickly and effectively as possible. Anxiety, LeDoux teaches, is what we feel when we worry about a future threat without being able to confront it directly. As LeDoux puts it, anxiety is "unresolved fear."

The benefit of both emotions is that they prompt us to pay attention to things that may endanger our well-being. The problem with them in modern life is that, while relatively few things pose mortal dangers compared to the days when humans lived in caves, our emotions are still wired by evolution to respond to risks with all-hands-on-deck alarms. Indeed, these fear circuits can often run out of control, as happens with Post-Traumatic Stress Disorder (PTSD), panic attacks, phobias, and other chronic psychological conditions. These specialized disorders require clinical intervention, so I will not be discussing them here. But the ordinary fears that may accompany conflicts over values at work can be surprisingly manageable. In fact, dealing with most workplace fears is a bit like stepping into the waves at a beach first thing in the morning. It is cold and uncomfortable at first but, if you are willing to jump in, you will get used to it.

To start, as LeDoux demonstrates, it is important to realize that the word "fear" is an *interpretation* we give to a set of strong, automatic bodily responses that happen *just before* we consciously perceive a threat. Modern neuroscience has shown that, by the time you consciously "see" a snake ahead of you in the grass and feel fear, your body is already being flooded with adrenalin and the process of backing away has started. Your brain is that fast. In non-human animals, LeDoux explains, the usual response to danger includes an initial "startle," followed by "orienting, then freezing or fleeing or attacking."

We humans respond the same way. In addition to the startle response, the bodily sensations we feel that signal a threat include, according to LeDoux, "taut stomach, racing heart, high blood pressure, clammy hands and feet, and dry mouth." This is what we mean when we talk about "sweating out" a situation that makes us anxious.

Consider this report by Cynthia Cooper, the internal auditor at WorldCom, Inc. who blew the whistle on CEO Bernie Ebbers and CFO Scott Sullivan for their massive accounting fraud—a story we saw unfold at the beginning of the last chapter. Part of Cooper's success stemmed from her professional courage: she was able to work through the physical symptoms of fear and stay on task in highly stressful circumstances.

At one point in the story, recounted in her book, *Extraordinary Circumstances*, Cooper was about to meet with Controller David Myers to find out whether a crucial accounting item worth hundreds of millions of dollars had any documented justification. She knew the fate of the company might turn on his response.

As she waited outside Myers's office, she reports, "My heart was racing and my palms were damp with sweat." She could have walked away and relieved her stress, but her professional sense of duty propelled her forward. Once the meeting began, Myers quickly admitted to her that no justification existed. Cooper's fear for WorldCom's future was realized, transitioning her from a state of anxious uncertainty to a focus on next steps. "My heart sinks," she continues in her account, switching to the present tense. "All of the anxieties that have been building over the previous weeks culminate in these few dreaded moments. I know that something is terribly wrong." Cooper's personal role in this scandal reflects so many dimensions of the Conscience Code that we will revisit her story in detail when we investigate Rule #9 ("Hold Them Accountable").

Understanding that fear is the by-product of an involuntary biological process that produces a standard set of physical symptoms can remind you that these sensations are seldom 100 percent accurate as indicators of danger. They are just signs that your body is having a "threat response." Your next move should be to examine your situation more closely to see if the threat is real, imagined, underestimated, or exaggerated. Stanford University psychologists have discovered that you can handle emotional stresses much more effectively if you adopt what they call a "stress mindset"—the belief that you can mitigate the effects of fear and anxiety by talking back to them.

Two time-tested tools can help you cope.

Talk Yourself Down. Your body may be treating an upcoming meeting with your boss as if it were an encounter with a saber-toothed tiger, but when fear finally pops into your consciousness, use your judgment to talk yourself down. What, after all, is the worst-case scenario for this meeting? What can you do to reduce the chances of that result? Once you remember that your life is not in danger, you can refocus on your goal, take a deep breath, and knock on the door.

Put your situation in perspective. A workplace conflict over values is probably not even the most dangerous thing you face on an average day in a modern city. Merging at high speed onto a crowded freeway on your morning commute is more dangerous to your physical safety than any meeting you will ever attend. But you do it every day because you have practice working through the fear in that situation. In the same way, you can learn to live with fear in the context of workplace conflict by stepping outside yourself and looking at what is happening from a more objective point of view.

Recommit to Your Values as Goals. When fear strikes, remember the reasons you are taking action. One simple way to do this is to fill in the blanks of these sentences:

> "I am anxious about having a meeting with _____
> because I fear that _____. But this meeting is worth
> the effort because I care so deeply about _____
> [identify the core values you are standing up for]."

To summarize: fear and anxiety are normal parts of personal and professional life. As someone committed to being a person of conscience, you need to develop emotional stamina. Cynthia Cooper's example shows that speaking up for your values can be stressful, but she did not let herself be defined by her fears.

Neither should you.

A Final Word about Courage

Once you understand fear, courage becomes less daunting. "Courageous" is not what Keanon Lowe and Cynthia Cooper actually felt when they took action; it is what other people called them because they behaved well in spite of feeling fear.

This gets us back to character habits and values. You can "tame" even mortal fears by acquiring situationally based habits that allow you to function when you feel threatened. Soldiers, firefighters, and police officers feel fear when they go into action, but they have learned to cope with it through training. They practice redirecting their attention to what needs to be done next, sustaining themselves with professional pride, loyalty to teammates, and their missions. Similarly, people of conscience can calm their fears by carefully rehearsing with friends or colleagues for upcoming encounters. Role-playing before a crucial meeting does not eliminate fear. But it helps keep your anxiety in perspective. And the more practice you get handling defensive bosses and wayward peers in real-world settings, the calmer you will get.

Second, as I suggested above, you will cope with fear better when you focus your mind on what is really important to you—your values. Consider the remorse you will feel if you let those values down. Many people of conscience report they "had no choice" but to act. Recall Anne Frank's rescuer, Miep Gies, whom we met in the last chapter. "My decision to help," she said, "was because I saw no alternative. I could foresee many sleepless nights and an unhappy life if I refused."

SELF-DECEPTION:
HOW RATIONALIZATIONS UNDERMINE CHARACTER

Even bad people think well of themselves. Thus, a boss or colleague who is pressuring you to do something wrong very likely believes that they are nevertheless a good person. This requires them to be adept at various forms of self-deception, especially denial and rationalization. Psychologists have many names for this: "moral disengagement," "motivated reasoning," and "self-concept maintenance." But they all describe the same basic human tendency to license self-interested behavior—up to and including cheating—by covering it up with a thin veneer of logic. The wise Benjamin Franklin once quipped, "So convenient a thing it is to be a Reasonable creature, since it enables one to find or make a Reason for everything one has a mind to do."

Forewarned is forearmed, so below I highlight a few examples of common workplace rationalizations. Treat them—and the many others like them—as red flags, warning you that you may be dealing with an acute case of self-deception. And of course, if you hear the quiet voice in your own mind whispering these things, it is time to renew your commitment to character.

The Rules Don't Apply to Me

The United States Navy fired 150 commanding officers between 2002 and 2012 for serious breaches of Navy regulations. The Navy's inspector general conducted a special, intense review of one five-year period during this span, examining in detail the records of eighty commanding officers who had been relieved of their command for misconduct. They wanted to see if any patterns emerged to help them understand why the Navy was facing this leadership crisis.

They found several. First, the #MeToo era seems to have gotten an early start in the Navy. This time period saw a spike in sexual misconduct complaints by women on active duty. As a result, roughly half of the officers were sanctioned for violating Navy rules against adultery, inappropriate relationships with people under their command, sexual assault, and sexual harassment.

Second, many of these officers allowed their authority to dull their character. In the words of the inspector general's report, the officers "felt they had the power to conceal their misdeeds." Psychologists have a special name for the phenomenon. They call it the Bathsheba Syndrome, after a famous episode in the Hebrew Bible in which King David (of David-and-Goliath fame) abused his kingly powers by sending one of his generals to a certain death so he could have an affair with the man's wife, Bathsheba.

Leadership scholar Donelson Forsyth summed up the syndrome this way in an interview with a military publication called *Stars and Stripes*: "Powerful people feel that they are entitled, that they get more of the group's resources and that the rules the group has established for the rank-and-file members do not apply to them." Navy vessels are floating dictatorships. The person in charge is sometimes surrounded with compliant staff officers who don't challenge their decisions. Before long, commanders start thinking they are above the rules.

A Navy warship presents exceptionally favorable conditions for this form of self-deception. As a result of the inspector general's investigation, the Navy War College now requires would-be commanding officers to understand this syndrome as part of their training.

But make no mistake: the same risk exists in every organization where the systems reminding top leaders of their accountability are weak, and those around a leader are unwilling to speak up on behalf of core values. Especially vivid instances of this blindness occur when billionaires ensnare others in insider trading rings and pressure accountants to help them cheat on their taxes. They don't need the money. But they see it as there for the taking: they are above the law.

Nobody Will Notice

My students report that their bosses sometimes tell them, when deadlines loom, to go ahead and leave false data or inaccurate analyses in reports to clients and customers. "Don't worry," the bosses say. "Nobody will notice."

The case of Jonathan Burrows provides a window into this mindset. Burrows was making over one million British pounds per year in the London office of BlackRock Asset Management, one of the world's largest financial institutions. He had more money than he needed, but he could not resist cheating to get a little more when he discovered a way to avoid paying the full fare on his commuter rail journey. By getting on the train at a little-monitored station in his rural area outside London, he saved nearly £15 per day. He exploited this loophole for seven consecutive years, ultimately cheating British Rail out of tens of thousands of pounds.

Then British Rail launched a major enforcement initiative to stop fare cheaters and caught Burrows in its net. His fine, with interest and penalties, came to £43,000, nearly $67,000 at the 2014 dollar exchange rate for pounds. Burrows's case stood out for the sheer scale of his theft, so the rail company referred it to the UK's Financial Conduct Authority, which oversees the financial services industry. The FCA interpreted Burrows's actions as evidence of a "suspect moral character" and applied its moral-behavior standard to ban him for life from holding any future job in financial services.

Burrows was outraged at the penalty. Surely, he said in a public statement, "the FCA has on its plate more profound wrongdoing than mine in the financial services sector." Perhaps. But if Burrows had brought a mask and a gun to the British Rail headquarters and robbed it of enough money to pay for a new BMW, the financial scope of his misconduct would be roughly the same. The fact that he thought "nobody would notice" if he stole the money a little at a time just reflects his lack of awareness that, as Durant said, "You are what you repeatedly do." Character, bad as well as good, is a habit.

Be a Team Player

In the last chapter, you saw how WorldCom's CFO Scott Sullivan and Controller David Myers persuaded accountants Betty Vinson and Troy

Normand to join their conspiracy by arguing that what they were doing was for the greater good. Sullivan appealed to their team spirit, telling them their help was required to save the business. Normally, it is great to be a team player. But when your team is cheating, you become a cheater, too—unless you summon your character and stand up for your values.

Just This Once

As Clay Christensen taught us when we talked about Rule #2 ("Commit to Your Values"), "It is easier to hold your principles 100 percent of the time than it is hold them 98 percent of the time." This is a powerful response when someone tempts you with the rationalization: "Just this once. We'll never do it again."

In the WorldCom scandal, Sullivan assured Vinson and Normand that their help was needed "just this once." Then "just this once" became every quarter and the pair was trapped in a criminal fraud. British Rail cheater Jonathan Burrows probably told himself "just this once" on the day he first discovered how he could beat the fare system for his commuter trip. The next day, he said it again. By the third day, he stopped telling himself anything at all. Cheating had become a habit that eventually ended his professional career.

Everybody Does It

This rationalization comes up more often in my Responsibility course than any other. Students refer to it as the "reason" they have engaged in everything from expense account abuse and falsifying sales reports to backdating documents and lying to investors. The habits built on these random bits of bad behavior set the stage for bigger problems later in a career.

For example, Doug Hodge, the former CEO of the giant investment firm PIMCO, was recently sentenced to nearly a year in prison for fraud. As a corporate leader, he had called on the finance industry to get its ethical house in order after the 2008 Wall Street crash. It was up to the people at the very top, he argued, to "personify trustworthy values."

But he failed to follow his own advice when it came to getting his children into elite colleges. Fearing that his kids might not be good enough to gain admission on their own, he allowed himself to be swept up in the college admissions bribery scheme run by Rick Singer (whom we met briefly when we discussed Rule #3, "Know Your Enemy"). With parents' help, Singer falsified wealthy kids' high school records to suggest that they were star athletes. He then used his clients' money to pay college coaches for "tagging" these kids to be specially admitted.

Hodge went along with Singer's scheme because he bought into a pervasive cynicism about college admissions. It's a game, Singer assured Hodge. Everybody does it. With this rationale to comfort him, this former CEO who advised others to "personify trustworthy values" doctored the pictures of one son playing football to make it appear that the other was a star football player worthy of special admission.

In the end, someone tipped off federal prosecutors about Singer's scheme—which had expanded to include hundreds of wealthy families—and "Operation Varsity Blues" was launched. Singer began secretly taping his conversations with his clients, including Hodge. Guilty pleas and jail time followed for film stars, managing partners at some of the best law firms in America, and top business leaders such as Hodge.

After he was sentenced, Hodge wrote a *mea culpa* essay for the *Wall Street Journal*. "In the 11 months since I answered that [first] call from the FBI," he wrote, "I've experienced all the confusion, anger, fear, regret, and remorse you'd expect." But most confusing of all for him was how to square his self-image as a "good person" with the fact that he was now a convicted felon. "I was raised with a strong moral compass," he asserted. "I've tried hard to live an ethical life."

He slipped all too easily into self-deception because, when "everyone" is cheating, you think of yourself as a "sucker" if you play by the rules. But Hodge knew what he was doing was wrong. In his essay, Hodge reflected that he would have been fine if only, at Singer's first mention of falsifying his children's high school records, he had listened to his "conscience."

I Deserve This

A few years ago, my students reported in class that virtually every junior employee at a well-known consulting firm falsified their expense accounts. Many requested reimbursement for take-out meals they had eaten at home or taxis they had used for personal reasons. Still others collected receipts from friends for restaurant meals and taxis and submitted these as their own for business-related expenses. It was standard practice when visiting firm offices in distant cities to submit expense claims for $39 every day even when they had no expenses at all. Why $39? Because they were not required to submit any receipts for expense claims of less than $40.

They felt little remorse for their actions. Instead, they blamed their employer because the firm under-compensated them for the ninety-hour weeks they endured. They felt they deserved to "tip themselves" with tax-free cash. Thus, "everyone does it" combined with "I deserve this" to create a corrupt office culture.

A moment's thought would have revealed that the actual victims of the fraud were the firm's clients. And some of these clients were government agencies, nonprofits, and even charities. The same rationalization can lead to everything from tax evasion to falsifying hourly bills in service businesses such as law and consulting. When people let a self-serving sense of "injustice" about their compensation take over their professionalism, it is easy for them to lose sight of their character values.

Once this rationalization locks in, larger frauds can appear less "wrong." Scott Capps, a longtime manager at a large mutual fund company, was sent to jail for stealing over $2 million from the firm by pillaging "dormant" accounts held in the names of dead and long-inactive customers. These assets were part of an area of operations he oversaw, and as his resentment grew over his failure to get the raises he felt he deserved, he eventually came to see the money as a justified supplement to his modest $65,000 salary. He felt like a "cog in a machine," Capps later told an interviewer. "They squeezed too hard." His brother-in-law (and co-conspirator) eventually could not stand the stress of the guilt he felt over the theft and confessed the whole scheme to the police. Both went to jail.

I'm Just Following Orders

In the wake of the atrocities committed during World War II, the time-honored "I was following orders" rationalization lost some of its force when Nazi war criminals were not allowed to rely on it. But it remains alive and well in organizational life. Take, for example, UBS banker Bradley

Birkenfeld, who was arrested as part of the largest tax fraud investigation in US history. UBS was seeking new business from ultra-wealthy clients, and one of its premier programs was helping clients hide their assets in secret Swiss accounts. They became very creative at this work. As part of his job, for example, Birkenfeld was asked to carry clients' assets bought with money from offshore accounts back into the USA to avoid taxes. In one case, he stuffed a customer's expensive diamonds into a toothpaste tube.

Eventually, sensing that the scheme was unraveling, Birkenfeld reported UBS to the US authorities, triggering a major investigation of both UBS and the Swiss banking system. But prosecutors found he had failed to cooperate fully with their investigation by withholding key evidence against one of his clients. So, despite his whistleblower status, they prosecuted him vigorously for his own part in the crime. As he was being sentenced to a federal jail term, he pleaded that he had simply been carrying out firm policies. As he put it, "I was incentivized to do this business." The judge was not impressed with his excuse and ordered him to jail for thirty-one months.

In the end, however, he got his revenge on everyone. Based on his testimony, UBS paid a $780 million fine and was forced to release the names of its formerly secret list of tax evaders. Ever the opportunist, Birkenfeld then applied for "whistleblower" status under the federal False Claims Act—a statute that allows whistleblowers to be paid a percentage of what the government collects in a corporate crime (more on this in Rule #9, "Hold Them Accountable"). The courts ruled that he was entitled to collect a $104 million award, the largest whistleblower bounty ever given. He now lives the luxurious life of the ultra-wealthy clients he once served—as an ex-felon.

A MOMENT FOR PERSONAL REFLECTION

As you think about the role of character in personal conflicts you have faced, look back on occasions when you may have let a rationalization overwhelm your conscience, leading you to do something you now regret. Did you really believe the rationalization that it was OK to do something just because "Everybody does it"? The Chinese have a saying that pushes back on temptations of this kind. It goes like this: "Never do evil just because it is a small evil." Can you commit to that as an ethical rule? Here are a few mantras that my students use to pierce through rationalizations so they can summon their true character:

- What would my grandmother (or Jesus, Buddha, or Muhammad) do in this situation?
- Assume everyone will eventually know everything. How would I feel if my conduct was revealed on the front page of the *Wall Street Journal*?
- Real winners don't cheat.
- Who may pay a price in the future if I rationalize this behavior now?
- Would I be proud to tell my children or grandchildren about what I have done (or neglected to do)?
- I am what I do. Are my actions building or breaking good character habits?

Now consider an occasion when you felt the tug of a rationalization but your character came through for you. Perhaps it was tempting to lie concerning something you were embarrassed about, but you caught yourself in time and took full responsibility for it. What helped you make that decision—the one you now look back on and feel good about? How can you bring that self-discipline to more moments that matter in your life?

NEXT UP: THE ROLE OF PERSONALITY IN ETHICAL CONFLICT

Your moral motivations can help you recognize the ethical problem you face, and your character will help you overcome your fears about taking responsibility for the situation. Another factor that will strengthen your willingness to step up and own the conflict: your personality strengths. How assertive are you? Can you hold your own in a confrontation with someone? To what extent do you feel you have the power to shape your social environment? The Oracle of Delphi in ancient Greece had one piece of advice she recommended to all who consulted her, no matter what question they brought: know yourself. Rule #5 ("Channel Your Personality Strengths") of the Conscience Code includes three self-assessments that will help you do just that.

RULE #5: CHANNEL YOUR PERSONALITY STRENGTHS

"You must bake with the flour you have."

—Danish proverb

The virtues that collectively describe your "character" stand against a broader background of your "personality." Rule #5 highlights three dimensions of personality—conscientiousness, conflict management capability, and confidence—that come into play as you decide to speak up for what's right. For some people, these traits are natural and effortless. For others, one or more may require special effort to summon. For yet a third group, the best solution may be to form alliances with other people who have these traits in more abundance, creating a value-based team to take on a challenge. This chapter will help you figure out which of these camps you fall into for each of these traits.

Personality springs from both genetic origins and socialization—nature and nurture. Psychologists sometimes label the genetic aspects of our behavior as "temperament." Your temperament became apparent when you were a very young child and, for most people, remains relatively stable throughout life. Social scientists have likened temperament to the foundation of a building. The behaviors you build on top of that foundation (including virtue habits such as honesty and loyalty) reflect your unique social experiences—in your family, community, schools, and culture. In short: add formative social experiences (nurture) to temperament (nature), and you get personality.

Personality is not a straitjacket. Rather, as I suggested above, it is a measure that defines your ranges of *relatively effortless action*. Industrious people focus naturally on meeting deadlines. A person who normally procrastinates is more challenged to do things on time. But even the most industrious person can set their to-do list aside to enjoy a day off. And a procrastinator will put in the effort to meet a deadline if the stakes are high enough. So, as you read this chapter, think of it as a chance to become better aware of the way your personality strengths can make it easier (or harder) for you to step up to "own the problem" posed by an ethical conflict.

This chapter is organized around several customized self-assessments I have developed in my work on negotiation and achievement. In the pages to come, we will examine three "Cs" in your personality that are especially relevant in ethical conflicts: conscientiousness, conflict management capability, and confidence. Awareness of your strengths and weaknesses in each of these domains will help you better meet the challenge when situational pressures push against your values.

Let's start with an example of the difference *conscientiousness* can make in the all-important choice to take responsibility for addressing an ethical conflict at work. Very often, "doing the right thing" is a simple matter of "doing things right"—something conscientious people do every day. Our story concerns an oncology nurse in an emergency care setting whose professional eye for detail and her initiative in taking one extra step that went "above and beyond" helped save the lives of hundreds of patients. When you are at the right place, at the right time, with the right attitude, the actions of a few minutes can set an entire organization on a better path.

REPORTING SETS YOU FREE

It was a routine day for Renate (her last name is protected by German privacy laws) at her hospital in Delmenhorst, a city in northern Germany.

While making her rounds in the intensive care unit, Renate glanced into the room of a lung cancer patient who had been in the ICU for several days. There she saw one of her colleagues, a highly regarded male nurse named Niels Högel, standing near the patient's bed. Renate was about to turn away when she noticed an oddity: the patient's life support monitor and IV drip was switched off. *Perhaps the patient was doing better*, she thought. Högel gave her a professional nod as he left the room.

After Högel left, Renate stepped closer to see if the life support system was working properly. As she stood by the patient's bed, she glanced down and noticed a second oddity: the trash receptacle next to the bed contained four empty medication vials. The vials were labeled for a heart medication—something she knew the patient was not taking. Renate's professional values concerning patient safety flashed to red alert.

She paused to think for a moment. Högel had come to the intensive care unit with sterling references. His former colleagues at the hospital in the nearby city of Oldenburg had described him as capable of working "independently and conscientiously." He was good, they said, in the crisis atmosphere of an ICU and treated patients with consideration while administering technically expert care. But Renate had also heard rumors and jokes circulating around her own hospital about him. Some of her nurse colleagues called him "Resuscitate Rambo," given the large number of patients he cared for who seemed to require the emergency resuscitation techniques he was so skilled at providing. That was enough of a doubt for Renate to take ownership of the situation.

She decided she should file a report about the incident. That was standard practice, after all. Indeed, the nurses at the hospital had a saying: "Reporting sets you free." If you filed a report, the responsibility for whatever might have gone wrong shifted to others in the chain of command at the hospital. It was the MRA—the minimally required action.

Still . . . as she thought further about it, she recalled that Högel had looked strangely startled when she showed up at the door. A flash of furtiveness? She had never been a fan of the "reporting sets you free" mantra. That was for the benefit of the nurses, after all—not the patients. She took one more precautionary step—a step that would move this case from "report" status to "investigation" status. She located a blood draw kit, took several vials of blood from the patient's arm, and sent them to the lab for analysis. Then she filed her report, referencing the blood draw.

The next day, Högel's cancer patient in the ICU died. The blood sample analysis came back an hour or two later showing that cancer had not been the cause. Instead, the patient had been injected with a lethal overdose of the heart medication Renate had observed in the trash receptacle next to his bed. The report forced the hospital's hand; the ICU's medical director and chief nurse immediately escalated the matter to top officials at the hospital. These leaders, in turn, referred the case to the city prosecutor.

A larger investigation followed. It turned out that Renate and her colleagues had not known everything there was to know about Högel. Nurses at his former intensive care unit at Oldenburg had reported some troubling suspicions. They wondered if he might be artificially inducing life-threatening heart attacks in ICU patients—then stepping in as a hero to rescue them. Several of his ICU patients had died of heart-related emergencies. The nurses filing these reports had been warned to stay silent unless they had rock-solid proof of their allegations. The reputation of the hospital could be implicated. "People often die in the ICU," the nurses were told. That did not mean they were murdered. If the nurses were uncomfortable with the high mortality rate in the ICU, administrators told them, they should transfer to another unit.

Oldenburg officials ultimately barred Högel from direct interactions with patients. But they were delighted to recommend him for his new position at Renate's hospital in Delmenhorst. As one of Högel's former colleagues said in his court testimony, "A culture of looking away and keeping your head down" allowed Högel to (literally) get away with murder for years. Eight doctors and nurses at the Oldenburg hospital ended up facing charges that they covered up the lax system that allowed Högel to perpetrate his crimes. One nurse, upon taking the stand in Högel's murder trial, pleaded with the judge, "I do not want to be sworn in. I do not know what to say. . . . I am scared that I am to blame." Such is the weight of guilt and shame for otherwise decent people who become so caught up in surviving at work that they fail the test of upholding basic human values.

Niels Högel was ultimately convicted of murder based on the blood sample Renate took. He also confessed to killing forty-three other people. According to the *New York Times*, as many as three hundred patients may have died at his hands, making him one of the most prolific serial killers in modern history. He is currently serving multiple life sentences for these killings.

A FINAL TRAGEDY

The same day the original cancer patient died and Renate's blood sample came back from the lab showing the cause, the ICU medical director faced another choice. He had escalated the issue of Högel's conduct to the hospital's leadership, but Högel was still on duty that day. Should a nurse suspected of murdering a patient be allowed to finish his shift or be escorted off the premises? The medical director decided to avoid making a scene and let him stay. During those few brief hours, a final patient died under Högel's "care."

Renate's story is extraordinary, but the type of conflict she faced is not. I have taught hundreds of nurse executives in management training courses, and they tell me that values conflicts are a daily occurrence in critical care situations. Nurses must deal not only with misconduct by fellow nurses, but also (and more commonly) by physicians who outrank them in status but may be incompetent, suffering from addiction, or stubbornly refusing to take account of crucial new information about a patient's condition.

Renate's example also illustrates how rapidly the four stages of the values-to-action process can speed by. As a seasoned professional, Renate *recognized* that the value of patient safety might be at risk when she initially noticed that an ICU patient's emergency equipment had been turned off. She was prompted to *own the problem* when she discovered the empty vials of heart medication that had no business being there. She quickly *analyzed her options and came to a decision* that a report was required. Finally, the *action plan she designed* included one extra step before leaving the room—gathering the blood sample evidence that would provide the proof needed to back up her report. This entire episode lasted only a few minutes, but led to saving untold lives, and helping reinvigorate a culture of patient safety in the German health-care system.

BRINGING YOUR PERSONALITY TO WORK

In the last chapter we noted that when people exhibit self-discipline in the face of fear, we call them "courageous." The traits that Rule #5 requires you to summon are more common patterns of behavior that reoccur across many more situations in your everyday life. Renate's careful attention to detail on her ICU rounds appears to have required no special effort or self-control; it was just part of "who she was." She probably took responsibilities in her personal life to pay her rent and balance her checkbook as seriously she did her nursing duties.

The sections below will help you measure the three aspects of your own personality I mentioned above—conscientiousness, conflict management capabilities, and confidence—examining how each can affect your ability to step up and take ownership in a conflict over values. We begin with the one Renate exhibited: conscientiousness.

THE FIRST C: CONSCIENTIOUSNESS

Research from multiple studies suggests that conscientiousness is crucial when it comes to ethical behavior at work. Conscientious people tend to be industrious, responsible, dutiful, and dependable—traits that Renate exhibited in the example above. By contrast, people who lack these qualities will need to exert more intentional effort to defend the professional standards that so often form the crux of values conflicts.

Below, you will find a short self-assessment to measure your conscientiousness as a personality trait. Place an "X" on the horizontal scale closest to the descriptor that best describes how you behave most of the time. Of course, situations and incentives can prompt you to act in out-of-the-ordinary ways, but try to honestly rate your typical pattern of behavior.

Conscientiousness Assessment

1. **"Orderly"** people make sure things find (and stay in) their proper places. This helps them ensure their peace of mind. The orderly person keeps their work and living spaces relatively neat, maintains organized notes on complex projects, and periodically tidies up. An orderly person is relaxed when they are in an organized environment. **"Disorganized"** people, by contrast, are happy to surround themselves with what looks to others like a chaotic environment. But they have their own unique way of navigating successfully through what appears to be the disorder around them. As they see it, super-tidy homes or offices do not stay that way for long anyway. So why spend so much time keeping them neat? They consider orderly people to be a bit compulsive.

Orderly				**Disorganized**
100	50	0	50	100
Highly Expressed	Moderate	No Preference	Moderate	Highly Expressed

2. "Industrious" people get things done. They live for their work. They are passionate about staying busy and working toward their goals. They tend to measure success in terms of accomplishments. **"Laid-Back"** people are less intense and achievement-driven. They have jobs to make money so they can have time to relax, enjoy themselves with friends and family, and take in the pleasures of life. A comfortable early retirement sounds good to someone who is laid back. They tend to measure success more in terms of overall quality of life rather than career accomplishments.

Industrious				Laid-Back
100	50	0	50	100
Highly Expressed	Moderate	No Preference	Moderate	Highly Expressed

3. "Deliberative" people take their time making up their minds among various alternatives, weighing all possibilities thoroughly and carefully. They want to get decisions right the first time, not through a messy process of trial and error. **"Spontaneous"** people like to make decisions quickly based on the information at hand. They are biased toward taking action to see what happens, learning, and then changing direction if necessary. It is easy for them to both make up their mind and change it.

Deliberative				Spontaneous
100	50	0	50	100
Highly Expressed	Moderate	No Preference	Moderate	Highly Expressed

4. "Dutiful" people are good citizens—at work, in their community, and within their families. If it is their turn to do the dishes, you can count on them to get everything washed. If they have to work overtime to make a deadline, they will find a way to do it. In short, they take their social roles very seriously and do whatever it takes to fulfill those roles. **"Entrepreneurial"** people "do their own thing." They are less defined by the social roles they occupy and more driven by the opportunities of the moment. The expectations that may come with a job description concern them less than finding their own way to address problems. They tend to do what they see as most urgent and important, worrying less about what others think they "should" be doing.

Dutiful				Entrepreneurial
100	50	0	50	100
Highly Expressed	Moderate	No Preference	Moderate	Highly Expressed

5. "Prompt" people stick to their deadlines. They make lists of their daily chores and tasks and check these items off as they complete them. Indeed, they often do unpleasant things first to get them out of the way. If they are unable to complete their list, they start with leftover items the next day. If the list gets too long or they fall far behind in what they need to do, they feel a bit anxious about it. **"Procrastinators"** are more relaxed about deadlines. What is important is doing the most important things—eventually. They are more likely to put off unpleasant tasks, enjoying the distractions that can make life more colorful and interesting, rather than letting their schedules define them.

Prompt				Procrastinator
100	50	0	50	100
Highly Expressed	Moderate	No Preference	Moderate	Highly Expressed

If you placed marks to the left of the "No Preference" point on three or more of the scales above, you are relatively conscientious. The further to the left you made your marks and the closer you got to staying on the left side for all five items, the greater the chances that conscientiousness is a defining trait your friends, family, and work colleagues would recognize in you. Researchers have found that conscientious people seem to have better-than-average abilities to defer short-term gratifications to achieve longer-term goals. Their sense of order, industry, and duty help them maintain their priorities without extra effort when it comes to core values.

Of course, conscientiousness alone will not prompt you to see or address a given values conflict. Indeed, extremely achievement-oriented, conscientious people may be at special risk of missing a value conflict through "Inattentional Blindness" (Rule #2, "Commit to Your Values") when they are leading the charge to achieve some deadline-driven goal. Finally, even the most laid-back, spontaneous procrastinator will stand up for a value if they also happen to be endowed with a strong sense of duty regarding it. But, assuming two people both embrace a given value and observe that it is at risk, the more conscientious one may be better equipped by personality to instigate a values conflict and see it through. Implication: less conscientious people will often benefit from combining forces with other, more conscientious allies.

THE SECOND C: CONFLICT MANAGEMENT CAPABILITIES

The next important dimension of your personality to consider relates to managing conflict. How reluctant are you to confront others when you have a dispute? Few people relish personal confrontations, but some find them harder to handle (and recover from) than others. For example, research from the negotiation literature shows that some people are so conflict-averse they are willing to pay a premium to buy a new car from a "no haggle" dealership. The disagreement inherent in a price negotiation with a salesperson makes their heart race.

Even those willing to engage in a dispute (or haggle over the price of a car) can be reluctant to push their point of view too hard. Such people seek quick compromises or accommodations that will resolve the matter amicably—as friends might. They view relationships as almost always more important than winning an argument or saving a few dollars. Such personality traits have important implications for the ways you approach value conflicts.

To help you explore your personal conflict styles, our next assessment measures them relative to five approaches: advocacy, problem-solving, compromise, avoidance, and accommodation. The profiler below has been adapted from one I use in my negotiation workshops. Take it, add up your scores at the end, and then we will investigate in more detail what those scores might mean.

Conflict Attitudes Assessment

Without giving the matter too much thought (and without revising your answers for any reason!), please select ONE STATEMENT in each pair of statements below. Select the statement you think *more accurately represents your attitude* when you face a conflict or dispute with someone else—even if you think neither of the statements are especially accurate or both are very accurate.

Think about such situations in general—not just ones at work or in your personal life. And don't pick the statement you "ought" to agree with—just pick the one your gut tells you is the more accurate attitude you bring to these situations most of the time.

Record the letter (A, B, C, D, or E) associated with each statement you pick in the space provided. Some statements repeat, but do not worry about answering consistently. Just keep going. All answers are equally "correct" in some circumstances so be as truthful about your genuine attitudes as possible. Summarize your selections at the very end.

ASSESSMENT

1.   E. I do my best to find out what is bothering the other party so I can fix it.
     D. I tend to stay away from conflict situations whenever possible.
     I select ____.

2.   C. I seek a middle ground between our positions in a dispute.
     B. I search for the deeper problems underlying our disagreements.
     I select ____.

3.   C. I look for a simple compromise to settle our differences.
     E. I do whatever I can to preserve the relationship.
     I select ____.

4.   D. I work hard to defuse tense situations.
     A. I speak out forcefully so others can see where I stand.
     I select ____.

5. D. I am skilled at tactfully avoiding most disagreements.
    C. I find that giving in a little usually prompts the other side
    to do the same.
    I select ___.

6. A. I clearly communicate my goals and explain my
    justifications.
    B. I focus my attention on solving the problem underlying
    the dispute.
    I select ___.

7. D. I prefer to put off confrontations with other people.
    A. I assert my point of view by making strong arguments.
    I select ___.

8. C. I am usually willing to compromise.
    A. I find that confrontations can sometimes serve a useful
    purpose.
    I select ___.

9. B. I fully discuss all the problems between us.
    E. I care more about the relationship than winning the
    argument.
    I select ___.

10. D. I avoid unnecessary personal conflicts.
    C. I seek fair compromises.
    I select ___.

11. C. I concede some points in order to gain something on
    others.
    A. I make my points forcefully so others understand my
    principles.
    I select ___.

12. A. I find it helps to be candid about our disagreements.
    E. I strive to maintain the relationship.
    I select ___.

13. E. I preserve the relationship by accommodating others' needs.
     D. I leave disputes to others whenever possible.
     I select ____.

14. E. I try to address the other person's needs.
     A. I always stand up for my principles, even it means a confrontation.
     I select ____.

15. A. I make sure that others know exactly where I stand.
     D. I emphasize areas on which we agree.
     I select ____.

16. E. I am always looking out for the relationship.
     C. I think give-and-take works better than trying to win every point.
     I select ____.

17. B. I identify and discuss all our differences.
     D. I avoid confrontations.
     I select ____.

18. A. I make sure I am heard.
     E. I strive to maintain relationships.
     I select ____.

19. B. I focus my attention on solving the problem underlying the dispute.
     C. I look for the simple compromise to put the dispute behind us.
     I select ____.

20. E. I always strive to maintain good relations with the other party.
     B. I work hard to solve the problem.
     I select ____.

21. C. I look to resolve conflicts quickly and fairly.
    A. I believe disputes help people identify their legitimate differences.
    I select ___.

22. B. I identify all our disagreements and look for solutions.
    D. I try to avoid unnecessary conflicts.
    I select ___.

23. E. I accommodate whenever possible to preserve the relationship.
    C. I usually find the middle ground between us.
    I select ___.

24. D. I try to emphasize the issues on which we agree.
    B. I uncover and explore the issues on which we disagree.
    I select ___.

25. A. I work hard to make myself heard.
    B. I try to address everyone's needs.
    I select ___.

26. C. I try to put the conflict behind us by finding a fair compromise.
    B. I take my time so we can identify all the underlying problems.
    I select ___.

27. D. I avoid explicit disagreements whenever possible.
    E. I think the relationship is usually more important than who is right.
    I select ___.

28. A. I do not mind confrontations if they serve a purpose.
    B. I work hard to address everyone's needs.
    I select ___.

29. C. I usually try to find the middle ground.
    D. I dislike conflicts because they leave people with bad feelings.
    I select ___.

30. E. I work hard to preserve the relationship.
     B. I try to identify the underlying problems, even if it makes people uncomfortable.
     I select _____.

RESULTS

NOW ADD UP ALL YOUR "A", "B," "C," "D," AND "E" ANSWERS ON THE PREVIOUS PAGES AND PUT THOSE TOTALS BELOW:

As = _____ (Advocate)

Bs = _____ (Problem-Solver)

Cs = _____ (Compromiser)

Ds = _____ (Avoider)

Es = _____ (Accommodator)

_____ TOTAL (Should equal 30)

Evaluating Your Scores

The Conflict Attitudes Assessment is constructed in such a way that each style is pitted against each other style twelve times. Thus, the highest score you can achieve for any single attitude is 12 and the lowest is zero. Scores of *7 or higher* suggest relatively strong impulses to respond to conflict situations using that style. Scores of *3 or lower* suggest weaker impulses to respond to conflict situations in these ways. Scores in the middle—4, 5, or 6—indicate moderate, functional impulses to use these styles appropriately in particular situations.

My Stronger Styles (circle yours):

Advocate	Problem-Solver	Compromiser	Avoider	Accommo-dator

My Weaker Styles (circle yours):

Advocate	Problem-Solver	Compromiser	Avoider	Accommo-dator

Below are thumbnail descriptions of each style to help you reflect on your conflict-relevant personality strengths. Once you have had a chance

to read them, think back on some conflicts and disputes you have experienced, and ask yourself if you behaved in ways that reflect your scores on
this assessment. Then read on as I explore the challenges each trait may
present. We will look first at the more assertive Advocate and Problem-
Solver styles. Then we will talk about the potential difficulties posed by
the more cooperative styles—Compromiser, Avoider, and Accommodator.

Advocate. Someone using the Advocate style steps boldly to the front
lines in a conflict. Although they may be concerned about the consequences of speaking out, they do not fear confrontation as such. They
take a strong position, make their arguments forcefully, are candid in
their opinions, and present the relevant evidence for their point of view
without holding anything back. The other party's feelings or sensibilities
are less important than the principles at stake. Someone who scores low
in this style tends to use it only as a last resort and feels stressed when
they do so. They greatly prefer other approaches described below.

Problem-Solver. Someone using the Problem-Solver style seeks ways
to transform the "either-or" aspect of a dispute into an "everybody wins"
solution. This approach can take more effort, time, and political skill to
carry off, but when it works, all parties are able to advance toward their
underlying goals without violating any core values. This style can lose its
effectiveness when the other party is unprincipled or unreliable and has
no interest in problem-solving. In addition, some ethical conflicts really
are "either-or" in structure, so creative work-arounds are not feasible.
Someone who scores low in this style tends to favor structured rather
than open-ended processes for engaging with conflict. They become
more impatient, more quickly, than those with higher scores.

Compromiser. Someone using the Compromiser style seeks a fair,
rapid resolution of a conflict under which each party agrees that the
other is "right" about some aspect of the matter, each is willing to concede something to the other, and both can put the dispute behind them.
This is a very functional approach when the stakes in the dispute are
relatively small and/or the time available to resolve the matter is short
due to a looming deadline. On the other hand, those who resort to this
style (as well as the next two) when core values are in serious danger may
appear unprincipled. Those who score low for this style may be seen as
argumentative (and uncompromising) about minor principles. But such
people can be counted on to be steadfast, stubborn defenders of their
positions whenever a key value is at risk.

Avoider. Someone using the Avoider style places a high priority on smooth social interactions. They seek tactful, diplomatic ways to eliminate interpersonal conflicts before they arise and tend to withdraw or fall silent when confrontations erupt. They see sharp, emotionally charged communication as a sign that something is wrong that cannot be fixed. They want no part of it. People who score low for the Avoider style are often seen as blunt and "politically incorrect." They endorse "radical candor" and say exactly what is on their minds. This can create problems in some organizational cultures. Those who score low in the Avoider style sometimes also score high for the Advocate style, as these two can easily fit comfortably together in a single personality.

Accommodator. Someone using the Accommodating style sees maintaining good relations with the other party as a paramount concern. In my negotiation training, I have observed that this conflict style is a favorite of people who also exhibit high levels of Agreeableness on the "Big 5" personality trait inventory, a trait that reflects high levels of trusting, cooperative, and deferential behavior. In disputes over values, Accommodators often see the problem as one of conflicting loyalties—on the one hand to an important, ongoing relationship with a boss or peer, and on the other hand to a relevant principle. Because their personality is wired to always place high importance on relationships, they can more easily rationalize deferring or setting aside a value conflict. At the extreme, they can be "pleasers"—people who too often seek social reassurance that all is well in their relations with others even when they are being imposed upon. People who score low in this style tend to be more "problem focused" than "people focused." They have a lower aptitude for empathy and may ignore emotional signals as they analyze problems, arrive at what they consider the right answer, and then advocate their solution. They share with low Compromisers a tendency to become stubborn when others fail to agree with their well-reasoned explanations.

GOING ALONG TO GET ALONG: HOW COOPERATIVE TRAITS CAN PROMPT YOU TO BACK AWAY FROM ETHICAL CONFLICTS

Compromise, avoidance, and accommodation are wonderful traits in the ordinary course of organizational life, when good relationships smooth the way to productivity. However, these traits can be a problem if they prompt you to look away from bad behavior simply to avoid potential conflict. In Renate's case we saw the potential costs when conflict avoidance becomes the hallmark of an organizational culture. Administrators at Högel's former hospital, worried about provoking a conflict, left him free to commit mass murder.

Another consideration: there can be significant personal penalties for failure to speak up. For example, the honor code at West Point, the US Army's military academy, is simple. "I will not lie, cheat, or steal," it reads. But then comes the hard part, "*or tolerate those who do.*" The refusal to "tolerate" includes the duty to report violations of the code whenever and wherever they occur. A failure to report leads to sanctions that include dismissal.

The duty to report sometimes places people in the awkward position of choosing between friends and professional responsibilities. It can also run afoul of people's desire to avoid being labeled a "snitch"—a dislike drilled into us as children when kids who "told on" others were socially ostracized. For these reasons, reporting wrongdoing can often feel like a no-win situation. Can't you simply be silent and be safe?

Sometimes. But if the rules being broken involve the highest stakes (as they did in Renate's case), become signs of systematic corruption (as they can with corporate frauds and accounting scandals), or involve reputational risks for the organization (as they can with all forms of sexual misconduct, hate speech, and rule-breaking by top leaders), the final point of the West Point honor code—refusal to tolerate—becomes a salient standard.

For example, not long ago, Richard Schulze, the founder, former CEO, and chairman of the board of the big retailer Best Buy, Inc., was forced to step aside by his board of directors for his failure to report an ethical violation by the firm's new CEO, Brian Dunn—his handpicked successor. Schulze received a written report of an inappropriate relationship between Dunn and a younger female executive in the leadership training department. Dunn denied anything untoward was going on, and Schulze let the matter drop without informing the rest of the board. When the board later received an anonymous tip about the situation, it launched a formal investigation, which uncovered evidence of special treatment and favors. It turned out that the relationship was an open secret inside Best Buy, leading many employees to conclude that workplace conduct rules applied to everyone except the CEO. The board asked both Schulze and Dunn to leave.

The duty to report (and escalate if necessary) can also extend far down into the rank and file of an organization. Consider the following example, which shows what can happen when the wrong person sets the moral tone for a unit—and decent people look the other way.

Case Study: Accommodating the Office Bully

A secretary at the West Virginia Bureau of Training and Staff Development (her name is not revealed in any reports of this incident) was compiling packets for an upcoming graduation ceremony for newly minted prison guards. As she gathered the materials, she was surprised and offended by the official class photo, which showed nearly all of the thirty-four graduates giving the Nazi salute (seven used a raised fist gesture instead). She asked the unit's instructor, a woman named Karrie Byrd, "What are you all doing in the picture?" Byrd replied that she had staged the group's graduation picture as a joke, reflecting what had become regular practice during the unit's training. It seems that one trainee had given her the Nazi salute early in the training and others had picked up on it. Byrd relished it because, as she told the secretary, "I'm a hard-ass like Hitler." Byrd felt that because the class members giving the salute included Blacks and women, there was no problem. She asked the secretary to photoshop the picture so the words "Hail Byrd" appeared as a banner behind the group.

Worried about what she was being asked to do, the secretary took her concerns to Byrd's supervisor, Captain Annette Daniels-Watts. But Byrd was apparently well known for being an office bully, because Daniels-Watts declined to confront her over the issue. "Since you have [the photos] all already printed," Daniels-Watts told the secretary, "you might as well go ahead and stuff them into the packets." The secretary complied. In addition to the secretary, two instructors at Byrd's level of seniority saw the picture before the final ceremony and advised Daniels-Watts against including it in the packets. Again, Daniels-Watts did nothing.

At the ceremony, the West Virginia commissioner of the Division of Corrections, a former federal prosecutor named Betsy Jividen (who is Jewish), saw the picture and immediately recognized how morally offensive it was and the danger it posed for everyone concerned. She escalated the issue to her boss, Cabinet Secretary Jeff Sandy (another former prosecutor), who immediately brought the matter to the attention of West Virginia governor Jim Justice. Justice ordered a formal investigation. Result: Byrd and Daniels-Watts, as well as the two instructors and the secretary who had seen the photo but did not press the matter far enough to stop it, were terminated. Four other instructors who had witnessed the salute during training and failed to report it were suspended. Finally, all thirty-four cadets were dismissed, including the few who had grudgingly participated in Byrd's ritual by raising a clenched fist instead of the Nazi salute.

Do the personality styles we examined above map on to this debacle? I think so. Byrd, with the worst values and most assertive personality, dominated her environment. She was a classic bully, claiming to be a "hard-ass like Hitler" and daring all those around her to prove her wrong. She was a high *Advocate*, who seemed to lack any aptitude for cooperative behavior. The secretary appears to have been a *Compromiser*. She had the good judgment to question Byrd about the photo but lacked the follow-through to do more than report her concerns to the next level. Meanwhile, supervisor Daniels-Watts appears to have been an *Avoider*, someone unwilling to take Byrd on even though she had the authority to do so. Byrd's fellow instructors had the good judgment to know how inappropriate Nazi salutes are for prison guard trainees, but nevertheless *Accommodated* Byrd's wishes to allow the practice (and the picture) to go forward. Finally, the few cadets in the photo who refused to give the Nazi salute also took a *Compromiser* approach—making a less insulting "power" gesture that did not overtly confront what the rest of the group was doing.

When I encountered this story, I felt that the dismissal of the secretary and cadets who gave the "power gesture" might have been overly harsh. After all, the secretary had elevated the issue to her boss, and Byrd was obviously an over-the-top drill instructor who had ordered the cadets to participate under an implied threat of discipline.

So, as part of my research for this book, I spoke to Jeff Sandy, West Virginia's cabinet secretary for the Department of Homeland Security. I asked him why he had thought it was necessary to terminate the cadets who refused to give the Nazi salute. His answer combined principle and pragmatism. First, he said, he felt all the cadets had a moral duty to proactively speak up against this practice, even if they were being ordered to engage in it. He referred to the Nazi war trials after World War II and the precedent they set for holding people morally and legally accountable for their actions even though they claimed to be only "following orders." When these state employees were ordered to give a Nazi salute, he strongly believed that "I was just following orders" did not constitute a valid defense.

On a more practical level, he reminded me that these cadets were going into service in correctional facilities. The nuances of who gave what gesture would quickly be lost in that context, fatally compromising the cadets' credibility in their future professional roles. The publicity surrounding the salute photo (it was widely circulated in the media and on the internet) crippled their ability to be effective witnesses in any future litigation regarding prisoner treatment. More ominously, their personal safety and the safety of others in their workplaces could be at risk based on their association with this inflammatory event.

As for the secretary? Secretary Sandy had no comment on her case. But I surmised that it was a question of complicity. She knew that her boss had done nothing about the issue and yet remained silent. On a matter this egregious, she had a duty to press the issue further. Thus, everyone involved was held accountable: some for instigating and participating in the practice, others for failing to report it, and still others for failing to pursue the matter after reporting it when the person in authority refused to take action.

Lesson: personality traits favoring compromising, avoiding, or accommodating behavior ordinarily help groups avoid unnecessary conflicts and remain on task. But when an ethical conflict arises, confrontation may become a necessary part of the solution. These same traits can then hinder people's responses, allowing the problem to get worse. When the principle at risk is as obviously important as it was in the Nazi salute case, otherwise decent, cooperative people need to step out of their comfort zone to take on the wrongdoer.

The Assertive Styles: Problem-Solving and Advocacy

In the Nazi salute story, three of the players modeled the more assertive styles that could have solved the problem before it became a national news story: Commissioner Betsy Jividen, Secretary Jeff Sandy, and Governor Jim Justice. Secretary Sandy told me that he had been out of state for a family event honoring his father, a World War II veteran, when Jividen called him from the graduation ceremony where the photo became public knowledge. The juxtaposition of what his father had fought for and what his colleague was reporting to him about a Nazi salute galvanized him into immediate action. And the subsequent steps taken by Governor Justice reflect an equally assertive approach to this incident.

While both the Advocate and the Problem-Solver are more assertive than the three more cooperative styles I analyzed above, they are assertive in different ways. The chapter on Rule #8, "Engage the Decision Maker," explores problem-solving, interest-based strategies for handling ethical conflicts. People who score high in the Problem-Solver style instinctively bring a more politically nuanced approach.

The Advocate style tends to be blunter and more stubborn—and riskier in terms of career interests. Obvious tensions can arise between the impulse to make the strongest case possible for a principle and the need to maintain amicable relationships. But it is sometimes necessary to upset people if they refuse to hear an important warning about a core value.

Case Study: An Advocate Stands Up for Auto Safety

Consider the case of a South Korean automotive engineer named Kim Gwang-ho, who decided to speak out about dangerous safety lapses at his employer, Hyundai Motor Co. As you read Kim's story, you will see an attempt at problem-solving, followed by a determined Advocate approach coupled with low Avoider, Compromiser, and Accommodator attitudes. Combined, these traits can result in an especially assertive, persistent, and blunt conflict style.

Kim joined Hyundai in 1991 as an expert in precision mechanics and made a career of working on engine testing and planning. After decades of work and many promotions, he was transferred to Quality Strategy, the unit that decided when a model recall was needed to address a safety concern. In 2015, Hyundai issued a recall in the United States of five hundred thousand sedans, allegedly for manufacturing problems that could cause the engines to stall. But Kim had inside information about what the Quality Strategy report on these issues revealed, and it was a much deeper and more pervasive problem than the recall suggested. It was an engine design problem, not just a manufacturing one. And it affected more models and markets than one sedan in one country. It would require a very costly recall.

His wife was worried about his career if he spoke up. But, as Kim later told the press, "I'm stubborn and I persuaded her that the problems would be buried forever" if these events went unreported. He decided to take action.

His campaign to address these larger safety issues began with a problem-solving strategy inside Hyundai. He used the existing channels to make his case, but he did not attract support from the people with authority. The firm rejected his evidence and his conclusions. His "stubbornness" now kicked into high gear as he pivoted to an Advocate approach. He flew to Washington, D.C., to meet with the US regulator that handles recalls, the National Highway Traffic Safety Administration. In violation of company policy, he brought more than 250 pages of the Quality Strategy team documents detailing the engine design and other problems and handed them over to the agency. When he got back home, he went public with his complaints to local South Korean media and government officials.

Hyundai responded by terminating Kim and, shortly thereafter, instigating a government investigation against him for potential trade secret theft. Police raided his home, seizing documents and a computer drive. Undaunted, Kim countered by invoking South Korea's whistleblower protection laws. Hyundai was forced to reinstate him. Within months, even as Hyundai's legal actions against Kim were continuing, regulators in the United States, Canada, and South Korea had announced extensive, additional recalls, including a rare "compulsory" one for vehicles in South Korea.

Kim's warnings were completely vindicated when, a few years later, Hyundai engines began failing in larger numbers. Regulators found themselves reviewing more than three thousand cases of engine fires, injuring some one hundred drivers. They feared as many as four million vehicles at both Hyundai and its sister brand, Kia, might be affected. More recalls were issued, prosecutors opened a criminal investigation into Hyundai's recall practices, and Hyundai was forced to set aside $760 million to settle consumer class action lawsuits.

Kim's remarkable story demonstrates how even a single stubborn Advocate, with the facts on his side and documents to prove it, can hold one of the world's largest companies accountable for violations of safety standards. If "Advocate" was one of your lower-rated styles, take note. In some circumstances, these are exactly the right people to add to your team.

THE THIRD C: CONFIDENCE (LOCUS OF CONTROL)

Our final personality trait concerns your overall confidence when it comes to influencing your social environment—a trait that Kim Gwang-ho obviously had in abundance.

One of my students ("Mary") highlighted the importance of this personality facet to me when she described how her former employer—a global consulting firm—cultivated the habit of being proactive as a key part of its corporate culture. The firm had a special name for this attitude: being "at cause." Employees were encouraged to seek ways to help their teams and their clients by anticipating and fixing problems before they arose. Operating "at cause" was especially important when employees encountered ethical issues.

As Mary put it, this "at cause" culture "encouraged fantastic levels of responsibility." Staying inside your own silo, minding your own business, and waiting for people in higher positions to structure problems for you were never enough. "At cause" employees looked out for one another, their values, and their customers. The opposite of being proactively "at cause" was being reactive (the firm labeled this as being "at effect"). Reactive employees allowed problems to fester while awaiting permission to act from higher authority.

Management guru Stephen Covey thought so highly of this trait that he made "Be Proactive" the very first habit in his book *The 7 Habits of Highly Effective People*. Psychologists have a name for such proactivity: Locus of Control. Those with an "internal" Locus of Control see themselves as having the power to act "from the inside out"—to take steps that can alter their situations. Those with an "external" Locus of Control more often see circumstances *outside themselves* as dictating their options. They don't waste time trying to change things that cannot be changed, focusing instead on a shorter list of priorities they know they can control.

You can readily see how this factor might be relevant when bosses and peers are applying situational pressures to behave unethically. If you have an internal Locus of Control and are used to taking the initiative at the first sign of trouble, you may launch more quickly into action against such pressures.

If your Locus of Control is more external, you may be more inclined to accept the status quo your bosses present to you.

Note: The Locus of Control factor says nothing about how effective you will be in a given conflict. Launching headlong into action (the favorite move of Internals) may limit your options, as others identify you as a troublemaker and work to minimize your influence. Waiting for the situation to evolve (as Externals are inclined to do) can sometimes help you clarify the problem and identify the allies you need to help you stand up for your values. Thus, as with all personality-based impulses, they are most effective when combined with good judgment.

Here is a rough-and-ready Locus of Control test to give you an idea of how formal assessments for this personality facet work. Answer True or False to the following statements, even if you would pick "it depends," were that choice available.

1. When I was in school, my grades were often determined more by which teachers I was assigned than how hard I worked.
    ___ True (External LoC)   ___ False (Internal LoC)
2. My plans generally work out, even if not quite the way I expected them to.
    ___ True (Internal LoC)   ___ False (External LoC)
3. Getting a good job usually has more to do with being in the right place at the right time than education or qualifications.
    ___ True (External LoC)   ___ False (Internal LoC)
4. People get the government they deserve. It is important to vote so your voice can be heard.
    ___ True (Internal ToC)   ___ False (External LoC)
5. Luck plays more of a role in success than hard work.
    ___ True (External LoC)   ___ False (Internal LoC)

Did you respond to three or more of the above prompts with either an Internal or External Locus of Control? The more you picked for one or the other, the stronger that impulse is as an aspect of your personality.

Locus of Control is a sufficiently important personal variable that some employers rely on it in recruiting. For example, Teach For America—a nonprofit group that places recent, high-performance college graduates in teaching positions in some of the nation's poorest public school districts—once used something similar to a Locus of Control assessment as a screening tool for recruiting teachers. The founder of the group, Wendy Kopp, was quoted in an interview with the *New York Times* saying that "the number one predictive trait [for success in the program] . . . is what we would call internal locus of control." She explained that people with this trait were much more likely to "own" the problems of the low-performing students in their classrooms rather than "blame everyone else in the system."

Years later, one of my MBA students who had worked for Teach For America reported that screening for this trait had not worked out as planned. Internal Locus of Control recruits, used to being able to take action that affected their environments, burned out (and sometimes dropped out) of the program more often than expected. In the challenging communities where they worked, nothing they could do altered the structural disadvantages their students suffered from—and their relentless efforts to help their students in the face of these conditions exhausted them. Teach For America began searching for recruits with more balance, patience, and resilience.

Although an internal Locus of Control can be a disadvantage when situations require collective rather than individual action, most value conflicts reward being proactive. In my work with students and executives, I have heard many stories of employees who have needlessly put themselves "at effect" (more reactive than proactive) where values are concerned—and later regretted it. To conclude this section, therefore, I want to offer a few examples they have shared with me. The phrases below are what your "at effect" voice may say to you. Be prepared to talk back.

Voices of the Disempowered

"I Was Only an Intern." "Joanne," an information technology summer intern, discovered that the internet startup she was working for had a charity component to its website. When users made a purchase, they were given the opportunity to donate a dollar to one of several well-known charities. One day she ran a test of the charity option functionality and was shocked to learn that the money was not going to any charities at all. Instead, it went straight into the firm's own account, where it became part of its profits. She was aghast, she later told me.

But what could she do? "I was only an intern," she said. "I felt I had no choice." She did nothing and left at the end of the summer, determined never to work there. Could she have done better by being "at cause"? She might have reached out to others at the firm, some of whom might be equally appalled to learn of this problem. Perhaps she would have discovered the firm meant well but a recent coding error had undermined its program. Perhaps she could have reported the issue to a mentor who would have taken steps to end the deception, even if this occurred after she left. By doing nothing, she let an unethical situation persist—and felt badly about it for years afterward.

"I Felt Powerless." "Jake," an employee at a large venture capital fund, was put in charge of organizing its annual conference for top executives, clients, and investors from around the world. As part of his job, he helped facilitate the process for selecting guest speakers and eventually came up with a list of five names. A week before these names were to be announced, one of the speakers was publicly accused of making a racist comment—one of several examples the media was covering as part of the Black Lives Matter movement. Jake did not think his firm should be inviting someone with this cloud hanging over him, so he asked one of the senior partners involved in the conference for his advice. To his surprise, the partner brushed aside his concerns, saying he knew the speaker personally and was sure the allegations were false.

This left Jake with a problem. He had scheduled a conference call with the executives on his off-site organizing team to make the final decisions on the event. Should he directly challenge the senior partner's position about this speaker or defer to his judgment? "I felt powerless," Jake told me. He did not raise the issue for discussion by the team, and the speaker was invited. Again, Jake was left with a memory of letting himself be "at effect" when he could have done better by being "at cause." Had Jake considered the matter further or consulted more widely, a number of arguments—both principled and practical—might have occurred to him to sway his organizing team. He could then have taken these back to the partner to explain the team's ambivalence about this speaker. A compromise solution: defer the invitation for a year to allow the facts underlying the allegations to come out.

"Someone Else Will Speak Up." When people observe a violation of values taking place on a team, they can remain "at effect" by waiting for others to take on the stress of confronting the situation. But sometimes,

nobody does so until it is too late. "Olivia" worked in the advertising unit of a digital marketing firm in Europe. At a weekly meeting where employees shared especially vivid and inspiring ads they had encountered from other companies, she showed an animation ad created by a major tech firm.

A month later, another ad team at her company—some of whom had attended Olivia's presentation—began bragging about a snappy new concept they had created for a client. When Olivia saw this video on her company's internal review site, she immediately felt uneasy. It appeared to be a clone of the ad she had shown, with a similar look, feel, and even musical content. At the very least she felt it was unethical to pass this off as original work. At worst, it might be in violation of copyright law.

But she hesitated to speak up, she later told me, because she was sure the appropriate creative director or account manager would flag it. But nobody did. Luckily, a few days before the team presented the ad to the client, her CEO (who had heard some buzz about the ad) personally viewed the video. He immediately recognized it as a rip-off of a rival's concept and came down hard on the head of advertising—Olivia's boss. The client presentation was canceled, and the firm's reputation suffered as a result of the delay. Olivia could have prevented all of this from happening in the first place (while advancing her credibility within the firm) had she been fully "at cause" in this situation instead of "at effect."

A MOMENT FOR PERSONAL REFLECTION

As you reflect on the role of your personality in ethical conflicts, take stock of your strengths and weaknesses. Can you recall an occasion when you stepped up to defend someone who was being unfairly treated or belittled? What prompted you to stand by them even when it was socially unpopular for you to take their side? How about asserting a political position that ran against what the group you were with seemed to endorse? Were you stressed by doing this or did it feel like you were stepping into a role that felt "natural"?

If you are a conflict avoider, consider the steps you can take to make sure ethical issues are dealt with—but without your having to endure a direct confrontation. Rather than withdraw from the conflict, can you delegate the problem? Rally a coalition? Report the issue to a higher authority for them to handle it? Perhaps the answer may be as simple as how you communicate. It will be easier for you to voice your opinion on email than in a one-on-one meeting. But be careful you do so diplomatically. People often read even a simple request made on email as an aggressive demand.

NEXT UP: RALLYING YOUR ALLIES

Your character and personality provide inner strengths. But it is harder to win battles when you fight alone. Research shows that this is especially true when you are called to defend your values by standing up to pressures from peers and bosses. Rule #6 of the Conscience Code is one of the most important of them all. It introduces you to a force that will help you prevail in even the toughest conflict over values: the Power of Two.

RULE #6:
LEVERAGE THE
POWER OF TWO

"We must, indeed, all hang together or, most assuredly, we shall all hang separately."

—Benjamin Franklin

A student, "Caroline," once spoke in class about an all-too-common experience in business today: being the only woman on a male-dominated team. Before coming to graduate school, she had a job at a high-tech consulting firm in Australia. Her family was proud of the prestigious, brand-name firm where she worked, and her friends envied the apartment her paycheck made possible. But the work was intense. Employees often had to be at the office until two or three in the morning. She was tipped off early about the scarcity of women at the company when, during the first break at the company's new-employee orientation, a line quickly formed down the hallway outside the men's restroom. There was no such line outside the women's bathroom.

On one project team, Caroline was the only woman in a group that worked together for just over a month. As she settled into her role, one of the issues she found herself confronting, on an almost daily basis, was the humor a few of her male teammates relied on to relieve stress during their late-night work sessions. Some of their "jokes" revolved around the ways various women in the office dressed and carried themselves. "Jake" and "Yannick" became the most relentless critics of female colleagues' appearance.

Caroline could have said something when these jokes first started, but she chose not to. Her gender seemed to be invisible to her male colleagues, and she found it easier to keep it that way. The jokes were inappropriate, but they never crossed the blurry line she had set in her mind between bad taste and sexually explicit disrespect.

Then, one night, Jake went too far. He began speaking in very sexual terms about what he wanted to "do" to the office manager, and Yannick immediately took Jake's comment even further—into graphic, offensive territory. Caroline felt a full flush of anger, as if she, herself, were being assaulted. But her earlier silence made it hard to speak up. She was a junior member of the team, and she felt outnumbered. She preferred remaining "invisible" by looking distracted and busy, even as the jokes escalated. Eventually, the project concluded, and the team broke up.

When she told her story in class, she ended on a note of regret. By allowing her fears to smother her moral outrage, she had let herself down. Even years later, she still regretted remaining silent.

Caroline let peer pressure narrow her choices to three poor options: remain silent (the one she chose), single-handedly confront Jake and Yannick (a daunting challenge), or report these two (and perhaps the whole team) to higher authority. As a conflict-averse person, only the first path—the one allowing her to evade owning the problem—appealed to her.

But by trying to handle this situation alone, she violated Rule #6 of the Conscience Code: Leverage the Power of Two. Before surrendering, she should have sought out an ally. As you will see below, when it comes to resisting the five situational pressures (peers, authority, incentives, roles, and systems), 1 + 1 = much more than 2. Having a whole cadre of allies is great, of course, but adding that first partner to your side makes you exponentially stronger.

An ally can bolster your confidence, help you think more clearly about next steps, and keep you grounded when the people applying the pressure try to make it look as if *you* are the problem. Psychologists report that the best workplace allies are those who help you better understand the situation you are in and then provide the confidence boost you need to manage it.

Were there potential allies for Caroline? We can only speculate. Was there someone on her team who seemed less than enthusiastic about Jake's and Yannick's sense of humor? Psychologists have a concept called "pluralistic ignorance" that may describe her team's silence about the out-of-control jokes. Everyone goes along with a dominant person because everyone thinks they are the only one with reservations about this person's ideas. Perhaps nobody spoke up on Caroline's team because everyone assumed (incorrectly) that the others found the jokes funny.

By testing out her viewpoint in private with one other person, perhaps a quieter one who might be open to hearing her perspective, she could have popped this bubble and created an alliance. If that was too risky, how about reaching out to the person who recruited her, a mentor, or a female colleague who had been at the firm longer than she? Research shows that women and minorities often find strength by conferring with one another in the face of sexist and racist attacks launched at them by fellow workers.

As Caroline told her story, I was reminded that sexism remains a pervasive, structural problem in male-dominated fields such as high-tech and financial services, so it is possible that nothing would have worked, even with an ally. But by proactively seeking an ally, she would at least have claimed her voice, gaining confidence that could have helped her next time she faced a similar situation. She could have cast off the burden of the regret she obviously felt about this incident when I met her.

To be clear: Caroline may have lost this battle had she chosen to fight it. But what was the downside? Embarrassment and resentment at having taken on an office bully only to be outmaneuvered by him. But I think she may have underestimated the power of her position in a workplace primed with the new norms of the #MeToo movement. Jake and Yannick were walking time bombs waiting to go off for the organization. Caroline might well have discovered that the people of genuine influence in her firm would be grateful to her for calling out this type of behavior—and admired her courage for doing so. That could have advanced her career.

The sections below are organized as follows. First, we will look back at the seminal research studies on peer, authority, and systemic pressures I introduced when we discussed Rule #3 ("Know Your Enemy"). It is now time to explore key findings about how to "escape" these social influence traps through alliances. Next, we will examine three sources of social influence that can lead you either toward or away from your core values: the Close, the Many, and the Powerful. We'll look at research on animal behavior and habit formation that underlines the connections between your social environment and your values. We will close the chapter with a case study of the Power of Two in action. It involves the famous scandal that brought down the medical device company Theranos, Inc. Many factors contributed to uncovering the fraud at this firm, but the actions of two twenty-two-year-old "people of conscience" were key. Their story illustrates how allies help you advance both your values and your career.

THE POWER OF TWO

Earlier, I introduced you to three social psychologists who demonstrated the surprising effects of peer pressure (Solomon Asch), authority (Stanley Milgram), and role-based, systemic forces (Philip Zimbardo) on human behavior. I promised then that we would look at some of the experimental conditions they discovered that help people resist these pressures. This section delivers on that promise.

The True Partner:
Escaping Peer Pressure in Asch's Experiments

To review: Professor Solomon Asch's work on peer pressure showed that, when everyone in a group says that "X is true," the final holdout will go along with them more often than you might expect—even when they know that "X is not true." Most do this to avoid the awkwardness of dissent. Others actually become believers in the falsehood they hear the group endorse.

Asch used a simple, visual test in his experiment. He presented people with two pieces of paper. On the first piece was a single straight line; on the second were three lines, one of which was the same length as the line on the first paper. The task was to match the two lines of equal length. In control groups, when subjects compared the two papers while sitting alone in a room, they made the correct matches ninety-nine out of one hundred times.

But when Asch had his subjects do the line-matching task in a group setting in which everyone else confidently named the same, *incorrect* line as the match, performance declined. Seventy-five percent of Asch's test subjects succumbed to peer pressure at least once during the experiment, and 5 percent—a dedicated set of "go along to get along" types—picked the unequal lines every time the crowd did. Subjects explained their behavior in a variety of ways. One theme was their desire to avoid the embarrassment of being a dissenter in a large group.

Asch's subsequent work revealed a stunningly simple way to help his subjects escape/resist peer pressure: provide subjects with a single ally. By adding a voice in the room that spoke the correct rather than the incorrect answer, Asch caused his test subjects' willingness to tell the truth jump from 65 percent to 95 percent. Asch called this ally the "true partner."

Caroline's experience with her team's sexist jokes lines up well with Asch's social conformity work. Early on, she was willing to go along with the team's unanimous definition of what a "joke" was even though she did not consider them funny—just as Asch's subjects sought to avoid the embarrassment of disagreeing with their groups about which lines matched up.

Now imagine if she had had someone she trusted on her team who shared her sense of outrage about sexist humor. Jake's and Yannick's jokes were, after all, genuinely inappropriate. With another voice speaking out, Caroline would have felt less isolated in her position and more confident in asserting her point of view.

The Dissenting Peers:
Escaping Authority Pressure in Milgram's Experiments

An ally can help you not only when you face peer pressure but also when you must stand up to authority. Professor Stanley Milgram's experiments, described in the "Know Your Enemy" chapter, were designed to investigate why ordinary German people had gone along with the Holocaust in World War II. In addition to the insight (discussed in Rule #2, "Commit to Your Values") that subjects who spoke directly to the victims were more likely to break off the experiment, Milgram designed a variation of his experiment that yielded results in line with Asch's "true partner" finding.

Recall that in Milgram's work, white-coated experimenters posing as "scientists" demanded that subjects give "victims" fake electric shocks, up to and including a "lethal" one. In many of the experiments, the victims cried out in pain as the shock levels increased. When his subjects could hear the screams of the victims (but not see them), twenty-five of forty subjects delivered the lethal shock level three consecutive times before the scientist ended the experiment.

In Experiment 17 of his series, Milgram took his basic setup and changed its conditions to test whether "group influence can release the subject from authoritarian control and allow him to act in a direction congruent with his values and personal standards."

In this version of the experiment, three people (rather than just one) were brought into the lab and formed a team to administer the "shocks." Two of them were Milgram's confederates and were given support roles while the test subject delivered the shocks. As the experiment proceeded, one of these confederates dropped out as soon as the person receiving the shocks gave their first vocal protest. A few shock levels later, the second confederate quit, saying, "I'm not willing to shock that man against his will. I'll have no part of it."

With the two "dissenting peers" breaking off during the process, 90 percent (thirty-six of forty) terminated the experiment prior to the lethal shock level—with twenty-five of them quitting at a level less than half that. As one subject said after walking away when the first confederate did so, "I was already thinking about quitting when the guy broke off." Another commented after he followed the two dissenting peers, "I thought they [the peers] were men of good character. . . . When the victim said 'Stop,' they stopped."

Lesson: No matter what your personality, having allies at your side can empower you to act on your values more quickly and decisively than relying on your inner resources alone. And having supportive peers may be especially important for those who, like Caroline, have more accommodating and conflict-averse personalities.

Zimbardo and the Power of an Outside Perspective

The third classic research study discussed earlier was Professor Philip Zimbardo's troubled Stanford Prison Experiment in which he placed randomly selected undergraduate students in roles of "guards" and "prisoners," attempting to prove that social roles and systemic pressures can distort the behavior of otherwise normal people.

Although, as I emphasized earlier, the experimental rigor of Zimbardo's work is now under a cloud, there is one facet of the case worth highlighting here. It took an outsider, PhD student Christina Maslach, to bring an end to the out-of-control proceedings. She brought both commonsense morality and the norms of social science with her when she began observing Zimbardo's "experiment." She was so disturbed by what she saw that she persuaded Zimbardo to end his experiment immediately on ethical grounds.

This aspect of the story was not an intended part of Zimbardo's design, but I think it teaches a lesson. My research on ethical conflicts revealed numerous instances of ordinary people swept up in wrongdoing by peers and bosses—but who were saved by a perceptive spouse or friend who could see more clearly than they what was happening. The Power of Two thus extends to people completely outside your workplace "bubble"—people who can point out how far you have strayed from your ethical commitments and bring you back to your senses before it is too late.

THE WAY IT WORKS: SOCIAL CONTAGION

The Power of Two underlines a critical fact about the connection between your social environment and your values: who you hang out with makes a huge difference in how you behave. As I mentioned earlier in our chapter on Rule #4 ("Summon Your Character"), success guru Jim Rohn once said that you are the average of the five people you spend the most time with. Stop and think about that for a moment. Do the five people you spend the most time with share your core values? I'm sure this is true for your personal life. But what about at work?

James Clear in his bestseller, *Atomic Habits*, points to three main sources of social influence: what he calls the Close, the Many, and the Powerful. Caroline faced all three—"the Close" because the team was working together in a tight-knit group for long hours; "the Many" by the simple fact that she was outnumbered; and "the Powerful" given Jake's and Yannick's outsized influence in the group. It can be a useful exercise to create an "influence balance sheet" using these three categories. If the balance seems to be favoring the people with the wrong values, as it did in Caroline's case, think about who you can add to the mix to tilt the scales the other way.

The Close

Proximity—in both the physical and relational senses—matters when it comes to influence. No less a historical figure than Henry Kissinger knew how important it was to occupy a White House office as close as possible to the Oval Office. When he became President Nixon's assistant for national security affairs, his office was no bigger than the cramped space he had used when he was a professor. But it was a few steps from the president, whom he saw in person almost every day for briefings—the kind of frequent contact few other government officials enjoyed. As he put it in his book *White House Years*, if you want to influence a powerful person, it helps to be "just down the hall."

Clear cites two studies that show just how much the behavior of those close to you can rub off. In one, researchers followed over ten thousand people for thirty-two years to track the effects of friendship on weight control. The study showed that having an obese friend increased people's odds of becoming obese themselves by 57 percent. Interestingly, the effects observed for losing weight are not as strong. If one person in a relationship drops a few pounds, the other person follows suit only about one-third of the time.

Social contagion can affect values, not just foreign policy and eating habits. Your family, of course, constitutes the closest of the Close when it comes to values. As I mentioned in "Rule #1 ("Face the Conflict"), my father exercised a tremendous influence on my sense of duty and responsibility. In tough situations, I often find myself asking what my dad would have done. My memories of him help me stay focused on the right issues.

But the Close can also be a source of pressure to violate values. Many of the students I teach are first- or second-generation US citizens whose parents legally immigrated to America from far-flung countries. Every year, they bring me tales of extended family members back home lobbying for help to beat the US immigration system by setting up sham marriages, falsifying documents, or engaging in other illegal maneuvers. When a family member asks you to break the law, it puts you in a bind. You are torn between traditional family loyalties and fidelity to the rule of law. My students report that these lobbying efforts almost always fail. After all, they are asking their US-based cousins to commit felonies, actions that would put my students and their parents in serious legal jeopardy. The conflicts these requests trigger rip the fabric of family bonds.

Are Your Friends Looking Out for You?

Just outside the boundary of family are those we consider friends. Once again, the influence from this source can be negative as well as positive. When a friend pressures you to behave badly, the resulting conflict of loyalties can be difficult to navigate. No less a moral authority than Mahatma Gandhi warned of this danger in his autobiography. He noted that friends exert powerful influences on one another. When you combine this influence with the insight that (as he put it) a "man takes in vice more readily than virtue," the stage is set for conflicts between loyalty to friends and commitments to core values. Gandhi, of course, always favored his values.

A student ("Ed") once shared an example of how a colleague, whom he also considered a close friend, led him, step by step, into behaving unethically. When Ed was employed by a consulting firm in Florida, he and his best friend at work, Jan, were assigned to a project for a private equity ("PE") company. PE firms buy companies at discounts, improve operations, and then sell them for a profit.

The PE firm in Ed's case had recently bought a company called "Atlas" that supplied parts for lawn mowers, household generators, and other small-engine products on a global basis. The PE owner wanted to standardize the prices Atlas was charging its customers. Ed and Jan (who was a year ahead of Ed and was being considered for a promotion to manager) were tasked with assembling a database of Atlas prices and providing this report to their partner.

The two friends had no trouble obtaining the standard "public" pricing for the parts in question—which was readily available from Atlas's rate sheet. But they knew that the real, off-the-books pricing included steep discounts given locally to loyal customers—and none of the salespeople at Atlas were willing to tell an outside consultant what these prices were.

To solve this problem, Jan came up with a bright idea that would allow him to complete the project and burnish his case for promotion. He built fake websites for nonexistent firms that looked as if they could be potential new Atlas customers. He then contacted Atlas local offices and negotiated with the local salesperson as if he were a buyer from one of these fake companies. It worked perfectly, and he uncovered the progressive discounts available for repeat orders. Ed was uncomfortable with this setup, but Jan appealed to him "as a friend" for his help. It would take both of them making these calls across the globe to fill in the database by their deadline. Ed went along.

The kicker came when they were done and the report was submitted. At the final meeting with their partner before the big presentation to the PE client, she asked how they had gathered the data. Jan lied, telling her they had accessed it through "relationship sources."

Thus, what started for Ed as a dubious way to gather data as a favor to a friend became a misrepresentation to their boss—a lie their boss repeated to an important PE client. Ed felt badly enough about this incident to tell me about it years later. He rationalized that he and Jan had not really committed fraud because the information they uncovered was true, and they collected it on behalf of the PE firm that owned this business. But if it was proper, why had he and Jan felt the need to lie about it? Ed never felt the same way about Jan after this. He sensed that Jan had used him to advance his own case for promotion.

Compare Ed's example to another, more edifying one involving two friends who proactively reinforced each other's values. I met Mike as an MBA student, but his story concerned a time when he was president of the Marketing Club at a state university in Georgia. He was recruited by some of the country's largest brand-oriented companies, and near the end of the summer before his senior year, he spent a week at one of the biggest and most famous of these firms, "Brand-It" (not its real name). At the end of his week, the Brand-It recruiter assigned to him called him into the conference room where she was doing final interviews and, out of the blue, accused him of trying to get an offer solely as leverage to obtain a position at Brand-It's biggest rival. She said she was tired of kids from his school playing this game and informed him that he would not be getting an offer.

Mike was shocked and told her that he already had an offer from the firm she mentioned. If he had wanted to take that offer, he said, he would not have bothered visiting Brand-It. She replied that the interview was over and walked out.

A few months later, as school was closing out its fall semester, Mike got a text from his friend Peter, a past president of his school's marketing club and current employee at Brand-It. Peter was furious at a social media posting he had just seen on Facebook that bad-mouthed their university. The posting said recruiting at Mike's and Peter's school was a waste of time because the school had only two types of students: slackers and morons. Mike and Peter dug into the posting and discovered that it had been put there by the same recruiter who had blown up Mike's interview.

Something needed to be done. But what? One of the advantages of having a trusted partner is the potential for collaborating on strategy. And that is what Mike and Peter did. At first, they considered escalating the matter to the career services office at their business school. Mike was president of the Marketing Club, and this recruiter's unprofessional attitude was insulting to everyone in their program. Mike was sure the school would take immediate action. But Peter argued that this strategy might tarnish Brand-It, which would be unfair. The problem, he said, was really a single employee. So they finally settled on a simpler, more targeted plan.

Mike had briefly met the overall head of recruiting during his summer experience and found his email address on the company website. Mike and Peter then drafted an email that attached a screenshot of the "slackers and morons" posting, and Mike sent it to this person using his university email account and identifying himself as president of the school's Marketing Club. Three days later, Mike got a short reply from an assistant to the recruiting boss. The employee in question, the message said, "was no longer employed at Brand-It." The assistant thanked Mike for his information.

Mike ended his story by wondering if he had done the right thing. He and Peter knew some action had to be taken, but they had never imagined that the company would act so quickly and decisively. I told Mike I thought he and Peter had handled this situation well. The information Mike sent was truthful, and he had provided his name and contact information. It had been sent to someone who ought to know about it and could take appropriate action. Finally, their strategy had, as Peter hoped, limited the damage by holding the individual recruiter accountable rather than smearing the whole company. My guess: Mike and Peter had given the head of recruiting the smoking gun needed to take long overdue action against a problem employee.

The Many

My advice about the Many is simple: be careful about the ethical values of the places where you work. The standards of the Many you are surrounded by have a way of rubbing off on you, normalizing values you would reject if you saw them only from the outside. The single most important decision you will make about values in your professional life, therefore, is choosing the organizations you affiliate with.

Social conformity is rooted in imitation. If you are walking down a city sidewalk and encounter a large group of people who are looking up at a nearby rooftop, what do you do? Stop, look up, and see what the fuss is about. When you observe widespread media attention to fashion trends, cultural fads, and, of special relevance to this book, issues such as the #MeToo and Black Lives Matter movements, you pay attention. The Many set the agenda for the rest, forcing people to decide where they stand.

Animal behavior scholars have a name for the tipping point when a group switches from one behavior mode to another. They call it the "quorum response." Different species have differently sized "quorums" that will cue a change in behavior. For example, as meerkats (a prairie-dog-like small mammal found in southern Africa) are foraging in groups for food, scientists have noted that it takes only about three members out of a group as large as nineteen to trigger a move to a new foraging area. One meerkat gives a special mewing sound signaling that a move might be a good idea, a couple of others echo the sound, and off the group goes.

In an interview with the *New York Times*, Professor Marta Manser compared the meerkat behavior to a group of people hanging out in an apartment. If someone says, "Let's go for pizza," and nobody picks up on it, then the group stays put. But if several people agree it's a good idea, then the idea becomes more persuasive.

Values are a lot more important than pizzas, but social momentum plays a key role in how these spread as well. For example, recent, rapid changes in our culture regarding such issues as women's rights and marriage equality (or, on the other side of the political spectrum, deep-state conspiracy theories) demonstrate what can happen when enough people turn in a new direction, tipping the balance to create a "quorum response." If you want to explore the powerful currents of social influence mechanisms in detail, take a look at my favorite business book of all time: Robert Cialdini's *Influence: The Psychology of Persuasion*.

The Close and the Many are connected. The people you have associated with most closely—family, community, and schools—are all nested inside larger social groups, the Many. And given everyone's desire to have more harmony than conflict in their lives, you have likely lived in a "bubble" occupied (mainly) by people and groups who share a common set of core values. As two Dutch scholars aptly put it, "Social groups provide people with moral anchors for their personal convictions." The group is both the source of the value and the mechanism for sustaining it within each member.

Here is the rub: the people you associate with at work will come from a broader cross section of social life than the ones you see most frequently in your personal life. This is bound to expose you to some uncomfortable conflicts as the people you encounter exhibit different assumptions about what rules "everyone" ought to apply. The conflicts become especially acute when your sense of self and social identity become bound up in your occupation. What do you do when you take pride in being an "investment banker" and then realize that the values held by many "investment bankers" in your industry condone behavior you used to consider fraudulent?

Add to this the problems that arise when you happen to find yourself swimming in what I call a "dirty pond." While many businesses apply higher ethical standards, others skate over the line into illegal conduct—as far as they can go without being caught, tried, and convicted of a crime. With the social influence of the Many pressuring you to accept this way of doing business, you may find your values slipping. Day after day, criminal conduct will be normalized by the rationalization that "everyone does it." Are you strong enough to resist that?

Finally, here are three sobering facts. My University of Pennsylvania colleague, behavioral economist Eugen Dimant, has shown experimentally that swimming in a "dirty pond" carries three dangers. First, anti-social behavior spreads faster in groups than pro-social behavior. So changing a bad culture into a good one is always a catch-up game. Second, the closer people work together, the stronger this "contagion" effect for bad behavior. So the intense, team-based work environments of high-paying-but-loose-morals firms are the perfect breeding grounds for the worst people to dominate. Third, people who are already inclined to behave badly pick up these corrupt group norms especially quickly. So they may set the tone before the rest of the group has a chance to establish the right norms.

Conclusion: To avoid having your values swept away by "the Many," do everything you can to avoid the "dirty ponds." Pick your workplace carefully, keep allies who support your values close at hand, and be prepared to exert extra effort to uphold the principles you believe in. When you hear someone say, "Don't worry; everybody does it," have your response ready: "Not everybody—I don't."

The Powerful

To some extent, authority pressure captures James Clear's notion that "the Powerful" exert strong influences on us. Bosses, political leaders, generals, and CEOs control the behavior of those around them by virtue of their positions at the top of their respective pecking orders. But that is not the whole story. When you allow yourself to be dazzled by the status of people you interact with—even when you do not work for them—you are at risk of "catching" their bad values (or being uplifted by their good ones) as you unconsciously imitate them in hopes of gaining some of their "magic" for your own life.

Take the case of former Ivy League basketball coach Jerome Allen—a good man who allowed himself to be drawn into a criminal conspiracy by teaming up with a corrupt business mogul. Allen was a highly respected member of a tight-knit community: the athletic department at my home institution, the University of Pennsylvania. Before he became a coach, he was an Ivy League all-star at Penn, and I fondly remember taking my sons to see him play.

At the time, I did not know Jerome's story. He grew up in poverty in a single-parent home in Philadelphia's hardscrabble Germantown section. As a professional college coach, he presented himself as a confident, competent leader, but he later admitted to a federal judge that he was "struggling with financial issues" on his modest salary.

When a wealthy, charismatic Miami-based health-care entrepreneur, Philip Esformes, began cultivating a relationship with him, Allen was literally swept off his feet by the vision of a future career in business. Esformes (who would later be convicted of massive Medicare fraud involving his chain of nursing homes and health-care facilities) introduced Allen to a high-status life of luxury with all-expense-paid trips to Florida—entertaining him at his multimillion-dollar home in Miami Beach. Being courted by the Powerful can be a disorienting experience for anyone, and Allen was an especially vulnerable target.

Then came the "ask." Would Allen endorse Esformes's son for admission to Penn's Wharton School as a special "basketball" admit? True, his son was not much of a basketball player, but in exchange, Allen would receive annual cash payments and a future in Esformes's Florida business empire.

Allen faced his moment of truth—and failed. "I had an opportunity to say no," Allen later told a federal judge when he pled guilty to fraud, "and I didn't." Allen's community came to his rescue, however, as a parade of character witnesses—former players, colleagues, and coaches—testified on his behalf at sentencing. His behavior was an aberration, they all said, not a pattern. He had always chosen the harder, straighter path before Esformes entered his life. The judge sentenced him to house arrest, fines, and community service—not jail. Jerome Allen, now an assistant coach for the Boston Celtics, got a second chance.

Pause for a moment to consider some of the Powerful people you admire. Would you describe any of them as a "person of conscience"? If so, take steps to make this person an even more vivid role model than they already are.

CASE STUDY:
TRUSTED PARTNERS THAT MADE A DIFFERENCE

We are now ready to put the concepts we have explored above to work in a real-world case study. The one I have chosen concerns a notorious corporate scandal, the demise of the medical device company Theranos, Inc. The outlines of the story are well known, having been the subject of a prizewinning book by *Wall Street Journal* reporter John Carreyrou called *Bad Blood: Secrets and Lies in a Silicon Valley Startup*. In addition, the story inspired a motion picture screenplay based on the book and two excellent television documentaries: HBO's *The Inventor* and ABC's *The Dropout*.

I have chosen the Theranos example for several reasons. First, the two heroes—Tyler Shultz and Erika Cheung—were young people in their twenties, the same ages as many of my students. Neither one wanted to be a "whistleblower" nor sought out media attention for their roles in bringing the scandal to light. They were just ordinary, clear-eyed "people of conscience" who cared about scientific standards, patient safety, and family. They were relatively powerless, but refused to be intimidated when their bosses pressured them to go along with the rest of their peers in a massive fraud.

The story also pulls together many threads from both this chapter and the book. As you review the story below, note the powerful role a "trusted partner" can play in a values conflict. And watch as the Close, the Many, and the Powerful all combine to pressure Shultz and Cheung to agree that "X is true" when they know beyond all doubt that "X is *not* true."

Elizabeth Holmes's Excellent Adventure

The story starts long before Tyler Shultz and Erika Cheung enter the picture, when a charismatic nineteen-year-old Stanford undergraduate named Elizabeth Holmes got a bright idea for a new approach to blood testing. Instead of drawing a tube of blood from someone's arm using a needle, Holmes envisioned a high-tech device that would take a single drop of blood from a finger prick and use it to run multiple tests. It was a simple, elegant idea that, when realized, would allow her to dominate the multibillion-dollar blood-testing market.

Holmes had limited skills as a technologist, but she was supremely gifted at persuading men many years older than herself to help her. In 2003, as a college sophomore, she convinced the dean of the Stanford School of Engineering, Channing Robertson, that her finger prick concept might work and enlisted him to join her firm's board of directors. He, in turn, helped raise her first round of funding. Theranos was born.

Between 2003 and 2011, Holmes raised nearly $100 million and was on her way to becoming a Silicon Valley celebrity. There was only one hitch: after eight years of work, she was no closer to realizing a working product. Indeed, such testing as the firm did was accomplished using traditional testing equipment. Her single-drop testing gadget—called the "Edison"—never came close to matching the picture she had of it in her head.

Her recruiting talents with older men never faltered, however. In 2009, she hired forty-four-year-old Ramesh "Sunny" Balwani, an acquaintance with a pugnacious, in-your-face management style, to oversee internal operations. Balwani was fiercely loyal to both Holmes's vision and Holmes personally. It was not long before they became secret lovers.

And, in 2011, she persuaded former secretary of state George Shultz to join her board. With his help, she added a number of other famous public luminaries to the board, including Henry Kissinger, Jim Mattis (a celebrated Marine Corps general and war hero), and former senators Sam Nunn and Bill Frist. Her star-studded list of investors ranged from the Walton family (retailer Sam Walton's heirs) to Rupert Murdoch.

A final 2011 event turned out to be significant only in hindsight. One day, George Shultz's grandson (Stanford junior Tyler Schultz) met Elizabeth Holmes at his grandfather's home in Palo Alto. The younger Shultz heard Elizabeth Holmes's pitch for Theranos, was inspired by it, and changed his college major from engineering to biology. He interned at Theranos in the summer of 2012 and started a full-time job there in the fall of 2013, soon after his graduation.

As it happened, he began work just as Theranos was struggling to deliver on a $100 million contract Holmes had signed a year earlier with drugstore giant Walgreens. The deal committed Theranos to delivering real-world, accurate blood tests at Walgreens' pharmacies. The rollout was scheduled for 2013 and 2014. By the time the younger Shultz started his job, the Walgreens rollout was already behind schedule and the pressure was on to save the deal.

The Power of Two

A few weeks after starting at Theranos in the fall of 2013, Shultz met another rookie, Erika Cheung. Cheung had just graduated from the University of California at Berkeley, but unlike Shultz, she had gotten her job the old-fashioned way: by attending a job fair on the Berkeley campus. Her dual degrees in molecular biology and linguistics and some good interviews had landed her something very close to her dream job—a well-paid position at a Silicon Valley startup doing work in her field that would "change the world."

With the Walgreens contract looming in the background, Shultz and Cheung worked side by side on a team that was testing the accuracy of the Edison. Outside the company, Elizabeth Holmes was doing her thing: dazzling the media with her youthful energy, black turtleneck outfits, and high-energy talks hyping the Edison. Admirers were calling her the next Steve Jobs or Bill Gates. Inside the firm, Shultz and Cheung were testing the Edison and wondering how something as klutzy as this could be the same machine she was describing.

Early on, Shultz and Cheung noticed that some of their data from testing the Edison machines did not make it into reports. Which data? The ones showing results that deviated too far from what had been expected. They inquired and were told that it was standard practice to ignore these "outliers."

They also became concerned that the firm was misreporting a variety of metrics on the Edison's accuracy for different types of blood tests. More concerning still, they saw that when the test results from the Edison were compared with results from traditional machines known to be accurate, the Edison was failing—big-time. Sometimes a blood sample tested on the Edison pointed to a severe illness. When that same sample was tested on conventional, accurate equipment, it showed entirely normal results.

Shultz and Cheung began to have lunch together every day, sharing evidence of what they saw going on. Cheung told her friend she was keeping careful records of all her tests, even if the data were being thrown out as "outliers." Shultz had his doubts that the company was even using the Edison to service the Walgreens contract. He had seen an area where Walgreens blood tests were being performed on ordinary, run-of-the-mill equipment.

But the two tried to keep the faith. In the super-secretive atmosphere at Theranos, it was hard to say exactly what was going on behind closed doors. Deep down, they both wanted to believe that they were just experiencing a badly managed startup trying to do too much, too soon. As Cheung later put it, "I was hoping that somewhere in that building there was something I wasn't seeing . . . a wonderful device that existed."

They were, in short, under the thrall of the three social influence sources discussed above. The people they worked with believed all was well, and Tyler Shultz's grandfather was a raving fan (the Close); the media bought into Holmes's vision—hook, line, and sinker (the Many); and the company was basking in the glow of support by celebrity investors and famous board members (the Powerful).

Over the Thanksgiving weekend in late 2013, something happened that disturbed Cheung more than anything she had seen up to then. She was running a standard quality control test on three Edison machines to see if they were working properly. She put blood samples with known properties into the machines, and the machines repeatedly failed to produce a report showing these known properties. It was like asking a computer to add 1 + 1 and repeatedly getting answers such as 5 and 8. She called the firm "help line" to find out what she should do, and eventually an employee from another unit came down to see what was going on. She watched as this employee tinkered with the quality control settings, ran a few more tests, threw out two of the results that did not conform to expectations, and sent out the report.

Cheung could hardly believe what she had seen: machines that had repeatedly failed quality control tests were being certified as accurate for use on real patient samples. She talked with Shultz, who had been getting a similar runaround when he challenged his bosses on the way data were being collected and reported. Cheung learned that Shultz had been to Elizabeth Holmes's thirtieth birthday party at his grandfather's house and had followed up this access to Holmes with a meeting to share his concerns directly with her. She had been polite, but had passed him off to a senior staff member. This executive had given him a few half-baked arguments before admitting that, "[S]ometimes Elizabeth exaggerates" the Edison's performance.

For her part, Cheung had made a bold move: calling a meeting of the senior scientists in her group to challenge the way quality control was being done. Everyone had been receptive to what she said, but nothing had been done.

Team Players?

Shultz and Cheung began to realize the pressure was on to ignore equipment failures and use the Edison to test samples from Walgreens patients, come what may. And they knew the pressure had a source: Elizabeth Holmes's enforcer, Sunny Balwani. In fact, after Cheung's meeting with the senior members of her team, she found herself summoned to Balwani's office, where he berated her for questioning the firm's testing methods. "He just sort of lost it," Cheung later told a reporter. "What makes you think we have problems?" Balwani said angrily. "What was your training in statistics?" He demanded that the testing group start producing results at a new, record pace. When Cheung and her colleagues said that it couldn't be done, they were accused of not being "team players."

It was now March 2014, and the final straw for the pair came over a technical issue called "proficiency testing." Under US law, clinical labs must undergo what amounts to an accreditation process three times each year. They have to show that the equipment they are using for blood testing operates within accepted regulatory standards. Theranos had not been using the Edison for real patient samples until the Walgreens contract came online, so the firm had always passed these tests by submitting data from the traditional equipment it used. But now the Edison, on at least a partial basis, was processing real patient samples submitted by Walgreens. The Theranos compliance team therefore conducted proficiency tests on Edison machines as well as traditional equipment. The Edisons performed very poorly.

Faced with this failure, which might have threatened Theranos's multibillion-dollar stock valuation (at this time, Elizabeth Holmes was worth some $5 billion on paper), Sunny Balwani ordered the lab to suppress the Edison results in the report to regulators. Shultz and Cheung were appalled. But when Shultz brought his concerns to his boss, he was told the legal regulations were extremely complex and that no laws had been broken. What to do?

Shultz decided to put his boss's assertion about the legality of Theranos's actions to a test. On Friday, March 28, 2014, he created an email account for an alias—"Colin Ramirez"—and sent a query to one of the proficiency-testing regulators Theranos had sent data to: the Clinical Laboratory Evaluation Program of the New York State Department of Health. He posed a detailed hypothetical. What if a firm did what Theranos had just done on a proficiency test? Would it be legal? The following Monday he got a reply. Such practices would amount to cheating, a top regulator said. The actions would be in violation of both state and federal law. The reply gave Shultz instructions on how to submit an anonymous complaint to state investigators, and he did so.

Shultz also sent Elizabeth Holmes a detailed email, complete with charts and numbers showing all the errors that he had picked up over his months at work. A few days later, Sunny Balwani responded with a blistering attack on Shultz's arguments and data. Balwani called Shultz's email "insulting" and demanded an immediate apology. It implied that, but for his status as George Shultz's grandson, Tyler would be fired.

That was enough for the young Shultz. He replied that he planned to resign and ended up being asked to leave that very day. As luck would have it, his security escort did not show up as he was leaving the building, so he carried paper copies of his email to Holmes and Balwani's reply with him as he departed. Within a few hours, he was headed for his grandfather's office to show him the emails and plead one last time for him to get clear of Theranos. George Shultz listened, had his secretary make copies of the emails to put in his office safe, and then asked Tyler to come back that night for dinner at the house. He had already gotten a call from Elizabeth Holmes, he said, who had warned him that his grandson was off the rails. George wanted a chance to show Tyler that he had the whole thing wrong.

For her part, Cheung was also feeling the stress. She had called her father (an executive at UPS) seeking advice. "I don't know what to do," she had told him. "I know I have a good job, I'm making really good money, I'm in Silicon Valley, but I can't do this anymore." He had expressed confidence in her judgment and reassurance about her family's support no matter what.

The day Shultz quit, Cheung had two conversations. The first was with Sunny Balwani, who called her to a meeting. He told her that he had figured out from Shultz's email that she was the source of some of her friend's proficiency-testing data. He came down hard on Cheung, telling her she needed to decide "if you want to work here or not." The second conversation was with Shultz, who told her he had quit and asked her to join him at his dinner meeting with his grandfather. Shultz explained that having two people testifying to the facts they had uncovered might help his grandfather come to his senses. Shultz may not have read Milgram's Experiment 17, but he knew that a pair of "dissenting peers" might stand a better chance of winning the day.

Cheung agreed, but the dinner meeting proved fruitless. George Shultz remained steadfastly under the thrall of the charismatic Holmes. He lectured them about what a great product Theranos had, even saying things they knew to be false about the Edison being used in hospitals and on medical helicopters. He advised the pair to find new jobs.

The next day, Cheung quit. Unlike Shultz, her backpack was checked as she departed, but she had, as she told Tyler earlier, been keeping careful notes and storing them at home. These would prove to be the detonating devices that ultimately blew up the company.

In late September 2015, after being threatened and harassed by Theranos lawyers about meeting with *Wall Street Journal* reporter John Carreyrou (Shultz had already been the target of similar intimidation), she filed a detailed, well-documented formal complaint with the federal Centers for Medicare and Medicaid Services about the fraudulent proficiency report and other misconduct she had observed. The complaint triggered a formal investigation, which, in combination with Carreyrou's series of front-page investigative stories (sourced in part by Shultz and Cheung) and Shultz's earlier anonymous filing with New York State regulators, brought an end to the Theranos story.

Criminal indictments against Elizabeth Holmes and Sunny Balwani were handed down on June 15, 2018. Theranos formally ceased operations a few months later, on September 4, 2018.

Wrapping It Up: The Power of Two vs. the Close, the Many, and the Powerful

It is impossible to say whether Shultz or Cheung, acting separately, could have brought about the result they did. But it seems clear that their collective power was more than the sum of its two parts. Shultz had hoped, when he brought Cheung to meet his grandfather the day before she resigned, that they might break the spell Holmes had cast on the stubborn, crusty former secretary of state. But that had not worked. All George Shultz had seen were two young, inexperienced idealists who did not grasp the "big picture" of the medical device business. Nevertheless, like Asch's subjects who benefited from a "true partner," they reinforced each other's confidence in the truth of what they could see with their own eyes. And with two voices on the side of this truth, they proved to be persuasive, reliable sources for the *Wall Street Journal*.

Their story demonstrates the power of an ally when you encounter the pressures of a real-world conflict. Shultz and Cheung fed off each other's energies, advanced each other's strategic thinking, and provided independent, credible information from the inner workings of a corrupt organization that could be used as evidence by the legal system. But they faced consistent opposition from George Shultz and were intimidated, at least initially, by the positive media coverage given the charismatic Elizabeth Holmes and celebrity status of many Theranos stakeholders.

In short, Theranos was a "perfect storm" of the pressures identified as the enemies of ethical conduct earlier in the book:

- Peer Pressure. Shultz's and Cheung's peers were passive players in the Theranos fraud, going along to get along. The weight of peer pressure was against them.
- Authority Pressure. The top officers at Theranos brought direct pressure on Shultz and Cheung to stop their questioning and go along with the herd. Balwani personally berated them both, threatening them with termination. Even after they left, the firm's lawyers and investigators stalked them and issued more threats to curtail their cooperation with the media.
- Incentives. The Walgreens contract with its urgent deadline requiring the Edison to be a working product provoked the entire scandal. Everyone was working feverishly to make the deadline, not to create a safe, useful medical device.
- Roles. Time after time, Shultz's and Cheung's junior roles in the organization were held up as reasons for them to stand down. They were told they were acting outside their areas of expertise and should let other, more senior people take responsibility for these important decisions.
- Systems. When an entire company goes rogue, people like Shultz and Cheung face more than individualized opposition. Investors, bankers, other employees, and even the media may have a stake in maintaining the illusion that nothing is wrong. Fearful of losses and embarrassment, they form a wall of opposition to anyone who might burst the bubble.

Against these pressures, our two heroes had three things going for them. They had each other as trusted partners in their work, powerful allies of their own at the *Wall Street Journal* and within the federal regulatory system, and, at the bottom of it all, the truth.

Coda

What became of Shultz and Cheung? Did they, in the words of this book's subtitle, advance their careers by keeping their values? I believe so. Three aspects of their story are worth noting.

Motivations. Neither Shultz nor Cheung aspired to be or thought of themselves as "whistleblowers." In a talk he gave at Lehigh University in 2019, Shultz said, "I never even thought of the word 'whistleblower' until I saw it written in a newspaper next to my name in 2016." Instead, he seems to have been motivated by two things. First, he was angry at the lies the firm was telling the public about a device that he knew did not work. Second, he wanted to protect his grandfather from the disgrace he could see coming.

As for Cheung, she seems to have felt a combination of guilt and shame at participating in an enterprise that was putting real patients at risk by providing their physicians with bogus blood test results. She consulted a lawyer after Theranos began stalking her, and the lawyer pointed out that she could file a complaint about Theranos with federal regulators. "I had no idea you could do that," she later told ABC News for a podcast series. It had been her first job out of college, after all. "That was never something I expected to sign up for, but it really started to eat me up inside, and that's what led me to file the complaint." In the complaint itself, she wrote, "I'm ashamed of myself for not filing this complaint sooner," and concluded with the hope that her filing would stop Theranos from ruining someone's life "by giving them a false and deceiving result."

Careers. Cheung and Shultz both found new jobs in Silicon Valley soon after they left Theranos. Cheung was doing lab work for a firm called Antibody Solutions when she first realized she was being stalked by Theranos lawyers. Shultz was working with a group at Stanford, trying to help a Canadian company win a science innovation prize, when he had his final visit with *Wall Street Journal* reporter John Carreyrou. Shultz went on to become the cofounder and CEO of a medical diagnostics software company called Flux Biosciences.

Cheung moved on from Silicon Valley to Hong Kong, where she became a program director at a technology accelerator called Betatron. With help from Shultz and a cofounder named Luke Finn, her next move was to launch a nonprofit called Ethics in Entrepreneurship, which became her full-time job. Her group promotes "speak up" cultures in startups and provides advice on ethical decision making in the tech industry.

Identities as People of Conscience. Their stories demonstrate that by doing the right thing, you can become the right kind of person. John Carreyrou summed up his evaluation of the two in his book *Bad Blood* this way: "I was . . . impressed with their sense of ethics. They felt strongly that what they had witnessed was wrong and were willing to take the risk of speaking to me to right that wrong."

One sign of having chosen the right path in a values conflict? No regrets. Cheung later told her college alumni magazine that, given a chance to do her life over, "I would have done exactly the same thing. It was stressful, but I couldn't even imagine another path." Shultz put it this way in a 2019 interview: "Luckily, I look back and have very few regrets. I'm pretty proud of myself for everything that I did."

Even Tyler's grandfather George Shultz eventually came around. In a statement given to the ABC news program *Nightline* when he was approaching ninety-nine years of age, George Shultz praised his grandson's "responsibility to the truth and patient safety even when he felt personally threatened and believed I had placed allegiance to the company over allegiance to higher values and our family. . . . I want to recognize and congratulate Tyler for his great moral character."

A MOMENT FOR PERSONAL REFLECTION

As you reflect on the role of friends and allies in ethical conflicts, try to recall an occasion when this asset was missing—when you had to stand alone against a bully or group that had turned on you, teasing or shaming you about something. Then expand that to moments when, to avoid experiencing these painful emotions, you went along with a group even though you knew it was wrong to do so.

Now fast-forward to a more recent time when you have been in a group that was advocating for values you believed in. That feeling of solidarity and empowerment is the Power of Two. Working with others in support of a cause increases everyone's courage and confidence. It often makes the difference between success and failure in conflicts over values.

NEXT UP: WEIGHING YOUR DECISION

The next chapter shifts our focus from using your character, personality, and alliances to take responsibility to thinking through your decision about how to respond. Ethical choices deserve careful consideration. Rule #7 of the Conscience Code ("Ask Four Questions") introduces you to the time-tested decision factors that have helped people make tough choices in social dilemmas for centuries. Think of yourself as having a set of scales on which to weigh the most important components of your problem. Four key factors deserve a place on those scales: consequences, loyalties, your identity as a person of conscience, and the principles you hold most dear.

RULE #7: ASK FOUR QUESTIONS

"Nothing pains some people more than having to think."
—Dr. Martin Luther King Jr.

An MBA student ("Ken") once concluded a story he had told in class by summing up the difficulties of standing up for one's values at an early stage in a career. As he put it, "It's difficult to disagree with a manager who is older, more experienced, and has direct authority over you. It's the same for resisting practices you disapprove of but believe to be commonplace in your organization. As I look back on the ethical dilemmas I have faced, I realize now that I did not give them as much thought as I should have. I should have spent more time weighing the consequences for me and my career. I should have thought more about the options I may have had."

Rule #7, "Ask Four Questions," is my answer to Ken's request for help. Until now, we have emphasized the "softer" sides of our natures, the perceptions and emotions that help you identify a challenge to your values and the character strengths, personality traits, and social ties that give you the courage to face this challenge. Now we are ready to explore the most distinctive feature of the human animal—our ability to reason. As you will see, your willingness to engage in genuine introspection sets you up for success at the decision stage.

In addition to prompting you to take your time as you work through ethical conflicts, reason helps you to grapple with the hardest cases—the ones in which your moral intuitions point in opposing directions. When you have the feeling that any decision you make will compromise an important value, reason is an essential ally. What is the best way to weigh these decisions?

This chapter takes up these challenges by examining a four-question framework. If you find memory devices helpful, you can call this one "CLIP." When you face a difficult values conflict, systematically consider four factors: Consequences, Loyalties, Identity, and Principles. Asking probing questions and consulting people you trust about these four items will help you better understand both the situation you are in and the options available to resolve it.

Ironically, the previous chapters have shown that your intellectual abilities can be a source of weakness as well as strength in many pressure-packed situations. Faced with strong impulses to keep your head down and avoid confrontations, your mind can play tricks on you, rationalizing instead of reasoning. Before you realize what has happened, you have made a fully "justified" decision based on reasons that will evaporate as soon as you are challenged to defend them. "Just this once" and "everybody does it" turn into "How could I have done that?" When this happens, you will join Ken in wishing you had more thoughtfully considered the consequences for yourself and your career. By taking the time to think things through, you improve the chances you'll get the balance right—making the decision that will stand the test of time.

Consider the case of Army Sergeant Joe Darby, the man who first alerted the US military command that prisoners held in the Abu Ghraib prison in Iraq were being systematically tortured and abused by their American guards. It all started one day in 2004, when Darby was writing home and discovered that the disk holding his photo album of camels, desert dwellings, and his buddies had melted in the desert heat. Needing a few shots to send his family, he asked his friend Charles Graner to let him use some pictures Graner had taken. When Darby opened Graner's photo disk on his computer, he found himself looking at prisoners being abused and tortured, the now-famous photos that would soon shock the world. And once Darby had seen these pictures, he found it impossible to forget them.

One of his core values, he later told a reporter, was a deep sense of loyalty to his fellow soldiers—"my comrades, my brothers in arms." My own father, a World War II veteran, taught me that there are few bonds stronger than those that arise among combat soldiers in war. It is a loy-alty that extends much farther and deeper than the ordinary loyalties of civilian life and includes an implicit pledge of secrecy regarding actions that people are not proud of. Darby knew firsthand that things happen in war that people later regret—and he, himself, later admitted that he had done such things. "I'm not a Boy Scout," he said. It followed that he was also "not the kind of guy to rat someone out."

Against that loyalty was the profound moral disgust he experienced when he viewed the photos. "I couldn't stop thinking about [them]," he said. The pictures depicted behavior that "crossed the line," giving him "the choice between what I knew was morally right and my loyalty to other soldiers. I couldn't have it both ways." He struggled with his decision for three days before turning the photos over to Army investigators, changing his life—and America's view of the Iraq War—forever.

Joe Darby's phrase is worth remembering: "I couldn't have it both ways." Call it the Joe Darby Test. When you have this sense, you are about to make a decision that will loom large in your memory.

Reasoned introspection, then, can help you question rationalizations and make wise decisions in really tough cases. In this chapter, I will offer a short primer on how experts advise us to think our way through these moral conflicts. The CLIP framework uses four pointed questions to advance your thinking. I will use these questions to analyze a compelling case one of my students brought to class about her work in Africa. Next, the chapter will take a look at the role that careful deliberation can play at each stage of the values-to-action process. We'll see how reasoning can help you better *recognize* that a value is at risk, take *ownership* of that value, *analyze your decision*, and *design an action plan*. A conclusion wraps up the chapter.

THINKING THROUGH TOUGH CASES: FOUR QUESTIONS

I'll begin with two disclaimers. First, if proper reasoning were all we needed to find the right answer to life's most complex problems, we would be living in a very different world. There would be a lot less hunger, racism, and social inequality, and we would be closer to solving the climate crisis. So let's agree that reason, as useful as it is, requires partners to advance the cause of moral progress—partners such as patience, courage, allies, political skills, persuasive arguments, and passionate commitment. No less a figure than the founder of modern psychology, William James, once said that, "The science of logic never made a man reason rightly, and the science of ethics (if there be such a thing) never made a man behave rightly." But James held out hope that reason could "help us to catch ourselves up . . . if we start . . . to behave wrongly."

Second, reasoning about moral questions is a profoundly complex field. In ethics and philosophy classes around the world, professors present their students with clever, otherworldly puzzles designed to keep them arguing late into the night. One favorite example involves a runaway trolley car. The trolley's driver has had a heart attack, and the car will certainly kill five people strapped to the track in front of it unless you pull a lever to divert the trolley to another track. The problem: the trolley will also kill a person if it goes down that other track—but only one instead of five. Would you pull the lever? The great majority of people say they would.

Then comes the twist: assuming there was no lever and no other way to prevent this accident, would you push someone directly in front of the trolley—thereby sacrificing them to stop the trolley and save the five people strapped on the track? In both cases, one person dies to save five, but the second case feels very different. Most people say they would refuse to push someone to their death. It's too personal and feels too much like murder. So which principle takes priority: the greatest good for the greatest number or the moral imperative that makes it wrong to deliberately push someone to their death?

Puzzles like this fuel academic debate and research about moral intuitions versus cost-benefit analysis. But few situations come with such clean lines.

So, instead of analyzing classroom exercises, the chapter offers four questions that you can use as a diagnostic checklist. This framework is by no means original. Over the centuries, the great moral philosophers—from Plato, Aristotle, and Confucius to Smith, Hume, Bentham, Mill, and Kant—have done the hard work of isolating the short list of issues you should think through in really tough cases. Scholars have long debated which of these factors takes theoretical priority over the others, but the rest of us are free to use them in any way that helps us solve real-world problems. My advice to students: treat all of them as touchstones for deliberation in a given situation, seek additional perspectives to protect yourself from bias and rationalization, and then apply your best judgment informed by your experience.

Below, you'll find the four questions. Note that each of them opens a large zone of inquiry filled with uncertainty. When applied to public policy debates over such things as poverty, hunger, and climate change, these questions are appropriate topics for extensive research. When used by someone like you facing a tough conflict at work, the goal is more modest: they will help you think through your situation responsibly in the time you have available. Answering these questions does not make a really hard case into an "easy" one. The Joe Darby Test still applies. But they can help.

1. **Consequences: What is the Balance of Harms?** What are the consequences for everyone concerned? Who pays what price? Is there a decision that minimizes these costs?
2. **Loyalties: What Duties Do I Owe to Others?** What duties of loyalty, if any, do you owe to people or organizations in this situation? Are these loyalties driving you toward or away from your true values? (*Note: this factor has a long tradition in Confucian thought but is less important in Western philosophy. Regardless, loyalty is usually considered a virtue, and the students and executives I work with uniformly take it very seriously in practical, work-related dilemmas.*)
3. **Identity: Can I Live with this Decision?** What will your decision say about who you are as a person? Are you at peace with that? Your identity is implicated at two levels: at the level of basic morality and at the level of your social roles. Questions such as, "What is my duty as a person of conscience?" can help you access the basic moral level, while questions such as, "What is my duty as a good parent?" or "What is my duty as a professional?" can be helpful at the social-role level.
4. **Principles: Is There a Principle at Stake That Must Not Be Compromised?** What core principles are at risk? The five value themes we have talked about capture many such principles: Compassion, Respect, Accountability, Fairness, and Truth. You may feel that some principles should never be compromised, no matter what the price.

In thinking logically about these four areas, you should identify the ones most relevant to your situation, seek information to clarify them, weigh them against one another, and test different scenarios by asking "What if?" Then you'll need to consult with "trusted partners" and advisors before finally reconciling yourself to a final decision that will often feel less-than-completely-satisfying. In Joe Darby's case, the tortured Iraqi prisoners (consequences), principles (war crimes), and duties (personal conscience as well as the duty to report violations of the Uniform Code of Military Justice) all pointed him toward reporting what he had seen. Only his loyalty to fellow soldiers pointed the other way. Even so, he felt this loyalty so strongly that it was a close call. He later commented that "the decision would have been harder if they [the guards in the pictures] had been different soldiers. But most of these soldiers I had doubts about already."

To see how the four-question process works in a less spectacular case, let's take a look at one a student brought to class. I'll tell her story, then ask you to make a decision based on your moral intuitions. Next, we'll walk through the four factors, and finally I'll reveal what actually happened.

The Bribe

The case involves "Nina," who worked as a project manager for a private foundation funded by an exceedingly wealthy family. The family had made its money in the pharmaceutical business, and the foundation focused on health-care initiatives in developing countries.

In this particular case, the foundation's executive director had been contacted by a friend who served as a partner in a European private equity group. The group had investments in Africa and had stumbled over a "special problem" in an African country just emerging from a brutal civil war. There was a hospital in a medium-sized city that was desperately trying to resupply its pediatric service. It had been looted during the war and was now restarting operations. The private equity partner who brought this to the foundation's attention said it required an "emergency response." The partner hoped the foundation could use its wide network of contacts to find a solution.

Nina was assigned to the case. While conducting her preliminary investigation, Nina told us, "I saw children die in front of my eyes due to lack of simple antibiotics and diarrhea medicine. It was one of the most compelling projects I had been asked to work on."

Nina was good at her job and was soon able to locate several large lots of pediatric medical supplies available at no cost through a government program in the United States. If Nina could solve the logistics of getting these supplies into the country within the next eight weeks, the US agency would release them to the foundation, and the hospital would receive the urgent items needed. The project was certain to save hundreds of young lives.

The final step in her logistics plan required Nina to obtain the signature of the country's customs minister on a set of key documents allowing the supplies to clear customs at its port of entry. This minister was new, having just been appointed by the government at the end of the war. Nina visited the Customs Ministry several times to collect the signed paperwork but was given a shifting set of excuses about "unavoidable delays" and mysterious "additional authorizations" that were necessary. After a week of this, her local contact informed her that this minister would not deliver the documents without a "commission"—i.e., a bribe—that would add roughly 5 percent to the costs of the logistical expenses of the operation, or roughly $15,000.

What to do? Time was short. Nina knew that bribes, though technically illegal, were a common feature of commercial life in some countries, especially those emerging from a period of social chaos. Moreover, the foundation could easily afford to pay this one, which came to little more than the executive director's travel budget for the quarter. Should Nina bargain to get the bribe as low as possible, pay it, and save the children? Or should she refuse to pay the bribe on principle and hand the project over to the country's poorly organized health ministry? The legal system in this war-ravaged country was as corrupt as the port system, so there was no use going to the courts.

Nina took this problem to her executive director, who contacted her friend, the private equity partner. A meeting was called and a debate ensued. Let's pause the story here for a moment. Then we will return to the outcome Nina reported in class.

Imagine you have a vote at this meeting. What would you recommend? You can assume that all the political pressure possible has already been brought to bear on the minister but with no effect. Circle your vote below, then read the following section.

My moral intuitions tell me I would (circle one):
Pay the Bribe . . . Not Pay the Bribe.

Thinking Through the Four Questions

I hope you will agree that this is, morally speaking, a tough case. You (and Nina) are between a rock and a hard place—you do not want to pay the bribe and you do not want to allow children to die. The Joe Darby Test applies: you cannot have it both ways.

Now—how should you think about this problem? Take each of the four questions, then explore, investigate, weigh, and debate them. Finally, sleep on it and decide. And remember, tough cases are likely to inspire sharply different moral intuitions, requiring you to prepare carefully to "talk it through" thoroughly and make your case persuasively (the subject of our next chapter).

Consequences—What Is the Balance of Harms? In Nina's case, as in most, the consequences of a decision should weigh heavily in the scales. Consequences are relevant, often dominant considerations in almost all tough cases. Indeed, the human mind seems to be programmed to inquire, "What will happen if I do this?" literally hundreds of times every day. In Nina's situation, children will die if she does not pay the bribe. This is a direct, painful, almost unthinkable factor. At the same time, the foundation can easily afford to pay an extra $15,000.

But these are not the only potential consequences of the foundation's decision. What happens if Nina pays the bribe?

As part of "thinking it through," it is wise (whenever possible) to consult with people who know more than you do about the type of tough case you confront. Nobody involved with Nina's situation had experienced a bribery demand in a developing country, and they were in a hurry. So they made a rookie mistake—they did not reach out to anyone outside their respective organizations to seek advice.

In reviewing her case, however, I shared Nina's problem with a Wharton colleague, Professor Phil Nichols, who writes on global corruption and has worked with a variety of organizations, large and small, facing this kind of dilemma.

His comment: "This group is going to face a lot of serious, perhaps crippling operational challenges if it pays the bribe." He noted that, having received one bribe, the Customs Minister might make Nina pay another and threaten to expose her as trying to "corrupt" him if she does not do as he asks. In addition, other officials at the port or on the police could begin viewing this group (and perhaps the private equity firm associated with this project) as lucrative sources of money—throwing up additional obstacles to this project as well as future ones. If all that were not enough, the local population, eager to celebrate the good deeds being done by the foundation, might become cynical about this project after they learn that a large amount of money has gone to an official they despise. Finally, Professor Nichols said Nina should consider what might happen if the bribe were to become known in the foundation's home country. He said he had seen bribery cases very much like Nina's in which donors, funding agencies, and government licensing entities had dialed back future cooperation with a group that had paid a bribe. "None of these are inevitable consequences of paying this bribe," he concluded, "but they could happen."

Note: When it comes to weighing the potential effects of a decision, a little investigation can help a lot. The obvious consequences will leap to your mind. The unintended ones require you to look harder.

Loyalties—What Duties Do I Owe to Others? The loyalty factor does not play an important role in this case—certainly not the role it played in Joe Darby's decision. One loyalty might affect the outcome, however: the one between the foundation's executive director and her friend the private equity partner. Suppose, for example, the executive director was inclined to pay the bribe, but the private equity partner spoke up against it due to legal concerns about his business dealings elsewhere in Africa? The personal relationship between these two might prompt the foundation director to defer to her friend, introducing a decision factor well outside the foundation's mission.

Identity—Can I Live with This Decision? Questions of identity arise at both the organizational and individual level. Nina's foundation has a mission to help in situations like this one. It has the motive, means, and opportunity to save these lives. But would you condemn it as acting "immorally" if the foundation turned away? I have my doubts. Had the foundation done something to create this situation, thereby putting an identifiable group of children in danger, its duty to rescue them might be more urgent. But it is not responsible for the war, the looting, or the greedy Customs Minister. All these factors create some moral distance between the foundation and the suffering it is trying to address. Furthermore, although the children living near this particular hospital will lose if the foundation moves on, other children in urgent need of help living elsewhere in the developing world will benefit as the foundation redeploys its resources, assigning Nina to solve another, perhaps even more urgent, health-care crisis.

What about Nina as an individual? There is little doubt about how she will feel if she has to abandon the project. She is the only one on the team who has seen the children's suffering firsthand. As Mother Teresa has said, "If I look at the many, I will never act. If I look at the one, I will." Especially if Nina believes the bribe is a simple, one-off transaction that will have none of the dire consequences detailed above, her personal identity as a person of conscience may prompt her to argue passionately to let the shipment go through. Indeed, with the institutional incentives lining up to cancel the project, one of Nina's most important roles at this meeting may be to advocate for the children whose lives will be lost through the greed of a local official.

Principles—Is There a Principle at Stake That Must Not Be Compromised? Emotions related to potential consequences will often tilt you in one direction or another, but your intuitions about that aspect of the decision need to be weighed with the other three considerations. There is an obvious core principle at risk in Nina's case—the need for honesty and transparency in the foundation's operations. Paying a bribe to a government official would have to be handled "off the books" and would clearly violate this standard.

A bribe would also be illegal under American law (where the foundation is organized) and probably the law of the country where the private equity group is headquartered (the British Anti-Bribery law is especially strict). Indeed, at least formally, it is probably illegal under the law of the country where the hospital is located, though this country appears to be so unstable that its bribery rules are being observed only in the breach. In some developing countries, however, governments take bribery quite seriously: they prosecute both the people taking them and anyone caught paying one. So, depending on the actual country involved, Nina could find herself facing a prosecutor, and the foundation could be fined.

You might think that a principled, legal argument one way or another would be enough to shut down any further deliberation in a really tough case. But consequences, duties, and loyalties are still relevant. For example, Harriet Tubman, American abolitionist and former slave, is honored in US history for her work spiriting over 70 slaves out of the

South prior to the Civil War. She used bribes to help her get the job done. And one of the moral heroes of World War II, German businessman (and Nazi Party member) Oskar Schindler, rescued some 1,200 Jews from certain death in German concentration camps by breaking multiple laws and paying a large number of bribes. For his efforts, the Israeli government allowed him to be buried on Mount Zion in Jerusalem—a unique resting place for a former Nazi.

Does paying the customs minister his bribe to get these medical supplies to the children fall within the precedent set by these notable examples? It would be a point worth discussing at Nina's meeting.

The Decision

The foundation decided not to pay the bribe, which the team saw as setting a bad precedent for foundation operations in the future. Thus, the medicines never made it into the country. Nina concluded her story by saying that she wished her team had pushed harder to make sure the customs minister understood they were walking away. She thought that might have given the official a final chance to change direction.

Nina and her team may or may not have made the right choice. But at least they made a deliberate one. Tough cases are like that. A good deliberative process assures a more informed (though not always a "correct") decision in terms of right versus wrong. As we will see near the end of the chapter, consulting people who have deeper experience with your dilemma can also uncover surprising solutions that allow you to get outside the moral box that is limiting your options.

REASONING AT EACH STAGE OF THE VALUES-TO-ACTION PROCESS

In addition to helping you work through difficult cases, the habit of careful deliberation using the four questions can also improve your decision making at each stage of the values-to-action process. Below, I'll review these stages in turn (looking again at some of the traps and rationalizations we discussed) and provide a few examples that illustrate how isolating the key factors can help you think more clearly about each step.

Stage 1: Recognize That a Value Is at Risk

New York University professor Kwame Anthony Appiah has written that, "In the real world, the act of framing—the act of describing the situation and thus of determining that there's a [moral] decision to be made—is itself a moral task. It's often *the* moral task." As I noted in the chapter on Rule #2 ("Commit to Your Values"), ethical issues can sometimes escape your notice. Some of the barriers that can hide values from view are: 1) inexperience in your professional setting, 2) ambiguity of your responsibilities in that setting, and 3) paying attention to a compelling feature of your situation—such as competitive pressure—that causes you to overlook an ethical value hidden at the edges of the problem (what my discussion of Rule #2 described as "Inattentional Blindness"). And, of course, even when our values raise an alarm, they can confront rationalizations that help us minimize them. Reasoned deliberation based on the four questions can help with each of these problems.

To illustrate this point, I want to return to a common dilemma we have touched on in earlier parts of the book: conflicts of interest. Conflicts of interest are, in the context of the four questions, often cases of "dueling loyalties" that spring from relationships. A friend of mine who runs a private equity firm once told me that having multiple conflicts of interest in business is actually a sign of success—"if you have no conflicts, you probably have no interests," he said. Standard conflicts-of-interest problems include selling land you own to your own company when you control the purchasing decision; giving sweetheart deals to close relatives and friends using company assets you control; and using a company asset you control (such as access to investors' financial capital) to favor one of your personal business ventures.

Organizations handle such conflicts by requiring executives to disclose them to their superiors. The person with the conflict then steps aside so disinterested people can take over the decision on behalf of the firm. Underlying these rules about conflicts of interest are important principles related to honesty and fairness in situations in which loyalties are divided. Being scrupulous about conflicts of interest is a sign of professionalism. However, recognizing them can delay decisions and put deals at risk. Careful deliberation can help you sort through all these factors to make better decisions.

Take the case of "Oliver," a student who gave the following example of a lesson he learned about conflicts of interest early in his career. He was working for a successful executive recruiting firm in the tech industry, "ExecTech, Inc." (not its real name). ExecTech made its money in the headhunting field, earning hefty commissions by finding and helping to hire top talent in the tech industry. Soon after arriving at the firm, Oliver was transferred to a new venture capital fund set up and controlled by ExecTech's two top leaders (its CEO and COO). This was a separate operation that had raised money from outside investors and was going to use this capital (along with the executives' own money) to invest in startups around Silicon Valley based on these two executives' extensive knowledge of the tech industry and their wide network of contacts.

Oliver got swept up in a conflict-of-interest debate between his two bosses when the fund's very first investment opportunity—a startup—turned out to also be an important, potentially lucrative head-hunting client for ExecTech. The outside investors in the fund, fearing that the two executives would serve their own interests by favoring ExecTech clients with sweetheart financing deals, had negotiated a special bylaw to take care of this situation. If the fund wanted to make an investment in an existing ExecTech client, a three-person committee made up entirely of outside investors would make the call.

The COO, who was bringing this opportunity to both the fund and ExecTech, was eager to avoid the delay (and risk of an adverse decision) involved in assembling the three-person committee. He and Oliver met to figure out how to get around the bylaw.

Oliver (who would have made a good lawyer) pointed out that the bylaw applied only to *existing* ExecTech clients. Thus, as long as the COO and CEO made the investment *before* the startup signed on as an ExecTech client, no three-person committee was required. The COO was delighted with this idea and brought it to the CEO for discussion, with Oliver in attendance.

The COO's reading of the bylaw was motivated entirely by one interest: money. He was so eager to make this investment and sign up this client that he had lost sight of the important values at stake in the situation—a form of Inattentional Blindness. Oliver, meanwhile, was so new to his job that he did not fully understand the conflict embedded in the deal. At the meeting, the CEO agreed that Oliver's solution "worked" in terms of technical compliance with the bylaw rules. But he strongly objected to the proposal.

The CEO's argument hit all four of the decision factors we have been using. First, he noted that the bylaw was there for a reason: to create trust and assurance among the investors. The *consequence* of this clever evasion would be to destroy that trust—and perhaps access to future investors. As he saw it, the *principles* at stake for the fund in this situation were honesty and transparency for the long term, not profits for the short run. He felt their duty of *loyalty* as general partners was to act as fiduciaries for their investors, a position he took very seriously as a matter of *personal integrity*. He advised—and the COO agreed—to disclose the entire situation to the outside investors and let them decide what to do.

In the light of the CEO's decision, Oliver realized that he had been so swept up in pleasing the COO and "getting the business" that he had missed an obvious set of ethical concerns. The CEO had taught him, in effect, that to be truly successful in business, you should always step back to get the bigger picture of how relationships will be impacted by short-term expediencies.

Stage 2: Own the Problem

It is not enough to recognize that a value is at risk—and investigate the matter if you are in doubt. You must also decide to take responsibility for it, as the CEO did in Oliver's case. This can be an especially hard test to pass when you have observed someone else committing a wrong and must decide whether or not to report it. Your *identity* as a person of conscience is often decisive as you debate what to do.

Here is an example. When Kathe Swanson, the city clerk in Dixon, Illinois, called the city's bank to obtain the bank statements she needed to prepare for an upcoming town council meeting, she got the surprise of her life. The city's controller, Rita Crundwell, usually handled these statements but she was on vacation. As Swanson looked over the documents, she noticed three mysterious deposits totaling $1 million in an account labeled "Reserve Fund." This was the first she had heard of such a fund, an unlikely event in the close-knit city administration office. Looking more closely, she found other oddities, such as frequent gas station charges for a "city vehicle" when the city owned and operated its own gas pumps.

Swanson wondered if she had uncovered a fraud being run by Crundwell and perhaps others. But were her suspicions enough to warrant reporting it? She knew the complications such an action would bring into her life. Plus, she was easily stressed in the best of times. Could she handle this? And if she did report it, whom could she speak with? She feared that other public officials, perhaps even the police department, might be in on the scheme. She folded up the bank statements, hid them away in her car, and spent three sleepless nights deliberating what to do. She finally decided she had to own the problem. She discovered, she later said, that "it's just not in my nature to turn and look the other way."

Invoking the Power of Two, Swanson spoke with the one person in the government she thought she could trust, Mayor Jim Burke. She handed the documents over to him, and he shared them with the FBI office in another city. Six months later, US marshals raided Crundwell's city hall office and home, carting away computers and records that revealed a multiyear, multimillion-dollar fraud. Over nearly two decades, Crundwell had stolen some $57.7 million, using the money to fund an elaborate lifestyle outside the city that included a world-class horse breeding operation complete with an outdoor arena and farmhouse estate. Now serving a nineteen-year prison sentence, Crundwell told the court that she was "truly sorry" for her crimes. Swanson had a different view: "Rita did not have a conscience."

Swanson went on to win the Cliff Robertson Sentinel Award, a prize given annually to people who make a difference by standing up for their values. The citation for her award praised her as an "unselfish hero" who, "without regard to personal or professional consequences, has publicly disclosed wrongdoing [in her workplace.]" The city was able to recoup over $40 million of its losses via litigation against Crundwell, its bank, and the city's insurer.

Stage 3: Analyze Your Decision

One of the toughest parts of making a moral decision is weighing four very different considerations on a single scale. How many negative consequences does it take to justify compromising one core principle?

How do you calculate the cost of losing even a small part of your moral identity? Modern philosophers tell us that, logically speaking, such comparisons cannot be made. And yet people make them every time they decide what to do in a difficult ethical conflict.

In his book *Moral Courage: Taking Action When Your Values Are Put to the Test,* Rushworth Kidder tells the story of Mike Saklar, the director of a community-based homeless shelter in the Midwest. The shelter, like most service organizations of its kind, depended on individual and corporate donors for its funding. A crisis arose when the corporate sponsor that provided the great majority of support for the organization's annual "walk for the homeless" suddenly went bankrupt. Without this corporate sponsor, the event was sure to fall embarrassingly short of the shelter's goals—potentially requiring layoffs and seriously compromising the budget for the rest of the year.

Into the breach came a new sponsor—a large beer distributor located in the city. It asked nothing more than to have its beer advertisements and logo displayed prominently at the event. A happy ending? Perhaps, but the shelter had an explicit mission: to help people get back on their feet by promoting a twelve-step sobriety program for clients who were addicted to drugs and alcohol. Did accepting these funds compromise that sobriety mission? Intuitions on Saklar's team ran in both directions. Some favored accepting the money from a perfectly legal, community-minded company. Others saw it as contradicting their core mission. Can a refuge that seeks to help alcoholics recover from their addiction be funded in large part by an alcohol business?

Thinking through the four questions, it was clear that *consequences* and *loyalties* lined up strongly in favor of taking the money. The shelter would remain operational on a sound financial footing, and the clients it served (to whom it owed a duty of loyalty) would continue to have a safe place to sleep. On the other side was the *identity* of the shelter (branding it with beer advertising would not help that) and the *principle* that the organization should remain true to its anti-addiction mission. Some on the board feared the organization would lose its "soul" if it took the money.

After a lengthy debate, Saklar's shelter turned the money down. But unlike Nina's case, there was a more satisfactory ending. Additional donors—some of whom were attracted to the shelter by the very fact that it had stuck by its principles in this hour of crisis—stepped up to provide the needed funding. The work continued.

Stage 4: Design Your Action Plan

In Saklar's case, the decision to reject the beer distributor's money ended the moral dilemma. Saklar had a practical problem remaining: how to fund shelter operations. But the values-to-action process had run its course.

However, let's assume for a moment that the board had decided that the greater good required them to accept the distributor's sponsorship. They would then confront Stage 4: Design Your Action Plan. The shelter's board would next need to consider how to carry out its decision in the most ethical way possible. This final stage thus requires you to combine strategic thinking about implementation with ethical considerations.

The most common strategies for taking action: meet with your decision maker to change their mind (taken up in Rule #8, "Engage the Decision Maker") or appeal to higher authority (one of the tactics covered in Rule #9, "Hold Them Accountable"). But a third path can sometimes open at this stage: discovering win-win solutions that avoid the either/or choice that makes tough cases so hard.

Thus, an important function of Stage 4 is to "get outside of the box" of your ethical conflict and search for practical, creative ideas to sidestep the moral question and solve the underlying problem.

Such win-win strategies can be found in a surprising number of cases if you consult with experts who encounter your situation more often than you do. Let's think back to Nina's bribe case for a moment. By failing to consult widely enough with informed experts, Nina and her team appear to have missed several opportunities that might have allowed them to thread the needle between paying the bribe and withdrawing their support. For example, nonprofits such as her foundation often cooperate with multinational business firms that do business in a given country. Firms such as Coca-Cola, Procter & Gamble, and even some arms manufacturers are known locally never to pay bribes and are sometimes willing to include in their cargoes the medical supplies and other social goods that nonprofits are trying to get into a country.

My colleague Phil Nichols reported an extraordinary case in which a nonprofit literally bluffed its way past an official demanding a bribe. Like Nina's foundation, this group was seeking to get medical supplies to a local health-care system and had run into a high-ranking, corrupt official with his hand out for money. It refused to pay the bribe but shipped the supplies anyway. Then, as the supplies were being unloaded at the port with this official in attendance, the group staged a large-scale press conference giving full credit for the operation to the very official who had demanded the bribe. Risky? Sure. But it worked.

PUTTING IT ALL TOGETHER: SOLVING ETHICAL CONFLICTS BY THINKING THEM THROUGH

I want to wrap up the chapter with a final illustration of an ethical conflict where the hero fell short of his goal—mainly because he did not think the situation through as well as he might have. This example comes from the startup stage of an entrepreneurial venture that one of my students was involved in. It is, my student told me, "typical" of the pressures entrepreneurs face as they struggle to raise capital. Formulating a good plan of action to solve a conflict over values is harder than it looks when you are faced with pressures related to incentives, deadlines, and conflicting loyalties.

"Aamir" was the CFO of a seventy-person startup before coming to business school for his MBA. He told our class that he had faced a lot of ethical dilemmas in his role, many of which, he now realized, he had not thought through very well. One of the toughest involved a conflict with the founder of the firm, Brett, who served as its CEO. The problem was simple: Brett had a habit of exaggerating the firm's performance numbers when he was delivering pitches for venture funding. Aamir became aware of this on the day before an important meeting to attract a $10 million investment. Here was the wrinkle: the person getting pitched for this investment was one of Aamir's personal friends.

As the CFO, Aamir was the "inside man" and did the detailed data analysis for the revenue projections, margins, and so on that went into the pitches. As he and Brett were going over the slide deck before the big meeting, Aamir realized that Brett had arbitrarily added substantial "improvements" to most of the key metrics.

At that moment, Aamir felt the full force of an ethical conflict within himself. He knew the pitch lacked integrity, and the padded presentation was going to be presented to his friend. What to do? Brett had recently fired the COO over a disagreement on strategy. Aamir was pretty sure that if he pushed back too hard on his ethical concerns, he would suffer the same fate.

So he tried to split the difference. He spoke up, but, as he later put it, he was not especially "forceful." He told Brett that he was uncomfortable with the exaggerations and warned that they could backfire if venture funds discovered what was going on. Brett responded that puffing up these numbers was a normal part of the VC process. "Everybody does it," he said. Brett told Aamir that he would take full responsibility for the pitches. "Just keep giving me the data," Brett said, "and I'll take it from there."

Aamir said that this had felt like a middle ground, so he agreed to it. And Aamir kept his end of this arrangement until he left to attend business school, making it a habit never to look at any of the final slide decks. Meanwhile, he privately kept a careful paper trail showing what the real numbers were.

As for the pitch happening the next day with Aamir's friend? Aamir gritted his teeth and attended, but he used a back channel to warn his friend that the CEO was not entirely trustworthy. The investment never came through. Aamir concluded his story by saying that this backdoor strategy had been potentially damaging to him and his company, but it was the only way he could feel "somewhat okay about myself."

Could Aamir have done better by thinking his strategy through more carefully? I think so. In his report to my class, Aamir made it sound as if Brett held all the cards in this conflict. But missing from Aamir's account is any effort to invoke the Power of Two. Were others at the firm uncomfortable raising money under false pretenses? Collectively, they may have had the power to influence Brett. Also, Aamir knew at least one venture fund executive; did he know others? It would have been worth consulting a few (perhaps through intermediaries) to see if Brett's "everybody does it" rationalization was true or false. If it was false, Aamir could have made his argument to Brett regarding consequences much more forcefully.

Finally, I think Aamir may have underestimated his leverage over Brett. Aamir could have reminded Brett that he had a personal relationship with the VC fund being pitched the next day. Aamir could not, therefore, stand by and let the pitch go forward with false data. That alone was a highly credible reason for Brett to change course—and an understandable one because it was based on Aamir's loyalty to a friend. If Brett nevertheless threatened to fire him, Aamir could have warned him that he had a broader relationship network that would be interested to know about Brett's fast-and-loose treatment of facts. In a sense, Aamir held Brett's credibility in his hands.

As a final move, Brett might have countered that Aamir had signed a nondisclosure agreement (a frequent provision in startup employment contracts), making it a breach of contract for him to go over Brett's head to reveal the truth about the data in the slide decks. But if Aamir were to consult a lawyer—a wise move whenever a conflict reaches the point where someone is talking about firing you—he would find that NDAs are unenforceable when it comes to reporting fraud to government prosecutors. And a false venture pitch using any form of electronic communication could constitute wire fraud, a federal crime.

None of this would have improved the relationship between Aamir and Brett, of course. But it would have empowered Aamir to stand up for himself and his values, giving Brett a choice about whether or not to conduct the business in good faith. When Aamir eventually left the firm, he would have done so knowing he had behaved with integrity instead of feeling merely "somewhat okay."

A MOMENT FOR PERSONAL REFLECTION

As you reflect on the role of reason in ethical conflicts, think back on situations you have faced that pitted one or more of the four factors we have discussed—consequences, loyalty, identity, and principle—against one another. Has a friend ever asked you to help cover up his or her wrongdoing? How did you balance your loyalty to your friend against the consequences to the people who were wronged? Are you proud of the balance you struck? Even if you are, could you have done a better job of minimizing the harm your friend had caused at the same time you remained loyal?

My personal feeling is that the identity factor—whether you can live with yourself after you make a decision—is the one that dominates when the four factors are in tension with one another. But many of my Wharton faculty colleagues feel that the cost-benefit analysis of consequences usually supplies the decisive answer. Still others view personal loyalty or "first principles" as the tiebreaker more often than not. Of course, the answer as to which is most important usually depends on the situation you face. But if you had to pick the single one of these four factors as your #1 ethical standard, which one would you pick? Why?

NEXT UP: FROM VALUES TO ACTION:
USING DIALOGUE TO PERSUADE

Aamir missed his chance to confront Brett more effectively in part because he lacked the strategic persuasion skills to win his point. To help you do better than Aamir did, the next chapter transitions to the "action" phase of the values-to-action process. We start with Rule #8—"Engage the Decision Maker"—using the art and science of effective dialogue. Dialogue usually beats accusation and confrontation when it comes to changing someone's mind on a sensitive issue related to personal values. Why? Because effective advocates know that showing people "the error of their ways" often leads to little beyond denials and defensive reactions. By contrast, a good dialogue begins by asking good questions, proceeds as you listen carefully to what the other person says, and then succeeds when you provide the other party with the arguments and information they need to *persuade themselves.*

RULE #8:
ENGAGE THE
DECISION MAKER

"When you see something that is not right . . . you have a moral obligation to say something, to do something."
— John Lewis, Georgia congressman and civil rights leader

The final stage of the values-to-action process—Design Your Action Plan—is the "payoff" stage. It calls on you to be a 1) skilled advocate, 2) an astute organizational tactician, and, ultimately, 3) an effective leader. The final three rules of the Conscience Code address each of these capabilities in turn.

Rule #8 asks you to "Engage the Decision Maker" by using dialogue-based communication tools. These are effective in many difficult conversations, but they are especially useful when you must confront people well above your pay grade on sensitive ethical issues.

Let's begin by listening in on a discussion between one of my former students, a consulting firm analyst in his mid-twenties named "Jeremy," and his boss, "Katherine," a demanding, impatient partner. It concerns a conflict over a recommendation in a corporate downsizing project.

Background: the recent acquisition of a competitor had prompted a large global internet retailer, CoreTech, to hire Jeremy's firm for advice. CoreTech was interested in consolidating operations to save money. It wanted to know how many customer service center employees it could lay off at the newly acquired firm without compromising the firm's core asset: its stellar reputation for customer satisfaction.

The scene opens as Jeremy sits down in Katherine's office to give a progress report.

Jeremy: I ran the numbers you asked about on the CoreTech project, and it's not what we expected.

Katherine: Really? It seemed like a pretty straightforward situation. What did you come up with?

Jeremy: I did all the interviews we talked about and reviewed the data for the past five years on customer queries, complaints, wait times, returns, satisfaction surveys, and so on. These people have a very efficient operation. It looks like CoreTech will be taking a big risk in terms of customer satisfaction if it lays off more than 15 percent of the service center workers.

Katherine: That can't possibly be true. When I pitched this engagement, it was clear to me that we could deliver a report calling for at least a 30 percent reduction in head count. That's a number the client mentioned to me, and I saw no problem delivering it based on the preliminary review I did with their team leaders. I'm sure you must have missed something.

Jeremy: I don't think so. But I brought my analysis so you can review it (hands over a five-page summary report).

Katherine (sounding irritated): Look, I don't have time to do your work for you, but I am certain you are wrong. Get Rashida [a more senior analyst] to look over everything again with you and get back to me next week. I can't sign up a client by talking about a 30 percent savings and then come in with a recommendation that delivers only half that. Take another look at the data—a very hard look.

[One week later, Jeremy and Rashida return to Katherine's office with a revised recommendation that justifies a 20 percent reduction in force.]

Jeremy: I went back over all my interviews and collected some new data. Then Rashida and I ran the numbers every way we could, and the most we can justify with a straight face is a 20 percent cut. Beyond that, we think customer service will definitely suffer.

Rashida: Jeremy is new, but he has done a great job on this project, and I'm with him on this. Twenty percent is the best we can do without seriously compromising the service experience, which was the main reason the client acquired this firm. In fact, I think 20 percent is pushing it.

Katherine: Well, I've been at this game a lot longer than either of you, and I know I am right. So here is what I want. I want you to deliver a report that calls for a 30 percent reduction. And I want it this afternoon along with a slide deck summarizing it. Just take the extra 10 percent in cuts and allocate them proportionately across all the functions you identified. I have a meeting in two days with the client, and I am not going to stand up there and go back on a promise I made. The employees left at the firm will be grateful to keep their jobs. We can assume they'll work twice as hard. Honestly, I thought I sent you a pretty clear message that the right number was 30. I guess I was not clear enough.

Jeremy and Rashida exchange glances.

Jeremy: OK. But the data won't support the recommendation.

Katherine: Make sure the data *does* support the recommendation. And bury all the adjusted numbers in an appendix. Nobody reads the appendix anyway.

Jeremy and Rashida exit. They deliver the revised report as ordered, recommending a 30 percent reduction in customer service center jobs. Jeremy left the firm before he heard anything about the impact this had on customer satisfaction, but when we spoke he noted that CoreTech itself had recently been mentioned in the press as underperforming and had become an acquisition target.

Jeremy struck a somber, regretful tone when he finished telling his story. "To this day," he said, "I regret how this project worked out. It inflicted real pain on about 350 people, hurting them and their families." Such is the cost when a boss overpromises results and lacks the humility and good judgment to admit being wrong.

We'll return to this dialogue at the end of the chapter when I provide a revised script for how Jeremy might have handled this conversation to defend his values. What Jeremy needed was a *persuasion strategy* to add to his data-based analysis. The values of compassion, accountability, fairness, and truth were all in play with this engagement, but he never hinted at them, much less pushed for them as priorities. Had he effectively talked it through with Katherine using standard dialogue techniques, he could have avoided delivering a fabricated report and perhaps saved the jobs of hundreds of hardworking, high-performing employees.

I have written two previous books that are relevant to this chapter: *Bargaining for Advantage: Negotiation Strategies for Reasonable People* and, with Mario Moussa, *The Art of Woo: Using Strategic Persuasion to Sell Your Ideas*. Both works explore the psychology of interpersonal influence to help readers become better negotiators and advocates. This chapter will draw on those books, as well as other works that more directly deal with conflict management, to address the very special problems that arise when you must have a tough conversation with someone over sensitive, core values.

The chapter is organized around a seven-step model for engaging with bosses and peers when you have a conflict over values. The process begins with searching inside yourself for motivation and ends with using a set of well-researched communication tools to achieve commitments to principled action. These seven steps bring together all the topics we have covered earlier in the book, from situational barriers, character, and values to personality, the Power of Two, and reason-based analysis. We advance from these foundations to the strategic aspects of persuasion, including decisions about whom to speak with, credibility, and the best way to frame your case. The chapter concludes with short sections on overcoming common objections and coping with office bullies.

SEVEN STEPS TO INFLUENCE

As we walk through the seven steps that prepare you for a dialogue, keep in mind the pressures that Rule #3 ("Know Your Enemy") introduced you to. They are what gave rise to the conflict in the first place. Easing them often opens the door to solutions. They include: *peer* pressure, demands from those in *authority*, perverse *incentives*, the expectations that people in particular *roles* feel driven to meet, and/or larger *systemic* forces that spring from corruption inside an organizational culture or the surrounding society.

Recognizing and labeling the forces pushing against you helps you gain a sense of control over your situation. Just as importantly, you will be sensitive to the pressures *the other party* is feeling, allowing you to devise plans for easing them—and thus make it easier for them to change course. Jeremy was suffering from authority pressure, but Katherine was feeling pressured to earn a fee (incentives) and deliver on a promise she had made as the engagement partner on the CoreTech account (role pressure). Jeremy needed to think about her situation, not just his own, to win her over.

The seven steps include:

> Step 1: Connect to Your Motivation
> Step 2: Remember the Power of Two
> Step 3: Identify Your Target Decision Maker
> Step 4: Assess Your Credibility
> Step 5: Consider Their Interests and Beliefs
> Step 6: Frame Your Argument So They Want to Buy It
> Step 7: Use Dialogue, Then Seek Commitment

In the pages that follow, we will dive into each of the steps in turn.

Step 1: Connect to Your Motivation

A successful values conversation always begins before you walk into the room: with a look inside yourself. Consider which of your core values are at risk in the situation (compassion, respect, accountability, fairness, or truth) and ask yourself why they are worth fighting for. At no point in dealing with Katherine did Jeremy motivate himself by reflecting on the norms she was trampling through her casual approach to the layoffs. Without such motivation, he was easily swept along by her assertive displays of authority and experience.

Consulting your "Why?" will help you check in with your moral emotions. Outrage and anticipated guilt or shame can propel you forward while fear regarding career consequences and a personality-based reluctance to engage in confrontations can hold you back. How can you summon your character and personality strengths to your aid?

One reliable way to boost your motivation is to put the potential victims of an unethical decision front and center in your imagination. Saving 10 percent of a workforce from unjust dismissal is a cause worth fighting for. Had Jeremy focused on this more vividly at the time, he might have found the energy to speak up forcefully.

There was another victim here: his firm's client. It was being given bad advice based on false data. Had he considered the question "Who are the victims?" more thoroughly, he would likely have realized that the firm as a whole might care quite a lot about holding one of its partners accountable for this sort of misconduct.

By explicitly reviewing his motivations for speaking up, Jeremy could have better balanced the anxiety he felt about pushing back against his boss with the substantial guilt that he would later feel from remaining silent. Some 350 invisible layoff victims needed an advocate to speak for them. Jeremy was their best hope.

Step 2: Remember the Power of Two

You have committed yourself to your values, but as we saw when I presented Rule #6 ("Leverage the Power of Two"), the path forward will be smoother if you bring allies into both your preparation and your action plan. Jeremy was given a gift in this regard when Katherine assigned Rashida to review his work. She confirmed his analysis, but he missed the chance to recruit her as a high-credibility ally for a value-based conversation with Katherine.

Compare Jeremy's experience with another, strikingly similar story brought to class by another former consulting analyst, "Isabella." She was working as the most junior member of a team handling a hydroelectric project in a developing country. Her team was charged with delivering on a contractual commitment her firm had made to accelerate the construction schedule of this project without increasing its costs. During her preliminary investigation, she realized that the contract had been signed on the basis of an incorrect factual assumption. The construction schedule problem did not stem from inefficiencies that could be fixed. Instead, they were the result of outdated equipment being used. She estimated it would cost $25 million to update the equipment needed to boost progress—a recommendation that violated the "no cost increases" clause of the contract.

She reported her findings to her project leader ("Ricardo"), who did not receive the news well. He had a large bonus riding on delivering the promised schedule gains. Her recommendation to spend $25 million on new equipment would eliminate his bonus. He devised an alternative plan: "borrow" newer equipment from a large, nearby construction site being managed by the same client and put this equipment to work on the hydroelectric project until it was completed. The older equipment would be moved to (and used on) the other site. The hydro project would thus speed up at no additional cost.

Isabella ran an analysis on Ricardo's suggestion and discovered that it would actually hurt the client's overall business. The hydro-electric project's gains would be more than offset by losses and missed construction deadlines at the other site. She presented her results to Ricardo, who responded that their consulting contract was concerned only with the hydroelectric project. He would recommend the other location be given priority treatment after the hydro project was completed.

More ominously, Ricardo warned Isabella to "stay in the background" and "be very careful what you say" about his plan when they presented it to the senior leadership team. She told me that after this conversation, "I was quite nervous about the position my boss had put me in."

In the end, she decided that she could not, in good conscience, be complicit in Ricardo's scheme to protect his bonus at the expense of the client's best interests. She was an "Advocate" in terms of personality, and could not stand by while a client's needs were ignored.

Ricardo led off the meeting with the senior partners by presenting his "equipment swap" solution without mentioning Isabella's ideas or analysis. When Ricardo's solution was opened for comments, however, Isabella spoke up and offered her full critique along with her $25 million investment recommendation. She stated forcefully that the overriding goal ought to be the client's best interests in the face of a consulting contract that was based on a faulty factual premise. Blindsided, Ricardo argued that Isabella's analysis was flawed and overstated the problems posed by an equipment swap.

The partners, impressed by the force of Isabella's argument, decided to resolve the dispute by assigning one of the firm's senior associates ("Peter") to review Isabella's work with her. The week that followed was, she told me, the toughest seven days of her consulting career.

Long story short, Isabella's analysis held up, and she converted Peter into her strong ally. With Peter taking the lead, they used the follow-up meeting to persuade the partners to overrule Ricardo, whose questionable motivations now became the focus of attention. Meanwhile, Peter recommended that Isabella take the lead in presenting both Ricardo's solution and her revised case to the client's CEO. The CEO, in turn, praised the transparency of her report and approved her suggested $25 million investment. He also approved a renegotiated consulting contract that included new incentives aligned with the realities she had uncovered.

Isabella spent an extra eight months on-site helping to lead implementation. After both construction projects came in on time, Isabella left for business school with glowing recommendations from her firm's top leadership.

She wrapped up her story in exactly the opposite way Jeremy had concluded his: with pride in her accomplishment. The difference? She showed conviction regarding the value of client accountability, was willing to escalate the dispute to Ricardo's bosses after he warned her to remain silent, and leveraged the Power of Two by recruiting Peter as her ally.

Step 3: Identify Your Target Decision Maker

Isabella's example illustrates the third step in your persuasion plan: identifying the decision maker. Isabella's boss had made it abundantly clear that he was not open to her more honest approach, leaving her only two options: concede or elevate the conflict to a higher level.

Isabella's personality style was very direct, but blindsiding Ricardo at the partners' meeting was risky. Had her facts and presentation been anything less than clear and convincing, she could easily have lost her job. But she was on solid ground with both. Indeed, her success provides evidence that an Advocate personality style can work effectively when a firm's culture rewards candid, fact-based persuasion strategies. Her confidence in her facts was apparent to the partners, prompting them to invest in having Peter review her case.

We will look at targeting decision makers in more detail in the next chapter, when we examine the full range of tactical moves available when your boss rejects your argument. For now, note that choosing whom to speak with and in what order is a key part of a successful persuasion plan.

Step 4: Assess Your Credibility

In every influence encounter, whether it involves a values conflict or not, there are invisible barriers that stand in the way of your success. One of the most important of these is your *credibility* with the person you are trying to persuade. Quite simply, if you lack credibility, the other person will not pay attention to, or believe, what you say.

Credibility is a footstool with four legs. The stronger the legs, the more secure the footstool. The first leg: your status or *authority* within your group. The lower you are in the pecking order, the less credibility you have. This poses a common problem for junior employees when they speak up for their values to a boss.

The second foundation is your perceived *expertise*—what others think you know. Have you read a lot of books on a subject? Gathered data and assembled it in reports? As analysts, both Jeremy and Isabella had "some" credibility for what they knew, enough to be heard and taken seriously. But not enough for this factor alone to carry the day.

The third leg of the footstool: *experience.* Credibility for experience relates to your judgment based on past successes solving similar problems. Although I have written books on negotiation and therefore have some credibility as a "negotiation expert," I have no credibility as a "labor negotiator" because I have no direct experience in this specialized field. Lacking experience, both Jeremy and Isabella were frustrated because their recommendations were (initially) discounted.

The final, crucial foundation for credibility is *trustworthiness.* No matter how much authority, expertise, or experience your audience thinks you have, they will question what you say if they think you are misleading them or will not deliver on your promises. Ricardo lost considerable credibility for trustworthiness with the partners when it was revealed that his plan for swapping equipment was ill-informed and self-serving.

Your overall credibility ultimately depends on *your audience's* perceptions of you, not on how you see yourself. As you prepare for your influence encounter, therefore, ask how your decision maker views your authority, expertise, experience, and trustworthiness. Then take whatever steps you can to improve these perceptions. As the examples above suggest, the simplest and quickest step can be recruiting allies your audience will see as credible.

Step 5: Consider Their Interests and Beliefs

If you want to be persuasive, it helps to understand how the other party views the problem. What are their motivations? How can you frame your proposal so it integrates into their existing interests and beliefs? Persuasion scholars have a name for this effort: perspective-taking. There are three main ways to accomplish it.

First, to get an emotional bearing, use empathy to ask, "How would I feel if I were in their shoes?" The more similar you are in background and the more experience you have in organizational roles like the one the other person occupies, the more likely this approach will yield insights. Some of the best corporate salespeople I have met came with experience in purchasing departments at competing firms. They have a visceral sense of what it feels like to be on the other side of the table, buying the product they now sell and comparing its price and features to the competition.

If you are a junior person with limited leadership experience, you may find it hard to gain this emotional perspective on your target, especially when you face a conflict. This gap provides yet another reason to consult more senior mentors for their input.

The second path is more deductive: Ask yourself, "What do I know about this person and their patterns of behavior? Given that, what are my predictions about their response?" This is an "if . . . then" approach to perspective-taking: "If I say X, what might they say? What about if I say Y?" Brainstorm with a trusted partner to game-plan different dialogue scenarios. Conversations rarely go exactly as you imagine, but an "if . . . then" method of preparing usually means there will be fewer surprises.

The third and best way to find out what someone else is thinking and feeling is the most obvious: use your meeting to ask them. Research suggests that this is both the most accurate and most neglected road into other people's mindsets. People rarely ask enough questions before making assumptions and leaping to conclusions. Step 7 of our model will give you some important conversational tools to use for this purpose.

In the meantime, focus your attention on two key areas as you prepare for your meeting: the other party's interests and beliefs.

Interests. Even when your credibility is high, you can run into a brick wall if your suggestion directly conflicts with your target's interests, i.e., it frustrates a desire or triggers a fear about giving up something such as compensation, opportunities, reputation, or status. The 19th-century banking mogul J.P. Morgan once said, "A man always has two reasons for doing anything: a good reason and the real reason." The "good reason" is usually something logical such as following the rules or deferring to the data. The "real reason" is more personal: a fear or desire.

Understanding the other party's interests is critical for several reasons. First, you may discover, as Isabella did with Ricardo, that your values are in direct conflict with their interests, leaving no room for persuasion. That is when you should begin devising a more political, power-based strategy designed to lead you to another decision maker. We cover this in the next chapter.

At the other end of the spectrum, you may be pleasantly surprised to discover that the other person's interests actually line up with your values. These cases typically fall into two buckets. Sometimes there is interest-value alignment, but *you* mistakenly think there is a conflict. Other times, you have to persuade the other party that their interests and your values can easily be harmonized.

You See Conflict When None Is There

One of my students, "Will," told me about a situation he encountered as a banker. He was negotiating a long-term joint venture with the government of a developing country, and his boss was growing increasingly frustrated with the time it was taking to put the deal together. He had begun to pressure Will to "do whatever it takes" to reach an agreement. One of the stumbling points in the deal was a request for a bribe by a local official. Will had taken a strong position against this request at the bargaining table. But his boss was now ordering him to abandon that position in order to reach an agreement, or so Will thought.

Will objected to paying bribes on ethical grounds, and he went to his boss to make his case. He told the boss he was prepared to resign as the negotiator if "doing whatever it takes" included paying off this official. The boss then began questioning Will more closely about the details of the partnership being contemplated. Eventually, the boss sat back and looked at Will thoughtfully. "I've done business in this part of the world a long time, and I don't share your principle about refusing to pay bribes in every case. But in the context of this long-term contract, I see now there would be no end to the trouble if we paid a bribe before we even signed this agreement." He told Will to go back to the bargaining table and hold his position. The boss had a new appreciation as to why the deal was taking so long—and he backed Will's "no bribe" stand with an additional mandate from the bank. The deal closed six months later without any bribe being paid.

This meeting might have been shorter had Will framed his argument around his firm's long-term interests instead of launching into a passionate defense of his beliefs about bribes. But all's well that ends well. His boss helped them both to discover that there was alignment between them.

You Turn Conflict into Collaboration by Harmonizing Interests and Values

Mary Gentile, in her excellent book *Giving Voice to Values*, tells the story of "Susan," a newly hired analyst working for a financial advisory firm. Susan devised an interest-based outcome to a moral problem when her new boss asked her to produce a misleading client report. The boss was taking over a group of high-net-worth clients and was disappointed to see that an especially important portfolio had underperformed relative to the average "growth stock" index it was appropriately measured against. Worried about looking bad in the client's eyes, the boss asked Susan to redo the report by comparing the investments against a lower-return, "blended" benchmark (for portfolios including more bonds) so the performance would look better.

Unwilling to participate in this deception, but lacking authority to explicitly push back on her boss, Susan hatched an idea for the boss's presentation that would help him look good without compromising the truth. The boss was new to this client, and the performance in the report reflected his predecessor's work, not his own. By leaving the report as is, Susan argued, the boss could suggest that he needed the year ahead to close the gap to the benchmark, with more gains to come after that. The boss agreed to her plan—without Susan ever mentioning that her approach had the additional virtue of being honest.

Beliefs. The toughest persuasion barriers arise when the other person either does not believe in your value or honestly thinks that they are doing nothing wrong. Recall Rule #2 ("Commit to Your Values"), when we talked about how beliefs connect to one another, forming a complex structure supporting a person's worldview. An attack on one of your decision maker's beliefs will often be seen by them as an attack on them personally, sparking an emotional, defensive response.

In addition, sometimes people's interests lead them to adopt self-serving beliefs that become resistant to change. For example, the first time someone cheats on their taxes, they may feel guilty but do it anyway because they need the money. Someone trying to talk them out of it might be able to appeal to their interests by arguing about potential penalties or showing them other, legal ways to solve their financial problems.

But after lying on their tax returns for a decade, tax cheats will likely construct beliefs about why doing so is legitimate, perhaps even principled. Their circle of friends will now include others who cheat, and this group may reinforce the belief that the tax system is a form of theft carried out by a corrupt government to favor special interests. It's not about money anymore. Persuading such a person to pay their taxes will require changing their political philosophy—or putting them in jail.

When you are up against a belief barrier, be realistic. You are unlikely to change the other person's mind. Instead, back off, return to their interests, and try to figure out a way to motivate the behavior you want without attacking their underlying belief.

The Case of the Backdated Documents

Take, for example, this case of a conflict that ran aground on the shoals of a conflicting belief. When a student, "Andrea," began working for a small private equity firm in Boston soon after college, her very first assignment was to create fake investment committee memos about deals the firm had closed the prior year. The backdated memos were designed to make it appear the firm had done its required due diligence (mandated by contractual terms with its investors) before making these investments. The problem: it had been a busy year, and the firm was doing deals so fast it did not have time to write up its due diligence. The investments had turned out to be sound, but the paper trail was a mess. Andrea felt very uncomfortable creating these reports, but she was the newest employee. She completed the assignment, said nothing about it, and was quickly staffed to other projects.

A year later, the firm's partners asked her to pull these memos out for inclusion in documents they were using to raise a fresh round of investment capital from new investors. Andrea decided she had to speak up. Including fake, backdated memos in a prospectus seemed dishonest to her. She approached her boss, expressed her discomfort (without using the word "fraud"), and offered an interest-based solution. She would restyle the memos as detailed, retrospective reviews, listing whatever due diligence steps had actually been taken.

"What's the problem?" the partner responded. "We do this back-dating all the time. It is how the business works. When we have time and the deals are big enough, we paper up the due diligence. Otherwise, it's just a headache. Everybody knows what's going on. Nobody cares."

Andrea then made a mistake. She said the memos were "fraudulent." From there, she reported, "the conversation went very, very poorly. I was shouted out of the room."

Two weeks later, she quit. "The partners saw themselves as good, moral people," she concluded. "But what they asked me to do was clearly unethical. Using backdated documents describing events that never happened was wrong."

Could Andrea have won this argument with a better persuasion strategy? I doubt it. She confronted a self-serving belief that backdating these memos was standard operating procedure, even if it might appear unethical. Had she looked for (and found) evidence that this practice violated the norms of the industry or, more alarmingly, was viewed as fraud by the investment community, she could have escalated the dispute, eventually blowing the whistle. But without such evidence, she had nowhere to go with her complaint.

Step 6: Frame Your Argument So They Want to Buy It

Framing a persuasion case involves summarizing a problem, offering your proposed solution, and providing arguments, reasons, and/or evidence to showcase your solution as the best one available. Skilled advocates spend a lot of time thinking about the first step in this process. Why? Because if you frame the problem well, you can show the other party how your solution advances rather than impedes their interests. This makes a huge difference in their willingness to go along with your recommendation.

As some of the examples above have shown, practical, interest-based solutions sometimes avoid the ethical conflict altogether, smoothing relationships and dodging awkward conversations about right versus wrong. In addition, you can often recast an ethical argument into one that discusses the legal risk of going down the wrong path. This gets your value on the table without necessarily implying a moral judgment about the other party.

Of course, as we have seen throughout the book, explicit appeals to moral and ethical values are often necessary. If your decision maker is unaware that a core value is at risk, it will be important to bring this fact to their attention. In addition, when two important values conflict, you will need to explicitly argue the merits of each. Finally, some decision makers are people of conscience who, in a given situation, will resonate more readily with a moral argument than an interest-based one. Many of the Jews who asked Germans to shelter them in World War II did so using appeals to values, not interests. These appeals worked, when they did, because they connected people who shared common bonds of humanity.

Step 7: Use Dialogue, Then Seek Commitment

As you have seen from the discussion above, the more you understand about the other party's interests and beliefs, the better positioned you will be to frame your proposal effectively. And, as noted earlier, the best ways to discover those interests and beliefs are to ask the other party to tell you. This requires engaging in a genuine dialogue based on active listening. The secret to such dialogue is mixing and matching the following conversational elements:

- seek a common purpose by focusing on shared interests,
- ask open-ended questions about the other party's point of view,
- listen,
- test for understanding,
- summarize what you have heard,
- advance your plan, seeking their feedback.

Then repeat this process until you can close in on an acceptable commitment.

I want to return to Jeremy's case now to see what a genuine dialogue about the layoff problem might have sounded like. I will begin by repeating Katherine's demand that Jeremy falsify the data to match her promised recommendation. Then I'll highlight the dialogue tactics as Jeremy uses them below.

Katherine: I want you to deliver a report that calls for a 30 percent reduction. And I want it this afternoon along with a slide deck summarizing it. Just take the extra 10 percent in cuts and allocate them proportionately across all the functions you identified. I have a meeting in two days with the client, and I am not going to stand up there and go back on a promise I made. The employees left at the firm will be grateful to keep their jobs. We can assume they'll work twice as hard . . . and bury all the adjusted numbers in an appendix. Nobody reads the appendix anyway.

Jeremy: It sounds as if the 30 percent layoff target is really important to you [*listening, focusing on interests, testing for understanding*]. That's your credibility up there, and I think I now understand how important that is [*summarize*].

Katherine: You bet it is.

Jeremy: Rashida and I were talking about this [glances at Rashida, who nods], and we are worried about your credibility, too [*establish common purpose based on interests*]. The data analysis for the presentation—even buried in the appendix—will likely be vetted by the client. They've paid a lot for our services, and we know the analyst on their side. He is pretty sharp. There are going to be inconsistencies between the analysis and the recommendations, and we are concerned that you could be embarrassed [*injecting urgency about protecting interests*].

Katherine [pausing]: I'll have think about that after I see your report.

Jeremy: What if we could deliver your 30 percent recommendation using the actual data we have? That would take less time to prepare and the data would back you up. Would you be open to that [*advancing a plan that meets her interests and protects his values, while also seeking feedback*]?

Katherine: How could we do that?

Jeremy: Well, it would take us back to the problem that brought the client to you in the first place [*including the client's needs as a common purpose*]. Could you remind us how they framed the problem [*open-ended question*]?

Katherine: They asked us to recommend a layoff level that could be achieved without compromising customer service.

Jeremy: So the problem is how to cut costs while maintaining great customer service [*testing for understanding*]?

Katherine: Right.

Jeremy: Well, we think that by framing the report around their customer service priority instead of the cost cutting, you could get your 30 percent layoff idea on the table and maybe even sell them on a follow-up contract for additional work [*advancing plan, adding another interest*].

Katherine: Keep talking.

Jeremy: The report can show a graph with a range of possible layoff recommendations—highlighting 30 percent but running from a very low number to one even higher than 30 percent. On the other axis, the graph would show our current predictions on the customer service effects at each level. You could then position the 30 percent as a target, with a rollout period of a year or two that would start with fewer lay-offs and use constant testing to see how customer service surveys are affected [*advancing plan*]. You could also add a recommendation that they monitor the remaining workers so they end up keeping the ones who are most efficient and effective, hopefully getting to 30 percent more quickly that way. In the meantime, you could lay out a follow-up contract to investigate how to save money in other parts of their operations in case they can't reach the 30 percent. It's a win-win-win. Nobody can challenge your data. Your credibility will be 100 percent protected. You may sell a follow-up contract. And you'll protect the client's customer service priority, which is why they hired us [*seeking common ground based on interests and beliefs*].

Katherine: Can you have that report ready for me to review today?

Jeremy: We have it right here [hands her the new report].

Note that this entire conversation pivots on interests. If Katherine refuses to accept Jeremy's plan, he might need to switch to a more explicit, principled tone. That discussion would use the same dialogue tools, but it would highlight the conflict between their views. Because such conflicts can more quickly escalate to confrontations, Jeremy and Rashida would need to have a plan for what they would do if Katherine keeps insisting that they be complicit in falsifying the report. They should be prepared to fight for their values.

To illustrate this "Plan B," I pick up the conversation where we left it above, with Jeremy handing Katherine the new report. Katherine takes a moment to look over it.

Katherine: Nice plan. But I would rather deliver my 30 percent recommendation and move on. There is no more business to be had from this client.

Jeremy: Rashida and I talked about that, and you need to know that we are very uncomfortable with that option. But we realize we are junior to you, so we wanted to be sure we are not misunderstanding something [*listening* and *testing for understanding*]. Can we ask a question [*seeking their point of view*]?

Katherine: What exactly don't you understand?

Jeremy: Basically, we've got two questions. Both come from the new-employee orientation materials we were introduced to when we joined the firm. Can you explain how your path lines up with the firm's duty, above all, to advance our client's long-term interests? Also, how does the report you are asking us to prepare reflect the standards of honesty the firm's "credo" talks about [*open-ended questions about the firm's interests and values*]?

Katherine: Are you accusing me of being unethical? I can't believe it. Look, you are hereby removed from this engagement. I'll find someone else. And if you talk about this to anyone, be warned: I have a long memory.

Jeremy: So, just to be clear, am I hearing you say that you refuse to talk about our ethical concerns with us [*testing for understanding* and *summarizing*]?

Katherine: I am saying you are off this engagement.

At this point, Jeremy would have a choice. He could leave the meeting and report the matter to his mentor and then, most likely, to the firm's ethics officer or supervising partners. Or he could engage Katherine further about his duty to report and see what her response might be. In the interests of using dialogue to go as far as possible with Katherine, I have continued Jeremy's conversation below—as it acquires a sharper edge.

Jeremy [getting up]: I'm afraid that gives us no choice but to take the matter to our mentors and the firm's ethics officer. You need to know that Rashida and I are in this together. We may also be forced to contact our counterpart at the client about the falsified data he will be receiving in this report [*advancing his plan, adding urgency, introducing Katherine to a new interest*]. But we would prefer to work it out with you here. Are you sure you are not willing to talk it through so we can come up with an acceptable approach to this report [*open-ended question seeking mutual interests*]?

That final piece of dialogue is what "hardball" sounds like when it is coming from a junior employee talking to a boss. Obviously, this takes courage, preparation, and confidence in the values you are standing up for. Note also that this approach leverages the firm's own mission statement and the integrity standards that new employees are trained to uphold as well as the underlying values of accountability and truth.

At this point, whether they elevate the matter directly to higher authority or talk with Katherine about this option, Jeremy and Rashida have put their jobs on the line. But if you are unwilling to stand up to someone who wants you to lie to a client about something as important as the core data they have paid your firm to produce, what kind of person have you become? And if your firm does not back you up on an ethical violation as clear as this, what kind of place is it to work?

My guess: in any successful firm, Katherine is an outlier who will be called to account by her more responsible partners (as Ricardo was in Isabella's case). And, far from hurting Jeremy's and Rashida's careers, their actions will advance their reputations as young people deeply committed to the firm's best interests.

Using dialogue instead of confrontation in a conflict over values gives you the upper hand in these sensitive situations. You position yourself as being open to new information, and you demonstrate a wider perspective on the situation than your counterpart. All this will enhance your credibility to third-party audiences.

A Word on Commitments

A final word on commitment. Obtaining an agreement to follow your plan is great. But what you want is a commitment to do so. Commitments are agreements with an added dimension: the other party stands to lose something important if they later back out. In business deals, that "something to lose" is usually financial: a down payment, deposit, or legal penalties for breaching a contract.

In organizations, the currencies are more subtle. The most important ones are potential losses of status, respect, or trust within the organization or with clients and customers. In the dialogue above, did you feel the power of Jeremy's argument that, "We may also be forced to contact our counterpart at the client about the falsified data he will be receiving in this report?" He was demonstrating that Katherine had something important to lose from insisting on her unethical course of action. Agreeing to Jeremy's plan (or something else they would collaborate on that preserved the integrity of the report) would be more than just a temporary promise she would later break. By holding Katherine accountable, these two young employees could be confident in her commitment.

OVERCOMING OBJECTIONS

It is impossible to anticipate all the objections you might get to a thoughtful proposal for resolving an ethical conflict. The examples already provided in this chapter feature a number of common ones such as, "I am more experienced," "That can't be true," and "This is the way the business works." Below I provide some general categories of objections you can anticipate.

Objections to Your Facts. These are relatively straightforward. The good news: a disagreement over facts may imply that the other party agrees with your values. Of course, the first step is to do your homework thoroughly so your facts are as solid as possible. If the other party nevertheless challenges your facts, you'll need to conduct further investigation, present both sets of facts to the ultimate decision maker so they can make their own determination, find a third-party expert to resolve the dispute, or agree on some other process to move the matter forward. No matter what options you use, be as transparent as possible.

Objections Based on Competing Values. As we saw in the chapter on Rule #7 ("Ask Four Questions"), tough cases arise when competing, legitimate values collide. The other party may object to your proposal because they believe another value is more important than the one you are putting forward. Be prepared to argue all four of the CLIP factors (consequences, loyalties, identity, and principles) on behalf of your preferred outcome.

Yes . . . But It Won't Work Out That Way. These objections rely on the speaker's superior experience and judgment about what the future may hold. If your credibility is low on this factor, seek allies with more experience who will endorse your case. Otherwise, try using the technique I illustrated in Jeremy's sample dialogue above: suggest phasing in your solution slowly so everyone can adjust to the future as it unfolds.

Rationalizations. This book has shown you just a fraction of the many self-serving rationalizations you may hear when you speak up for your values against others who have an interest in behaving unethically. If you hear phrases such as "everyone does it," "just this once," and "nobody will notice," be prepared to directly challenge the tenuous assumptions that underlie them. For example:

> **Everybody does it.** "Not everyone. I, for one, am unwilling to do it. And I'd like a chance to investigate how widespread the practice is before agreeing that it is as common as you say."

> **Just this once.** "Just this once is the first step on a slippery slope. It is easier for me to remember what I should do when I stick with my principles 100 percent of the time."

> **Nobody will notice.** "I will notice. As I see it, character is who I am even when nobody else notices."

Beyond meeting rationalizations with common sense, you can also (as noted above) suggest interest-based solutions that address the other party's needs while remaining true to your values. You do not need to embarrass them by calling them out on a rationalization. Sidestep it.

Mumbo Jumbo. Sometimes the other party will offer a string of complex, technical, hard-to-follow reasons why your objection should be dismissed. "This is not improper accounting," they say. "After all, the historical account averages divided by the net present value of the average fare on Siberian Railroads fully supports the number we have here." Intimidated by the mumbo jumbo and assuming they know something you do not, you back off.

Don't do it. If you cannot understand the other party's reasoning, ask them to explain it in plain English, get it in writing, and then take time to check with experts who know more than you do. If it is a genuine argument, they will be happy to accommodate you. If it is mumbo jumbo designed to intimidate you, they will find a way to dodge your request. Then you know what you are up against.

DEALING WITH BULLIES AND TYRANTS

In our sample conversations, I emphasized Katherine's role as a bully so you could observe how hard-nosed tactics can stifle dissent as well as how dialogue-based countermoves can help you cope with office tyrants. But bullies often make true dialogue impossible. What then?

A student, "Melanie," reported that she once walked into her boss's office a few minutes late for a meeting, triggering an enraged rant filled with expletives. She tried to speak, but her boss shouted her down. Shaken, she finally backed out of his office, hands held over her head in a "surrender" gesture. Thereafter, the boss avoided eye contact with her in the hallways and refused to acknowledge her at meetings.

She was leaving for business school within a year, so she tried to tough it out. But her boss's treatment began to affect her performance, so she went to her mentor and explained what was happening. He thanked Melanie for coming to him and revealed that she was by no means the first person who had complained about the bully's abusive behavior. The mentor arranged for her to report to a different supervisor during her final months at the firm. He then reported the matter to the management committee, which launched an internal investigation into the tyrant's conduct. She later heard that he had been asked to leave.

Dealing with bullies is worth a book of its own. In fact, there are quite a few already written (see, for example, Lynne Curry's excellent *Beating the Workplace Bully*). And even if you have mastered the entire beat-the-bully playbook, you will still lose these encounters as often as you win them. Bullies respect power—the subject of the next chapter—more than attempts at collaboration.

But I don't want to leave you defenseless, so I provide some helpful tactics below. As you read these, remember three priorities we have returned to over and over in this book: go into these meetings with as much motivation as you can muster; don't walk into the lion's den alone; and when you speak, be an advocate for all the victims of the tyrant's behavior, not just yourself.

Break the Conflict Cycle. A wise person once said, "Never wrestle with a pig. You both get dirty and the pig enjoys it." Trying to shout down an office bully is a loser's game. When the bully starts to rant, find a way to break the pattern. Let his temper run its course and then put your idea back on the table. If he keeps trying to intimidate you, offer to send him an email later on with your response. As tempting as it will be, avoid the two most salient options of getting angry or buying peace by giving in.

Claim the Protection of Organizational Rules and Standards. Bullies are breaking the basic rules of civility that govern the workplace. Most organizations have formal standards of conduct tucked away in employee manuals and orientation materials that embody these norms. Become familiar with this language, have them at hand for easy reference, and claim their protection whenever you are forced to deal with this issue.

Take Them On in Front of a Sympathetic Audience. Isabella advanced her goals by speaking up about Ricardo's plan in front of an audience (the supervising partners) that believed in her values. Bullies look especially unreasonable when they behave badly in front of a group that, like you, believes in dignity and respect. For this reason, you may find it useful to stage your meetings with a bully when others are present. If the bully starts acting out, quietly ask for a break and, when you return, begin by asking for the group's input on some "rules of engagement" to assure that everyone is heard. When a bully is outnumbered, it is often possible to reset the conversation so it is conducted with a more constructive tone.

Match Their Intensity, Not Their Style. Bullies try to get their way by being loud and emotional. If you try to out-shout them, you will lose. After all, this is their sweet spot. But you can sometimes best them on the conversational battlefield by going for intensity instead of volume. Remain silent. Eventually, they will ask what is going on. Continue to remain silent. Then, quietly and deliberately, make your point. This can be especially effective in a larger meeting, where your intensity will be felt by everyone in the room.

Flip the Script. An ex-dominatrix named Kasia Urbaniak teaches techniques for how to deal with sexual predators who use their positions of power and celebrity status to force themselves on victims. One of the tactics she has her students practice is called "flipping the script." The goal: steal the scene from the bully who thinks they are in control of it by completely changing the narrative of what is happening in the room. She gives an example of a would-be sexual harassment victim breaking into a loud song during a hotel encounter—then making her escape before her harasser could regain his momentum.

This is an admittedly outside-the-box approach to office tyrants, but if you have enough confidence and some skill at improvisational theater, you can break their illusion of control by doing something completely out of sync with what is going on. Take a book off a nearby shelf and page through it; walk to the window and silently point to something happening outside. The bully will eventually notice that you are living in a different reality than he is, opening the door for you to get the conversation back on track.

Reference the Grievance Process, Then Use It if Necessary. A final move is to warn the bully that you know how to hold them accountable to the rules by utilizing whatever formal grievance process is available. Give them a choice: change their tone now or answer for it later to someone else. With this eventual move in mind, email yourself notes on your various negative encounters with the bully. Copy a trusted partner, so someone else can testify to the stress and dysfunction you have experienced. Then be prepared to make your case.

In summary, bullying tactics are a values problem, even when they are deployed in the service of ordinary business objectives. Bullies show disrespect for other people by abusing the norms of civility that ought to govern professional interactions. Allowing a bully to intimidate you regarding any decision is bad practice. But permitting it in an ethical

dispute puts you and your organization in special jeopardy. Not only
have you empowered norm-busting conduct that can cause psychological
harm, but you have also become an accomplice in a tyrant's misconduct,
perhaps even their crimes.

A MOMENT FOR PERSONAL REFLECTION

Dialogue is a powerful conflict management tool. I first learned about
it when I was working with the Federal Bureau of Investigation's Crisis
Negotiating Unit and have subsequently used it myself at work, at home,
and even as a volunteer on a suicide prevention hotline. If you want to
learn more about it, I strongly recommend *Crucial Conversations: Tools
for Talking When the Stakes Are High* by Kerry Patterson, Joseph Grenny,
Ron McMillan, and Al Switzler. Asking open-ended questions, listening
carefully to what you hear, creating common ground with the other
person, and advancing toward a shared solution works to help resolve
conflicts between spouses, siblings, and litigation opponents, not just
parties in a workplace dispute over values.

Think back over your experience and try to recall the last time
someone genuinely *listened* to you. This is more unusual than it sounds.
Often people reach back to a beloved grandparent or mentor who had
the ability to set everything aside when you spoke with them. Do you
have a friend who pays careful attention to you in a conversation and
shows sincere interest in what you were saying? Do you play this role in
anyone else's life?

Bring dialogue tools to life by practicing them with people that matter
to you. They will be happy you did, and you will get better at using them
in the moments that matter at work.

NEXT UP:
ACTION STRATEGIES WHEN DIALOGUE FAILS

As Isabella's case shows, sometimes dialogue is impossible. When the
other party's interests and beliefs are in direct conflict with your values, it
may be wise to bypass them and find others who will be more sympathetic
to your cause. And even your best efforts at dialogue may fail to persuade

the boss or peer who is headed in the wrong direction. No matter what is stalling your progress, the task will now be to advance your values using other tactics. Rule #9 ("Hold Them Accountable") examines the options available, from whispering in the right person's ear and building effective coalitions to full-throated whistleblowing.

RULE #9:
HOLD THEM
ACCOUNTABLE

"It is not only what we do, but also what we do not do, for which we are accountable."

—Molière

Dialogue is a great option—if it is available. But what if you are too low in the pecking order to ask for a meeting? Suppose you fear retaliation from the powerful people who are behaving badly? And even if you succeed in having a conversation, what happens when the other party rejects your suggestions?

Four additional influence moves remain at your disposal:

- *Elevating the issue* to a higher-level decision maker,
- *Reporting the matter* to an ethics officer or internal committee specifically charged with protecting the value in question,
- *Escalating pressure* on decision makers using political moves, and when all else fails,
- *Blowing the whistle* by filing complaints with outside authorities and going public with your story.

The boundaries between these options can be fuzzy, and there is no established "order" for taking them. For example, later in this chapter, I will tell you the story of a low-level employee who outmaneuvered the powerful head of her organization by applying a single, well-targeted bit of political pressure. She lacked the credibility to elevate the issue, the status to report it to anyone, and the hard evidence to blow the whistle.

But with one subtle move, she solved a major corruption problem. That said, it may be wise in a given case to elevate the issue first, report it when you do not get the response you want, and only then resort to pressure and whistleblowing tactics.

The goal in using all four moves is the same: get the issue before a sympathetic audience—people who have the power, duty, inclination, and incentives to set things right. If the issue is important enough and your opponents hold most of the cards, you may end up waging what amounts to a "campaign" on behalf of your value. At the end of the chapter, we will examine a detailed case study of just such a strategy.

The discussions in this chapter will shed new light on the tactical choices made by the heroes of some notable stories told earlier in the book. For example, in the Theranos scandal (Rule #6, "Leverage the Power of Two"), we saw how Tyler Shultz and Erika Cheung *elevated* their concerns about the firm's fraudulent blood-testing device first to CEO Elizabeth Holmes and finally to George Shultz, Tyler's grandfather and a Theranos board member. These meetings failed to change anyone's minds, so they quit their jobs and *escalated* the pressure on Theranos by secretly cooperating with an investigative journalist from the *Wall Street Journal*. Meanwhile, Shultz had already filed a *whistleblowing* regulatory complaint under an assumed name, and, when company lawyers began threatening her, Cheung followed suit. Cheung's complaint triggered the formal legal investigation that exposed the fraud.

The chapter's organization is straightforward. First, we'll examine each of the four tactics separately, going from the relatively simple (elevating the issue) to the most complex (blowing the whistle to outside authorities). I'll provide examples to show how these moves work and what risks each entails. Then we will dive into a detailed case study that illustrates how one person used all four of these tactics effectively to hold her bosses accountable. Our heroine this time is Cynthia Cooper, vice president for internal auditing at WorldCom, Inc., who overcame every obstacle thrown in her path and proved that the company's leadership team was cooking the books. You heard about the WorldCom scandal earlier in this book (Rule #2, "Commit to Your Values"), and we met Ms. Cooper briefly when you learned how personal character helps you cope with your fears (Rule #4, "Summon Your Character"). Cooper's narrative weaves together many of the threads of the Conscience Code—from a commitment to values and personality strengths to the Power of Two.

When you are finished reading it, I hope you will agree with me that Cynthia Cooper belongs in the "Person of Conscience Hall of Fame."

OPTION 1:
ELEVATING THE PROBLEM TO HIGHER AUTHORITY

The most obvious way to advance your values after meeting initial resistance is an appeal to a higher authority. You will need to bring the persuasive dialogue skills you encountered in the last chapter to discussions at the next level.

Elevating with Permission

Elevating a dispute raises an immediate political problem. Will your boss or peer see this as an attempt to bypass them, undercutting their credibility? Perhaps. For that reason, your first step (when your relationship with the other party permits this) should be to seek their permission for your appeal.

Here is an example. One of my students, "Marta," worked as a senior director for a nonprofit group providing community health services in rural Africa. As part of her job, she recruited local villagers as paid "Health Advocates" to promote her group's initiatives. Nearly all of these advocates were women, and the work provided a modest but welcome source of income. The program had been operating successfully for two years when a new CEO took over Marta's organization. Following a strategic review, he and the board decided to change priorities and issued an order to close down her project. Her boss ("Eduardo"), the head of African programs, directed Marta to lay off the Health Advocates "immediately."

Marta strongly objected to this move. She knew each of the advocates personally and had seen firsthand the good work they were doing. She was distressed at the lack of respect her organization was showing toward this deserving group, and she asked for a three-month, paid "transition period" during which she could train them to continue their professional lives on their own. Marta set up a meeting with Eduardo to plead her case.

Eduardo was sympathetic, but he rejected her plan. He was under a mandate to wrap up the program, and he pointed out that no promises had been made to the advocates about how long their jobs would last. Marta then asked for his permission to take the matter to the CEO. Eduardo agreed, provided both of them could be present when Marta made her case. Marta said she was comfortable with that.

As Marta prepared for this all-important video conference with the CEO, she reconnected with the values that had led her to take this job in the first place. These included a love of the people she served as well as her belief in her organization's community-service mission. She felt this mission would be severely compromised by terminating the advocates in the way Eduardo planned. She also feared that this move would permanently damage the reputation of her organization in these rural communities, where relationship norms dominated all others. The more she thought about it, the more strongly she felt. She decided that, if the CEO upheld Eduardo, she would have to offer her resignation.

At the video conference meeting with the CEO, she and Eduardo both made their cases. Marta argued that the advocates were people of influence in their communities who deserved the training she could offer them. She concluded her pitch with an appeal to purpose. The termination plan was inconsistent with the values of the organization. She said that she would reluctantly have to resign if the plan went forward.

Eduardo was surprised by the passion Marta showed about the issue and expressed his support for her as a talented, dedicated team member. But he remained convinced that the dismissals were an economic necessity under the board's new policy. The CEO took the matter under advisement and a few days later emailed his decision.

He backed Marta's plan, modifying her proposed termination period to two months and providing Eduardo with supplemental funding to cover the cost. He thanked them both for bringing all facets of this decision to his attention, with a special nod to Marta for her display of commitment to the foundation's mission. He now realized, he said, that the organization might need the goodwill of these advocates in the future. They were well worth investing in.

Marta's appeal to higher authority had two effects. First, she was able to wrap up her project in a professional way consistent with her values. Second, by elevating this dispute with Eduardo's permission and arguing

her case with principled conviction, she strengthened her working relationship with Eduardo and won the respect of her new CEO.

Elevating without Permission

Asking for permission to elevate a dispute can work when you have a
solid relationship with your boss and a workplace culture that encourages
transparency. But what if you ask permission, and the other party objects?
Continuing with your appeal may now seem both disloyal and defiant.
For these reasons, many appeals to higher authority are made without
permission. When you take this route, however, be sure to bring your
diplomatic skills. It seldom pays to offend a boss unnecessarily.

Whispering in the Decision Maker's Ear

Take, for example, a technique I call "whispering in the decision maker's
ear." A student of mine ("Ali") worked for a global energy company and
was leading a process to hire five Arabic-language interpreters to serve in
its offices around the world. It was a rigorous review that included taped
interviews and a multi-factor rating system. Over sixty people applied for
these positions, and Ali was charged with providing the human resources
department with a slate of eight to ten qualified finalists, ranked in order
of their ratings. The head of HR would then make the final decisions.

Ali's team came up with eight names, and checked the list with his
boss before forwarding them. To his surprise, the boss added the name
of a candidate Ali's team had passed over. Ali protested that many other
candidates had higher rating scores than this person. His boss then
opened the candidate spreadsheet and revised this candidate's score so
she ranked third on the list. He ordered Ali to advance her name.

A few days later, Ali learned the reason for his boss's insistence on this
candidate: she was his niece. What to do? Confronting his boss directly
over his nepotism would trigger a high-stakes personal conflict, and
elevating the matter would put him in the vortex of a messy, personal
dispute. So Ali decided to solve the problem with a "whisper."

After forwarding the list of finalists to HR, Ali called the human
resources leader who would make the final decisions. He explained

that the process had surfaced some excellent candidates but he had a recommendation.

"Before you make the final decisions, I suggest you listen to the audiotaped interviews of the top six or seven people on the list yourself," Ali said.

The HR leader asked why.

"Let's just say we had some disagreements on the team about who ought to be listed as the top five," Ali replied. "A review of the tapes will help you decide which five you ought to hire."

The niece did not get an offer.

Delegate the Appeal to a Higher-Credibility Messenger

If you lack the credibility to elevate a matter yourself, look for someone better suited to do so and ask them to take the lead. Take the case of "Hiroshi," who told my class about a problem he encountered when his boss wanted to send out a misleading report to an important client. He and another analyst, "Fran," had worked for weeks on different parts of this document. With the deadline looming, Hiroshi reviewed Fran's work and found that it was filled with factual errors and analytic shortcuts. She obviously lacked industry expertise for this assignment. But when he shared his concerns to his newly promoted project leader, Roberta, she waved his concerns aside. There was no time to redo the report, she said. Besides, the work was "good enough."

Hiroshi's name was going on this document, so he decided to elevate the issue. But he had two problems: he felt sure Roberta would not agree to an appeal, and he realized he was too junior to approach the partner supervising the entire client relationship. So he contacted his mentor—a senior executive in the same office as the supervising partner—and explained the situation. The mentor reviewed the report and agreed that the problems Hiroshi had identified were significant and troubling. The mentor quickly set up a conference call that included the supervising partner, himself, Hiroshi, and the firm's top expert in the client's industry.

The result? The partner ordered Roberta and Hiroshi to work with the industry expert to revise the report before it went out—a process that involved twenty-four hours of intense work but brought the report up to the firm's standard before the deadline. Hiroshi concluded his story by noting that Roberta had resented his actions at first. But several months later they had a "good conversation" that cleared the air. She admitted that she had managed the deadline poorly by not leaving time to check with the industry expert. Ultimately, she gave him an excellent performance evaluation at the end of the year.

Overall, when you face a decision to elevate a matter without permission, follow Hiroshi's "start with the people you know best" strategy. Advance the issue first to someone with whom you enjoy a strong relationship of trust. Then seek insights about whom to talk with and in what order. That way, you can gain both information and a potential ally as you move up the chain of command.

OPTION 2: FILING AN INTERNAL COMPLAINT

Every organization has formal complaint systems in place to address specific issues. These can include everything from regulatory compliance matters to sexual harassment and conflicts of interest. As I noted above, hinting that you may be forced to make a formal complaint can often motivate a boss or peer to take your advocacy of a value seriously.

Unfortunately, as a practical matter, many such complaint procedures trigger complex rules and formalities that can delay decisions. In addition, they often operate to minimize legal and reputational risks to the organization rather than as neutral forums where you can obtain justice. Finally, as soon as you file one of these complaints, you may be tagged as a "troublemaker." The focus of the dispute may then shift from the issue you are complaining about to you personally. Although many human resource managers do their best to make these systems work, my students have repeatedly expressed dissatisfaction with invoking them as effective ways to hold people accountable.

Take, for example, the story a former student, "Amelia," told about filing a sexual harassment complaint. She worked for a Mexican financial services company and was assigned as the only female on a fifteen-member team. She was quickly targeted by the team leader, an old-styled chauvinist who had been at the firm for several decades. Comments such as "I wonder if you are as good in bed as you are with trading stocks" made team meetings a torture for her. Amelia put up with it for a few months, in hopes that the boss would grow tired of making such "jokes" at her expense, but instead he became ever more aggressive and explicit. At length she complained to human resources.

To her dismay, someone in HR immediately tipped her boss off that she had complained, and he fired her within two weeks for "poor performance." She refused to buckle to his retaliation and demanded a meeting with the boss to demand his proof that she had underperformed. He had none, of course, but he told her to "go quietly or I'll see that you never work in the industry again." She secretly recorded this meeting, then hired a lawyer and threatened to sue. The firm knew when it was beaten and paid her a settlement, but Amelia did not get her job back. It took over a year before another company hired her, and she ended up working in a different country.

Of course, many firms have internal complaint procedures that are managed with integrity. My advice: gather the best information you can on how the system operates in your organization and whose interests it is designed to serve. Then make a prudent decision about whether this option can help. At the very least, you should document your case *as if* it were going to be carefully reviewed by an internal tribunal. That will make you more persuasive and credible no matter which tactical option you ultimately use.

OPTION 3: APPLYING POLITICAL PRESSURE

Appeals to higher authority and filing formal complaints involve the persuasion skills we explored in the last chapter. Escalating a dispute by applying pressure calls on *political* insights. Recall the examples from earlier in the book when I described how Google and Wayfair employees used large-scale walkouts to bring about changes in company policies on social justice issues (Rule #2, "Commit to Your Values"). At a more nuanced, tactical level inside organizations, bosses generally want to protect their status, reputations, and power. These desires can provide you with political leverage to hold them accountable.

Remember: politics is often the art of managing appearances. You can influence bosses and peers by offering them ways to look good by doing the right thing or showing them how they may look bad if they continue on the wrong path. When you do this well, you can accomplish a great deal with a minimum of conflict.

The Boss and the Press Conference

Take, for example, the story of a Chinese student ("Chunhua"), who told her classmates how she was able to pressure the corrupt leader of her government agency to stop channeling public funds to his relatives and friends. Her lever: a single press conference.

Chunhua worked as an analyst on a team charged with distributing economic development grants to rural communities. A few months into the first year of this program, she noticed that all the grants were going to a single Chinese province—one that was the home base of the agency's leader. When she dug a little deeper, she thought she detected another pattern: many of the grant recipients appeared to have personal ties to her boss.

She was far too low on the organization chart to go to the leader directly. In addition, she lacked the documentary proof she would need to complain to outside regulatory authorities. Calling out a highly placed official was risky business. What to do?

Her social network included friends in the agency's press office. They, like her, cared deeply about the agency's mission and were upset about how the funds were being diverted. After a few brainstorming sessions, they hatched a subtle plan based on three strategic insights about the situation they faced.

First, and most important, the Chinese central government had recently announced a major anti-corruption initiative. Bribery and misuse of public money were hindering economic growth, so the government had made stopping it a national priority. This provided Chunhua and her friends with the basis for applying pressure on the leader.

Second, Chunhua's friends in the press office controlled access to an important influence lever: the Chinese media. In China, she explained to the class, mainstream reporters see themselves as *allies* of the government organizations they cover. They take their cues from government press offices to help them do their jobs. Her friends thus had cozy working relationships with the reporters who covered the agency.

Finally, Chunhua's press-office friends had already scheduled a press conference where the agency's leader would talk about the progress of the economic development program. They decided this would be the perfect stage to put their boss on the spot.

Chunhua's friends fed a reporter two pointed questions. The first: Could the leader comment on the strategy behind where the initial grants were going and why most had gone to a single province? The second: What was the leader's plan for vigorously implementing the new anti-corruption campaign in its grant-making process?

The boss, caught off guard by the first question, went on record saying this region was a "strategic test case" to iron out the logistics for administering grants. He assured the reporters that the program would now be rolling out to all regions in China. The second question prompted a lengthy speech about the importance of the government's new anti-corruption initiative. Chunhua and her team were delighted to hear him say that he and his staff would be reviewing "every grant" for signs of misconduct. They knew that senior analysts on his staff now had the ammunition they needed to hold him to that pledge.

The grants soon began flowing to the rest of the country. Chunhua and her friends returned to their jobs satisfied with a job well done. And her story received a round of admiring applause from her classmates.

Chunhua's use of political pressure was exceptionally crafty, which is why she won praise from her classmates. But it also demonstrated four smart tactics worth considering as you seek to resolve conflicts using pressure instead of persuasion. We have met some of these moves in earlier chapters.

Start with Allies. Chunhua used her allies in a different part of her organization who shared her values. The Power of Two helps in every conflict, but it has special application when you need to apply political pressure on an issue.

Leverage a Current, Widely Shared Organizational Priority. Chunhua and her friends linked their concerns about the leader's behavior to the Chinese government's well-publicized campaign against corruption. This was politically astute. At any given time, organizations prioritize certain values over others to accomplish specific goals. For example, if a firm has recently been rocked by a sexual harassment scandal, it will likely make the treatment of women a special priority. This sensitizes everyone to the issue, providing an especially persuasive argument against any decision or policy that might be seen as inconsistent with this priority.

I once used this tactic to help lead a successful campaign in my local community to stop my university from installing a high perimeter wall around our urban campus. Several university board members had proposed that such a wall, combined with a massive relocation of students to on-campus housing, would improve overall security. However, many graduate students, faculty, and staff would continue living in the surrounding community after the wall was built, so it was, at best, a poor way to address security issues.

Our campaign succeeded because we linked it to an urgent, citywide priority in Philadelphia—the creation of private/public partnerships for neighborhood revitalization. The wall was a sign that the university was withdrawing from the city while our revitalization campaign showed a way for it to engage more fully as an urban neighbor. In the end, we instigated actions to enhance local public schools, encourage home ownership, make loans to small businesses, and—on the issue of public safety—deploy campus security officers in the community more effectively.

Stage Your Meeting with Third Parties Present Who Are Sympathetic to Your Position. Chunhua won the day because she used a public gathering—a press conference—to commit her leader to the right path. We knew we had won our battle against the wall when university officials testified in favor of our proposals before the Philadelphia City Council, cementing it as a priority. Note: You do not need a public hearing to lock your priorities into someone else's decision matrix. Simply invite your decision maker to a meeting where you can appropriately highlight your priority before an audience that believes in or has a duty to advance it. Then tactfully nudge your target into publicly endorsing the value in question.

Keep a Low Profile. Pressure tactics, especially when implemented by politically savvy coalitions, are an excellent way for conflict-averse or vulnerable employees to join forces with other, more assertive people to advance their values. Like Chunhua, think of yourself as a strategist rather than a spokesperson. Delegate to others in appropriate roles the jobs of leading meetings and following up on implementation. In some cases, this may mean that others get credit for cleaning up an ethical mess that you identified and fixed. So be it. Your reward is the satisfaction of getting people to do the right thing without the risks of a confrontation.

OPTION 4: WHISTLEBLOWING

"Whistleblowing" is a specialized term. Elevating a dispute, reporting it, or launching a pressure campaign may, in a given case, be part of a whistleblowing effort, but the ultimate goal for whistleblowers is the *public exposure of wrongdoing*—not just the reversal of an internal decision. Three factors distinguish this option.

First, whistleblowers can come from both inside and outside an organization. We will look at some classic examples of employees (or ex-employees) using whistleblowing tactics below. But anyone can be a whistleblower, including enterprising lawyers, community activists, and journalists. For instance, one of the most famous whistleblowers of the modern era is Erin Brockovich (played in the film carrying her name by Julia Roberts, who won an Oscar in 2000 for her work in the lead role). Brockovich was a file clerk at a California plaintiff's law firm when she found documents suggesting Pacific Gas and Electric Company (PG&E) had released cancer-causing chemicals into the water in Hinkley, California. The ensuing class action lawsuit, brought with the cooperation of some of Hinkley's residents, triggered a financial settlement of $333 million for PG&E's victims.

Second, the typical whistleblowing story involves significant misconduct by either an organization or an individual. One of the more notorious whistleblowing cases of recent years involved an Indian generic drug company called Ranbaxy, Inc. Dinesh Thakur (whom we met briefly in the chapter on Rule #2, "Commit to Your Values") joined Ranbaxy from Bristol Myers Squibb as a high-ranking officer in the research and development department. Soon after joining the firm, Thakur's boss recruited him to do research on what the boss feared might be a major quality-control problem in manufacturing. The boss suspected Ranbaxy was saving money by fabricating quality control tests, thereby creating a major public health risk for consumers, especially the most vulnerable consumers of all—poor people in developing countries with weak regulatory oversight of the drug industry.

Thakur's research confirmed his boss's worst fears. Both men then brought their findings to the board of directors, which listened politely to their presentation but refused to act. The boss immediately resigned, but Thakur pressed on, trying to further develop the factual evidence that might persuade Ranbaxy's board to reverse itself. When Thakur finally realized the firm's leadership was corrupt, he quit, thinking that he, like his boss, could put this experience behind him.

But his conscience would not let him rest. Several months after quitting, he decided to become a whistleblower. He reported the matter to the Food and Drug Administration (FDA), the US agency with jurisdiction over generic drug manufacturing. As he later commented, "I just couldn't live with myself knowing what I knew and how it affected the poorest of the poor across the world."

Thus began an *eight-year* whistleblowing odyssey. It started with his filing a complaint to the FDA using an anonymous email account and ended with Ranbaxy pleading guilty to seven criminal counts brought by Department of Justice prosecutors for selling adulterated drugs with the intent to defraud. The company paid a $500 million fine and was eventually acquired by another Indian pharmaceutical firm. Thakur himself received a whistleblowing reward of nearly $50 million from the US government for bringing the fraud to light. The full story of the Ranbaxy scandal (and of corruption in the generic drug market generally) can be found in Katherine Eban's excellent book, *Bottle of Lies: The Inside Story of the Generic Drug Boom.*

The third distinctive feature of whistleblowing, well illustrated by both the Brockovich and Thakur examples, is the involvement of outside institutions dedicated to bringing wrongdoers to justice. Whistleblowers file lawsuits, complain to regulators, lobby for new laws, and use media campaigns to build public sympathy for their causes. The stakes are always high when the term "whistleblower" is used, and the press usually plays a key role.

For example, Michael Woodford, the CEO of Japanese company Olympus, Inc., blew the whistle *on his own board of directors* by exposing its misconduct to the press. Michael Woodford was a British citizen who had worked his way up the executive ranks at Olympus for over thirty years before becoming the first non-Japanese person to lead the company.

Soon after taking his leadership role, he discovered that Olympus had engaged in a major cover-up of billions of dollars in financial losses. When he brought these revelations to his board of directors, however, it refused to act. The board saw Woodford's investigation as an act of "disloyalty" to the firm rather than an attempt to protect its investors. Woodford's saga had many twists and turns, but the short version is straightforward: the board fired him, he returned to England, and he went public with his allegations. Within a month of his being fired, Olympus had lost 80 percent of its market value. In the end, he filed a lawsuit for wrongful dismissal, winning a multimillion-dollar settlement. He later said that it would have been all too easy for him to join in the conspiracy of silence around the hidden losses. But, as he told his wife,

"If I had walked away, I would have been complicit. . . . I would have been part of this." When asked if he considered himself a whistleblower, he said he did not. He preferred the term "Truth-teller."

There is an extensive literature on whistleblowing. I have listed a number of these works in the bibliography and especially recommend Stephen Martin Kohn's *The New Whistleblower's Handbook: The Step-by-Step Guide to Doing What's Right and Protecting Yourself*.

In addition, there are well-established organizations dedicated to helping whistleblowers survive the sometimes brutal experience of being one. These include such groups as the National Whistleblower Center, the Government Accountability Project, and the whistleblower protection program run by the US Department of Labor.

Importantly, a number of specialized law firms work with whistleblowers in hopes of sharing the statutory rewards that may come from exposing frauds. As Dinesh Thakur's case illustrates, such rewards can run to millions of dollars under "whistleblower laws" such as the US False Claims Act (for frauds committed against the government). For example, in just a few months between March and May of 2020, at the height of the COVID-19 pandemic, the US Securities and Exchange Commission received over four thousand tips from whistleblowers related to business-related frauds. And in calendar year 2018, the SEC paid out over $64 million in bounties from the fines collected based on whistleblower tips. The Internal Revenue Service and Commodity Futures Trading Commission also oversee whistleblower reward programs.

PUTTING IT ALL TOGETHER:
CYNTHIA COOPER AND WORLDCOM

We are now ready to use our understanding of the four strategies described above to track a complex values conflict from beginning to end. Our story features a determined midlevel executive named Cynthia Cooper who, drawing on her inner strengths and her commitment to professional values, overcame every obstacle her crooked bosses threw at her to expose one of the largest corporate frauds in US business history, the WorldCom scandal.

We visited the beginning of this story in the third chapter (Rule #3, "Know Your Enemy") when we saw WorldCom's controller, David Myers, and his boss, CFO Scott Sullivan, pressuring two reluctant bookkeepers (Betty Vinson and Troy Normand) into making the first false accounting entries. We then met our hero, Cynthia Cooper, in the following chapter (Rule #4, "Summon Your Character") as she sat outside David Myers's office, nervously awaiting the confrontation that would make or break her case.

I will now connect the dots between these two points in the WorldCom story so you can see how a dedicated person of conscience who takes her professional values seriously can successfully expose corporate corruption from the inside.

"Don't Ev-v-ver Allow Yourself to Be Intimidated"

To understand the WorldCom story, you have to start with Cynthia Cooper's character as a person. She grew up in Clinton, Mississippi, a community of around 25,000. In high school, she won the scholarship prize for outstanding citizenship because, her teachers said, she consistently volunteered for jobs nobody else wanted to do, such as clean up on Friday nights after football games. She took her scholarship to nearby Mississippi State University, where she majored in accounting, adding a Masters in Accounting a few years later from the University of Alabama. Her career then wound its way through major accounting firms and private companies, with the usual ups and downs. Eventually, at the age of twenty-nine, she landed a job in the internal auditing department of a high-flying telecommunications firm (Long Distance Discount Service, or LDDS) located in Clinton and led by a charismatic CEO named Bernie Ebbers. A year later, in 1995, LDDS renamed itself WorldCom, Inc.

Cooper was a quiet person, a confirmed introvert. As she put it in her 2008 book, *Extraordinary Circumstances*, "I'm circumspect and reserved. Sometimes I don't even want to answer my phone at home." But she combined her reserve with an effectively assertive conflict management style. Evidence for the latter can be found in the way she handled herself in WorldCom's male-dominated culture. Once, at a WorldCom company lunch with a group of executives, a large man at the other end of her table beckoned her, "Hey, Cynthia, why don't you come down here so you can sit on Papa's lap." The men around him, including one who reported to her, broke out laughing. Cooper gave the man an icy stare. "That's completely inappropriate," she responded. Ever the good accountant, she let people know when they had crossed a line.

Cooper's inner life was anchored in faith and family. Her grandmother, Nannie Ferrell, "had a tremendous influence on my life," she wrote. Ferrell's spiritual strength "helped her run the race well, live by her values, and stay true to her purpose." Cooper also benefited from strong female role models in her family. During one "down" period in her career, her mother told her that, "You come from a long line of strong women. Life may knock us down, but we don't stay down." One of Cooper's mottos, embedded in her memory in her mom's distinctively southern drawl: "Don't ev-v-ver allow yourself to be intimidated."

Her professional role model was Terri Hudson, a woman she worked for early in her career at a telecommunications company called Skytel and who inspired her to become an internal auditor. Hudson was a rare boss, a talented auditor who overcame the sexist culture she encountered at her firm, rose through the ranks, and ultimately became Skytel's CFO. Cooper's description of Hudson could easily apply to herself: "She's assertive," Cooper wrote. "[She] makes her career aspirations known, and asks her boss for what she feels she and her staff deserve. Nothing has been handed to her." As I researched Cooper's story, I often imagined her silently asking, when the pressure was on, "What would Terri do?"

You Don't Have the "Business Expertise" to Question These Decisions

WorldCom's fraud began in the fall of 2000. Its business had been declining due to seismic shifts in the telecom market toward digital technology and away from the traditional telephone products WorldCom specialized in. In the face of a sudden, steep drop in revenue in mid-2000, CFO Scott Sullivan and Controller David Myers (with Ebbers's approval) hatched their plot to "cook the books." The goal: produce quarterly reports that met Wall Street financial expectations so they could keep the stock price high until the business turned around. Ebbers's strategy for the company was based on that price. He had announced in 1996 that, "Our goal is not to capture market share or be global. Our goal is to be the No. 1 stock on Wall Street." By 1999, the year Cynthia Cooper was promoted to vice president for internal auditing, Ebbers's strategy was working. WorldCom's market cap was $115 billion, and it was the fifth most widely held stock in America. The leadership team's multimillion-dollar bonuses depended on meeting Ebbers's stock-price goals.

The conspiracy to falsify WorldCom's accounts had been running successfully for over a year before Cooper got her first hint that something was wrong. In March 2002, the president of the wireless division came to her office to complain that revenue reserves from his unit were being moved to cover losses in other parts of the organization. He wondered what was going on.

To make sense of what follows, you need to know where Cooper stood in her organization. As head of internal auditing, she reported to two bosses, one inside and one outside the firm. Internally, her boss was the CFO, Scott Sullivan (to whom Controller David Myers also reported). Sullivan set Cooper's salary, approved promotions for her team, and gave her performance reviews. But when it came to Cooper's work on accounting matters, she also reported to the outside auditing firm that certified WorldCom's financial statements (which was Arthur Andersen at the beginning of this story and became KPMG by the end). The top layer over everyone in this system was the four-member audit committee of WorldCom's board of directors, chaired by a telecommunications consultant named Max Bobbitt. Bobbitt was an Ebbers loyalist who had been a WorldCom board member since 1992. He had no formal accounting experience.

Cooper did not like what she had heard about the wireless division, so she elevated the problem to an Arthur Andersen partner named Kenny Avery. Avery told her he was already looking into it. He did not seem especially concerned.

A few days later, however, Cooper learned that somebody else was worried about the wireless division problem and not in a way she expected—Scott Sullivan. Avery had tipped Sullivan off about Cooper's query, and Sullivan was furious at what he considered an "end run" around him. As the next few days passed, Sullivan went on what Cooper would later call "the warpath," at one point shouting at her during a meeting that she did not have "the business expertise" to get involved in the revenue question at Wireless. Cooper, unsettled and fearing for her future, began moving some of her personal items from her office back to her home in case she got fired.

But she persisted. And at their next encounter over the issue, he switched from bullying Cooper to patronizing her. In response to her questions about the accounting treatment for Wireless, Sullivan told her the issue would soon be resolved by using an accounting principle known as "the rule of ten." Cooper had a master's in accounting and knew mumbo jumbo when she heard it. There was no such thing as "the rule of ten," but she decided there was nothing to be gained by challenging Sullivan directly on this. "He would never have talked to you that way if you hadn't been female," a colleague later said.

Cooper now knew something was wrong and that Sullivan and possibly Myers were part of it. But what exactly was going on? She kicked her internal audit team into high gear to figure it out. Normally, it is beyond internal auditing's mandate to investigate the financial accounting matters handled by the outside auditors. But evidence was mounting that people had things to hide, and she lacked confidence in Arthur Andersen, which had recently become embroiled in another accounting scandal at Enron, Inc. So she dove into a full review of WorldCom's financial record system. At one point, her group found itself mysteriously locked out of WorldCom's computerized financial record system. Undaunted, Cooper assigned a tech-savvy member of her team to hack into it so her work could continue.

"What Is Prepaid Capacity?"

The issue that would light the bonfire under WorldCom and its leaders emerged on May 29, 2002—a little over a month after the WorldCom board had forced Bernie Ebbers to resign based on the worsening condition of the company. Cooper and her team had learned that a former WorldCom financial analyst named Kim Emigh was blowing the whistle to his local Texas newspapers about capital spending abuses he had observed in the company. Emigh had been fired for asking one too many tough questions, a signal to Cooper that she should look into WorldCom's capital accounts (the values placed on physical assets like equipment and property).

At a meeting soon after this project got underway, a team member looked up from the reports they were poring over and asked everyone in the room, "What is prepaid capacity?"

Nobody knew. But the deeper they looked, the more mysterious it became. For example, while digging around in the accounts for "furniture and fixtures," the team found a $500 million asset labeled "prepaid capacity" that had been added to the books just a few months earlier. Soon they found similar entries popping up like weeds in a flower garden. WorldCom's balance sheet was being propped up by billions of dollars of "prepaid capacity." Controller David Myers was now sending urgent messages to her to stop looking at accounting matters outside her jurisdiction. An audit committee meeting was coming up, he said. She and her team ought to be preparing for it.

They were, just not in the way Myers expected.

By June 10, her team had found huge "prepaid capacity" entries for $743 million, $941 million, and $100 million. Overall, the total amount they had uncovered was $2.5 billion, a number that would soon balloon to some $3.8 billion. Cooper and her team began to carry their work papers home with them, making electronic copies of their research findings in case their bosses attempted to destroy the records.

Sullivan and Myers sensed that Cooper was on their trail. On June 11, Sullivan called Cooper to his office to try once again to warn her off. He told her he was holding up promotions for everyone in her office until he had a chance to review their work more carefully. Just as she was leaving, she turned and asked Sullivan the question that had sparked their entire investigation. "What," she asked, "is prepaid capacity?"

He fielded the question without a pause. "Prepaid capacity," Sullivan replied, "represents costs associated with no- or low-utilized Sonet Rings [a network transmission term] and lines which are being capitalized."

It was the "rule of ten" all over again. Cooper had a feeling this was nonsense, but Sullivan had rattled off his answer with such supreme confidence she said nothing. After the meeting, she asked her team if anyone had a clue what Sullivan's explanation meant. Nobody did. She decided it was time to bypass both her internal and external bosses and elevate the prepaid capacity issue to Max Bobbitt, chair of the board's audit committee.

Turning Up the Heat: Applying Pressure

On June 12, she spoke to Bobbitt about the prepaid capacity mystery. He listened carefully, noting that the Audit Committee would be meeting two days later on June 14 and suggesting she huddle with KPMG partner Farrell Malone (KPMG had now taken over from Arthur Andersen as WorldCom's outside auditors) about the issue. Bobbitt would then meet with them both on June 13. He advised Cooper, "Don't have any further discussions with David Myers or Scott Sullivan until we reach a consensus on how to proceed at the [Audit Committee] meeting." He was clearly worried that Cooper had found something, but she wondered about his loyalties. Which would he protect: WorldCom's leaders or the truth?

On June 13, Bobbitt met secretly with Malone and Cooper at a Hampton Inn in Clinton not far from WorldCom's headquarters. Cooper presented her information on the prepaid capacity issue, showing what WorldCom's income statements would have looked like without the suspect entries. Bobbitt hesitated. Sullivan was a wiz at accounting and had served WorldCom well for years. Did Cooper have enough proof that prepaid capacity was a fraud to present the matter to the audit committee? He did not think so. He decided not to raise the issue at the June 14 meeting and ordered her to speak with Sullivan again. Indeed, he told Cooper not to speak with anyone until she had met with Sullivan.

Cooper now suspected that Bobbitt might try to block the truth from coming out. A few days later, on June 17 and with Sullivan leaving messages to ask for a meeting, Cooper made a fateful decision. She decided to defy Bobbitt and start knocking on doors. It was time to confront the rank-and-file people in the accounting department to see if she could pry loose the proof she needed.

She and her top lieutenant, Glyn Smith, first double-checked with the outside auditors at KPMG. Did they have any information whatever on prepaid capacity? The answer was "No."

Next they visited bookkeeper Betty Vinson. Her name was on many of the prepaid capacity entries. Did she know what it was or have documentation for it? Vinson replied that she knew nothing. She got her orders to make these entries from her boss, Buddy Yates, and his boss, David Myers.

They walked down the hall to Buddy Yates's office. He denied knowing anything about it, directing them to David Myers.

Finally, they came to David Myers. As they approached his office, Cooper heard the phone ring. She was sure it was Yates warning Myers that they were coming. She also knew that if Myers denied knowing anything, she would be back to Bobbitt without the additional proof he was demanding—and possibly without her job. Heart racing and palms sweating, Cooper waited until Myers stopped talking on the phone and walked with Smith into his office.

The meeting began with some evasive back-and-forth about prepaid capacity as Myers tried to dodge the question. But Cooper pressed him hard, expressing disbelief that a professional controller could be uninformed about an asset worth billions of dollars on his company's books.

At last, Myers came clean. He later told Cooper that he had promised himself he would tell the truth if anyone asked him directly about the prepaid capacity issue. He could, it seems, rationalize the accounting, but he could not rationalize lying about it. He admitted he had no support for the fake entries, and there were no accounting principles to justify them. "[O]nce it was done the first time," Myers admitted, "it was difficult to stop."

"I Can and I Will"

Cooper immediately reported the news of Myers's confession to Bobbitt, assuming this was the smoking gun he had been looking for. But her problems were not over yet. On June 18, at Bobbitt's request, Cooper and Smith flew to Washington, D.C., to meet with Bobbitt and the KPMG accountants. Bobbitt had also invited Sullivan, insisting that Sullivan be given a chance to justify his accounting. Bobbitt remained reluctant to convene an emergency meeting of the Audit Committee.

On June 20, Cooper forced his hand. She told KPMG partner Farrell Malone that if Bobbitt would not schedule an audit committee meeting in light of Myers's confession, "I'm going to get on the phone and call one myself."

"You can't do that!" Malone exclaimed.

"I can and I will," Cooper responded.

She prevailed. With all parties present, including the outside auditors, Sullivan, Cooper, and the audit committee convened late in the day on Thursday, June 20. Cooper's report was presented and then Sullivan, flanked by an entourage of WorldCom executives ranging from David Myers to the firm's general counsel and a brigade of outside lawyers from WorldCom's law firm, launched into his defense. The meeting ended with him requesting a few days to further develop the factual and legal record before the committee made a decision. Bobbitt gave him until Monday, June 24, but the handwriting was on the wall.

On June 24, both Sullivan and Myers were asked to resign. Sullivan refused and was promptly fired. The next day, WorldCom issued a press release stating that it was restating its financials by $3.8 billion and laying off 17,000 employees. Civil and criminal actions followed as WorldCom's stock price sank from a high of $64/share in 1999 to $.09/share after June 24. Its assets were eventually sold off to Verizon. Sullivan, Myers, Vinson, and others pled guilty to criminal fraud. These co-conspirators then testified against Ebbers, who, for reasons best known to himself, refused to settle the criminal case brought against him. Ebbers was convicted and sentenced to twenty-five years in federal prison. Years later, a broken and nearly blind man, he was granted compassionate leave so he could die at home. He passed away a few months later, in February 2020.

As for Cooper, *Time* magazine named her as one of three "Persons of the Year" for 2002, and she went on to write *Extraordinary Circumstances*, the profits from which she donated to the cause of ethics education. Many WorldCom employees as well as some residents of Clinton, Mississippi, initially blamed her for WorldCom's demise. But that was shooting the messenger. WorldCom was a bankrupt business long before Cooper figured out that "prepaid capacity" was a phantom asset.

She now runs her own private consulting firm. I'll let her have the final word about what her WorldCom experience can teach us. "Above being loyal to your superiors," she wrote, always "be loyal to your principles." And the best way to prepare for the unwelcome day when your principles will be tested: "Practice ethical decision making every day."

A MOMENT FOR PERSONAL REFLECTION

Recall a time when someone held *you* accountable for doing less than your best. It might have been a parent prodding you to take your schoolwork seriously or a coach or teacher who caught you trying to take a shortcut and reminded you that real winners play by the rules. What impact did that have on your life? Were you resentful at first but grateful in the end?

Those memories are worth keeping in mind when you find yourself called to hold someone else accountable for their actions. In the WorldCom saga, Controller David Myers expressed enormous relief after

Cynthia Cooper forced him to reveal the fraud he and other WorldCom leaders had been perpetrating. He had been so stressed by the conspiracy that he had considered committing suicide. Her commitment to integrity actually freed him to return to being the person he wanted to be. He served time in jail for his actions, but he expressed the highest respect for Cooper's professionalism.

My point: it can be hard to hold people accountable for their actions, but it is sometimes your duty as a person of conscience. The West Point honor code does not just forbid lying, cheating, and stealing. It is also wrong to "tolerate those who do." When otherwise good people who have behaved badly are held accountable, it can be a wake-up call. It reminds them that fairness and honesty are the "better way." As for the truly evil bosses? Punishment helps protect us from them.

NEXT UP:
CHOOSING TO BE A LEADER FOR YOUR VALUES

The subtitle to this book offers the promise that by leading with values you can not only sleep well at night but also advance your career. The final rule in the Conscience Code, "Rule #10: Choose to Lead," thus points to the path that will take you to this goal: committed, integrity-based leadership. Cynthia Cooper's story inspires me because it so clearly illustrates how leadership on behalf of professional values can elevate ordinary people to distinguished careers in their chosen professions. You may not end up on the cover of *Time* magazine, but when you commit to working not only for a boss, but also for your values, you are demonstrating a positive quality that others will admire. Value-based leaders say, in effect, "I care enough about the people I work with and the mission we serve to hold myself and others to common standards of decency." Good things follow for people willing to make this commitment.

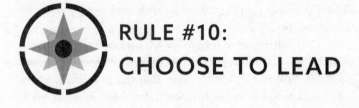

RULE #10:
CHOOSE TO LEAD

"Fight for the things that you care about,
but do it in a way that will lead others to join you."
—Ruth Bader Ginsburg

One of my favorite quotes from the research I did for this book is Durant's well-known summary of Aristotle's virtue ethics: "You are what you repeatedly do. Excellence, then, is not an act but a habit." As a person of conscience, you will bring your moral courage to work every day. Others will look to you as a role model for ethical action. You will remind them, when they are most tempted to forget, that everything worth doing is worth doing with integrity.

But you can also choose to be something more: a *value-based leader*. This requires you to seek out greater responsibilities and expand the scope of your influence. People of conscience strive to do the right thing, but the quote from Supreme Court Justice Ruth Bader Ginsburg encourages us to "lead others to join you." By choosing to lead with your values, you help create the right kinds of organizations and, ultimately, the right kind of society. Rule #10, Choose to Lead, thus invites you to take a longer-term perspective on the values-to-action process—a leadership perspective.

Our final chapter proceeds as follows. First, I'll share the story of how a young manager's decision to speak up for her values put her on the path to becoming one of her institution's top leaders. This will give us a final chance to review the dynamics of ethical conflict and see how each rule in the Conscience Code contributes to your ultimate success. Next, I'll extend the time frame within which to view value-based decision making from the "single event" to the longer arc of your career. Three well-documented leadership capabilities emerge when you acquire the habit of standing up for your values: character, initiative, and conflict management skills. We will reexamine stories from earlier in the book showing how people demonstrating these three capabilities seized their leadership moments to help create positive work environments for everyone around them.

I'll conclude the chapter (and the book) with a reminder of how value-based leadership contributes to a more fulfilling life. When you commit to infusing your daily work with the values that give your life meaning, you are moving beyond work-life balance toward work-life *integration*. You are on the way to transforming your professional career from a job into something more: a true calling.

LEAD WITH YOUR VALUES AND ADVANCE YOUR CAREER

A few years ago, I was teaching a negotiation workshop in Chicago for health-care professionals and had the pleasure of meeting several Chief Nursing Officers. CNOs are frontline nurses who have risen through the ranks to become the senior-most executives at their hospitals responsible for patient care. Over dinner between the two days of the program, I sat next to one of these CNOs, "Beth." She was on the top leadership team at a large Midwestern hospital and had raised some great questions in our class about the hardball tactics sometimes used in labor-management bargaining. She obviously knew her job. I was researching this book at the time, so I asked her how often ethical conflicts came up for her and her nursing colleagues.

Her response was immediate. "These issues come up almost every day," she said. "Patient privacy, end-of-life issues, pressures from doctors and other nurses to cover up mistakes, pushing back against sexism. I could go on and on. Dealing effectively with ethical challenges is an essential part of the job."

Then she volunteered a personal story about how an ethical conflict had impacted her career. It had happened soon after she received her first promotion—from nurse to nurse manager—at her hospital, "Midwest Memorial." I will try to capture the vividness I heard when she told me her story by retelling it below in her own voice. But I have, as always, disguised the context to protect everyone's privacy. The "20-20 plan" referred to below was not its real name.

Beth's Story

The problem arose when Midwest hired a new CEO. He came from a consulting background and was steeped in the analytics of facilities utilization and insurance reimbursement. He told us on Day 1 that his focus would be on a major reorganization. At first, everyone was excited about having a new, energetic leader to help take us to the next level. Midwest was one of the best hospitals in the state, and many of us wanted it to be *the* best. Sadly, we eventually figured out that he was a climber. He wanted to run a major health-care system, and he viewed his job at Midwest as a springboard to that position.

In his first few months, the CEO convened a number of employee stakeholder committees to study how hospital operations could be improved. Everyone participated enthusiastically, welcoming the chance to be heard. But then reality set in. It soon became apparent that ideas for saving money and squeezing more work out of fewer people were advancing to the next stages of discussion. Ideas for improving patient care and investing in staff development took a back seat.

Six months in, he released his final reorganization plan, and we all saw what his real agenda was. Basically, he was trying to put the entire hospital staff at the service of an untested information technology software platform his consulting firm had designed. The underlying concept was what he called the "20-20 principle." We could reduce overhead by 20 percent at the same time we increased revenues by 20 percent, making the hospital the most efficient health-care provider in a five-state region. Rumors started to fly about layoffs, morale began to sink, and people were getting their resumes ready. More than anything else, everyone—me included—was confused. Midwest's reputation depended on the quality of its care. Patient satisfaction was what had gotten us there. There was no mention of patient satisfaction in this plan.

I was caught in the middle as a new manager. I wanted to be a team player, so I tried to calm everyone down. Meanwhile, staff resistance among the rank and file started to emerge. Three of the most vocal critics on the nursing staff worked for me. They were among my best nurses, and I actually took them aside and counseled them to tone it down—but to no avail. They joined with people from other departments and started lobbying to stop the plan. They printed up flyers saying something like "20-20 Can't See Straight" and put them on all the cars in the parking lot.

At about the same time, anticipating board approval for his plan, the CEO asked each staff manager to "nominate" people for severance packages (i.e., layoffs). I had to send in a list of four names and, after a lot of soul-searching, I identified the three people whom I considered to be my group's weakest links and prayed that three would be enough. A few days later, I got my list back. Only one of the four names on the new list was a person I had nominated. The other three were the high-performing nurses who were leading the protest against the 20-20 plan. I was furious, but I had no idea what to do.

After a few sleepless nights and a heart-to-heart talk with my husband about my future at Midwest Memorial, I decided I had to speak up. I contacted the nurse supervisor for my area to ask his advice. He said there was nothing he could do. It was the CEO's call. He thought the 20-20 train had left the station and advised me to "keep my head down." The next day, I took a deep breath and went over his head. I asked for a one-on-one meeting with the Chief Nursing Officer.

I prepared my case, bringing the performance evaluations for the entire team. I told her I was ready to resign if these terminations went through. I was pretty passionate about it. She heard me, and a few days later invited me to a meeting with a member of the hospital board she knew and trusted. I explained what was happening, and he was genuinely surprised to hear about it. Apparently, the CEO had done a really good job of managing up, and the board had been told that the staff was enthusiastically behind the plan. The Chief Nursing Officer was great—she backed me up 100 percent.

The CNO's board contact took the issue to the board's executive committee. Long story short: the board conducted a confidential investigation of all the layoff lists. It turned out that the CEO had targeted virtually every employee who had spoken up against his plan—about thirty-five in all.

A month later, the CEO left to return to his consulting firm. The 20-20 plan was scrapped and the COO, whom we all trusted, was promoted. After everyone calmed down, he led a successful initiative that improved operations but also addressed patient care and safety issues.

About a year later, the chief nursing officer recommended me for promotion to nurse supervisor when my old supervisor moved to another state.

Beth wrapped up her story by saying that the chief nursing officer had publicly credited her for her courage in speaking up. That, in turn, had established her within the hospital as someone who would step forward in a crisis. It was no coincidence, I found myself thinking, that Beth now occupied the same office once held by the woman she had persuaded, years before, to champion her cause.

Values as the Pathway to Leadership

Beth's story could easily have worked out differently. The CNO she appealed to may have been less courageous or well connected. The board may have felt that the CEO it had just installed deserved its loyal support rather than an investigation. Beth would have quit, the unjust layoffs would have taken place, and what had once been a top-performing hospital would have become a distinctly unpleasant place to work.

I therefore offer Beth's story not as a guarantee that choosing her path will always win the day but rather because it illustrates the wisdom of an old saying in sports: you can't score if you don't shoot. Being a leader for your values always involves taking some risk. But if you want to make a difference, that's a price you must be willing to pay.

That said, is there an upside? I think so. Beth's commitment to her values and her administrative abilities landed her in the top nursing job in her hospital. But even if her appeal had failed and she had decided to quit, I think her choices would still have benefited her career in the long run.

First, she would have proven to herself that, faced with a moral crisis, she had the guts to stand on the right side of the conflict. That would have firmly established her confidence in her own moral courage and redoubled her commitment to nursing as a professional calling, not just a nine-to-five job.

Second, as unpleasant as career turbulence can be, the doors that close usually reveal others that you had not seen before. Beth was a talented nurse who would have found another place to practice her profession.

Beth's story also provides an opportunity to review each rule of the Conscience Code.

As the crisis at Beth's hospital unfolded, she:

- *Faced the Conflict.* Beth was not looking for a fight, but after a few sleepless nights she knew she had to engage with a decision maker about the layoff issue.
- *Committed to Her Values.* When Beth saw that the CEO was using the layoff process to punish his enemies—and that doing so would compromise patient care—she knew her core professional values were at stake. The most obvious sign of this commitment was her willingness to resign if her appeal failed.
- *Knew Her Enemy.* Beth was confronting pressure from the highest authority in her organization. Although she could count on many of her peers for support, they were looking for her to lead. This brought out her best.
- *Summoned Her Character.* Beth did not let fear paralyze her into inaction. Instead, she channeled her outrage into an effective strategy.
- *Channeled Her Personality Strengths.* Beth was assertive, but her story suggested she was more of a "Problem-Solver" than an "Advocate." She was persistent, able to create alliances, and willing to hand her problem off to people with higher authority.
- *Leveraged the Power of Two.* This was crucial. Beth knew she could not do this alone. When her supervisor told her to "keep her head down," she went to the CNO, who became her trusted partner.
- *Asked Four Questions.* This situation did not require complex moral reasoning. All four factors pointed Beth toward the action she took: the consequences of the 20-20 plan, her loyalty to her staff, her identity as a person of conscience, and basic principles of workplace justice.
- *Engaged the Decision Maker.* Persuasive dialogue was clearly something Beth did well. Her attempt to engage her supervisor failed, but the CNO was receptive. Beth's well-prepared case carried the day first with the CNO and later with the board member.
- *Held Them Accountable.* The CNO deserves credit for devising the final action plan that resolved the crisis. She had the relationships, credibility, and authority to elevate the issue to the board. But Beth gave her the motivational energy she needed to carry the dispute forward.

To sum up: hearing Beth tell her story renewed my confidence in the idea that those who do good can also do well. The crisis at Midwest inspired her to lead with her values, and, in doing so, advance her career.

VALUE CONFLICTS:
CRUCIBLE MOMENTS FOR EFFECTIVE LEADERS

Beth's story helps us look back over the ground we have covered in the book. But it also provides a bridge forward—to the more general subject of effective, ethical leadership. It is no accident that Beth was promoted to a top job. Her willingness to step up and defend her employees from unjust dismissal displayed three widely acknowledged leadership aptitudes: character, initiative, and conflict management skills.

Below, we'll look at the importance the leadership literature places on these three abilities and review examples from earlier chapters that connect value-based leadership with career success.

Character: The Courage to Do the Right Thing

Character is the foundation for a successful life. No surprise, then, that it features prominently in both the Conscience Code and modern leadership theories. John Maxwell's bestseller, *Developing the Leader within You*, identifies character as "the foundation of leadership." Stephen Covey's *Principle-Centered Leadership* lists character as one of the two "preconditions" for effective leadership practices (the other being skill at getting things done). And James Kouzes and Barry Posner state in their book *The Leadership Challenge* that one of the first and most important activities of the effective leader is to "set the example" for those who follow. The courage you exhibit in an ethical conflict demonstrates your character in an especially credible way: it shows you are willing to put yourself at risk for the greater good.

The most notable story of personal courage in the book was that of high school security guard and football coach Keanon Lowe (Rule #4, "Summon Your Character"). Lowe achieved national attention for his actions in disarming a stressed, rifle-wielding student at Parkrose High School in Portland, Oregon. His grateful community later awarded him its Civilian Medal of Heroism and declared May 29, 2019, the "Coach Keanon Lowe Day of Recognition." But Lowe displayed not only courage but also compassion for the student, who was trying to commit suicide when Lowe disarmed him. When these two virtues combine in a single, high-risk test of character, you know you are dealing with a true value-based leader. A year after this incident, Lowe's skill as a football coach and commitment to young people earned him a promotion to become the head football coach at a high school twice the size of Parkrose.

The whistleblower examples given earlier in the book, from Justin Hopson's work reforming the New Jersey State Police (Rule #2, "Commit to Your Values") to WorldCom's Cynthia Cooper (Rule #9, "Hold Them Accountable"), also illustrate character-based leadership in action. A traffic accident ended Hopson's work as a state trooper, but his record as a dogged, ethical professional set the stage for him to transition to a successful career as a private investigator, including a leadership position on the state Ethics Committee for his new profession. Dinesh Thakur's courageous work exposing the fraud at generic drug maker Ranbaxy (Rule #9, Hold Them Accountable") yielded an award of nearly $50 million as his whistleblower "bounty" from the fine Ranbaxy paid for its crimes. But he did not take this money and retire to a life of luxury. Instead, he has become a leader in public health policy and a crusader against fraud in the pharmaceutical industry.

Finally, Tyler Shultz and Erika Cheung, the two young heroes of the story about the Theranos blood-testing scandal (Rule #6, "Leverage the Power of Two"), have each gone on to careers as values-based leaders who run their own entrepreneurial organizations and speak widely on how to promote ethical cultures in business.

Initiative: Leading from Where You Are

The quote attributed to tennis legend (and social activist) Arthur Ashe that led the Introduction to the book captures the second leadership quality required of those who follow the Conscience Code: initiative. As Ashe put it, to make a difference in your life, don't wait for someone to give you permission: "Start where you are, use what you have, do what you can."

One of my students ("Pam") was being interviewed at the end of her summer internship at one of the most prestigious tech firms in the world.

She had performed well over the summer, and her boss had presented her with an offer to return as a manager on the logistics team.

"What do you expect your duties to be when you come back to us next spring?" her summer boss asked her.

"Given that I will be a manager, I expect to be responsible for allocating the resources you give me so the team can achieve the results you want," she replied.

"That's half the job," came her boss's response.

"What's the rest?" she asked.

"Managing me. We have hired you because you showed us that you can take the initiative. Your title may be manager, but you'll be evaluated on how well you perform as a leader. As I see it, I will work for you as much as the other way around."

The ethical conflicts we have encountered in this book have taken place at every organizational level—from the C-suite to those in summer internships. And all involve employees taking the initiative. When you step up to address a dispute over values, you are performing a notable leadership service to your organization. As the story about Beth and her hospital illustrates, you are bringing important information about reputational and perhaps even legal risk to people higher in the chain of command who can do something about it. When you do this skillfully (i.e., when you follow a strategic values-to-action process rather than simply launch a self-righteous campaign), you are displaying leadership abilities that will be visible to important audiences. These experiences also build self-confidence, a key leadership trait.

Over the course of the book, we have met a range of people who developed their leadership skills by showing initiative. Below are a few reminders about them.

Speaking Up for Professional Values. Many of the stories my students have reported in class involve an insistence on high professional standards when a boss or peer tried to compromise honesty or accuracy in client relationships. Not surprisingly, successful organizations reward employees who protect the integrity of professional work.

A simple illustration: Hiroshi's story in the last chapter about his project leader, who wanted to send out a client report riddled with misleading factual and analytic errors. Hiroshi went over his manager's head and got the expert support he needed to protect both the integrity of the report and his firm's reputation. As a result, his superiors (and eventually even his manager) applauded his leadership on behalf of the firm's values.

Our discussion of Rule #8 ("Engage the Decision Maker") highlighted a similar example involving my student Isabella and her battle with her boss Ricardo over a flawed recommendation to accelerate the construction schedule of a hydroelectric project. Ricardo recommended an illusory, short-term solution that would protect his bonus but that Isabella knew would not be in the client's best interests. Despite being warned to remain silent about her views, Isabella took the initiative, putting forward an honest, investment-based solution to the supervising partners. Result: Ricardo was taken off the assignment and Isabella was promoted to lead the project.

Speaking Up for Moral Values. When violations of professional standards rise to the level of moral failures, the people who speak against them sometimes risk their job security. But, as I have argued throughout the book, jobs and careers are two different things. The US Bureau of Labor Statistics reports that professionals change jobs, on average, roughly twelve times over the course of their working life. Given that reality, there is a lot to be said for measuring success in your career in terms of professional integrity rather than longevity with a single employer.

First, the good news. Taking the initiative to speak up about what you perceive to be a moral failure can, in fact, advance your standing within your organization. You may be educating your boss and others about ethical perspectives they had not properly appreciated. Recall the story about my student Marta in the last chapter. She protested when she was ordered to fire, without notice or severance, all the "Health Advocates" she had hired to help with her health-care initiative in rural Africa. By elevating this issue to her new CEO, she educated him on the importance of these community leaders to the future success of her organization.

Then there is the story of the German nurse Renate from Rule #5, "Channel Your Personality Strengths." By taking initiative, she ended a string of murders committed by her colleague, a serial-killer nurse named Niels Högel. The staff at his prior hospital had turned a blind eye to the irregularities of the "care" he delivered, preferring to cover up rather than confront the risk he posed. Renate found evidence proving Högel had given a patient a lethal overdose of unnecessary heart medication. Her initiative forced her bosses to confront and take action against this murderer. Although the record does not disclose the effects of all this on Renate's career, we do know that her actions spurred a systemic review of hospital accountability practices in Germany. When your initiative helps reset national standards for protecting patient safety, I call that career-enhancing, value-based leadership.

Marta's and Renate's cases are encouraging, but when the moral dispute targets organizational corruption, your career risk rises. Most large-scale whistleblowing cases end up with the person of conscience taking action from *outside* the organization after leaving (or being fired). Corporate wrongdoers will often do whatever it takes to cover up their crimes.

Only you can decide whether taking initiative to address a moral wrong is worth the career risk that goes with blowing the whistle. Two things are certain. First, when organizational lapses put public health or safety at risk, the urgency of speaking up skyrockets. Second, the decision to leave a corrupt organization for a job that pays less can be the best thing that ever happens to your career. The odds are excellent that you will find honorable work elsewhere—work you can feel good about with colleagues you respect. As a famous verse from the Bible puts it (in my own loose translation), "What shall it profit a person if they gain the whole world but lose their soul?"

Conflict Capability as a Leadership Skill

The third valuable capability practiced by people following the Conscience Code is their willingness to face conflict rather than run away from it. Corporate practice and the leadership literature both teach us that this is an important skill for effective leaders.

On the corporate side, many successful firms have built their cultures around skillfully channeling conflict. For example, Andrew Grove at Intel promoted "constructive confrontation" as a management mantra; at Google, leaders are encouraged to use "radical candor" in their interpersonal communications; and Ray Dalio's management philosophy at the hedge fund Bridgewater celebrates "radical transparency." Such workplaces are not for everyone, but they are an indication that conflict is an essential aspect of organizational life that good leaders must know how to manage.

The leadership literature also celebrates conflict capability as an essential skill for firms facing challenges in rapidly changing markets and social environments. Take, for example, Ronald Heifetz's "Adaptive Leadership" theory, laid out in his classic book, *Leadership without Easy Answers*. Heifetz places the ability to handle conflict at the very center of the leader's job.

As Heifetz sees it, leaders must master two types of problems: "technical" ones and "adaptive" ones. Technical problems require the traditional skills associated with authority-based leadership: substantive expertise, goal-setting, execution skills, and accountability.

Adaptive problems involve reconciling the conflicting values that arise within the organization (or between the organization and society) during times of social and technical upheaval. Examples of adaptive problems include responding to new demands for sexual harassment account-ability in the wake of the #MeToo movement; deciding, in the face of the COVID-19 pandemic, when and how to have workers return to their offices; and finding the right balance between short-term economics and the environmental challenges posed by climate change. Each of these problems is messy, involves the need to consult with multiple stakeholders, and may stir sharp debate among people with strongly held beliefs.

Heifetz recommends that organizations seek out leaders who have the ability to recognize values that may be hidden within operational disputes, the courage to push back against denial and avoidance mechanisms, and the willingness to protect whistleblowers and other dissenters so all points of view can be heard. Many of the case examples we have reviewed —from Beth, Tyler Shultz, Erika Cheung, and Isabella to Marta and Cynthia Cooper—illustrate how these skills are honed in ethical conflicts.

LEADING A VALUE-BASED TEAM

This book has focused primarily on how to speak up for your values when someone is pressuring you to compromise them. But as we conclude our journey, I'd like you to consider what happens when your leadership is recognized, your career advances, and you now supervise others. When you become the boss yourself, how can you effectively lead people to adopt your value-based approach to their professional work?

The Goal: A Positive Workplace

A leading business ethics scholar, New York University's Jonathan Haidt, once wrote that he had never observed a single instance of an ethics class improving the moral conduct of a business executive. He did, however, hold out the hope that business practices could be improved by leaders who harnessed the power of situational forces to channel behavior toward honorable conduct and "away from slippery ethical slopes."

Thus, one way to think about the leader's job is to consider the leader as a "values architect"—someone who designs social environments that make ethical behavior the norm. We know that the very same situational factors that push people to behave badly, which we explored in detail when we talked about Rule #3 ("Know Your Enemies"), can be put in the service of generating the positive behaviors you want to encourage. It is the leader's job to do this work.

There is a great deal of literature on how to create positive workplaces, much of which focuses on effective mentoring, coaching, and culture change. Some worthy titles include Aubrey Daniels's *Bringing Out the Best in People*, Edgar Schein's *Humble Inquiry: The Gentle Art of Asking Instead of Telling*, and Amy Edmondson's *The Fearless Organization*. Using the PAIRS framework I have presented in the Conscience Code, I offer some suggestions below on how you can harness situational forces "for good" as a value-based leader.

Peer Pressure. The ancient Stoic philosopher Epictetus once said, "Keep company only with those who uplift you, whose presence calls forth your best." It is hard to overstate the importance of personnel decisions in the creation of a positive workplace. Select team members not only for competence but also with an eye to their moral motivations and commitments. With a critical mass of the right people, peer pressure can bring the weight of social conformity down on the side of ethical behavior.

Authority. You are the boss now, so you must use your authority to set clear standards and insist on ethical accountability. To maintain your credibility, you must model the ethical behavior you talk about (more on this below) and celebrate the initiative of team members who take value-based stands, even when you disagree with them.

Incentives. Most organizational incentives are designed to drive economic outcomes. To these you must add value-based incentives that reward not just outcomes but also *the way things get done*. This means incentivizing behaviors that enhance qualitative measures such as employee engagement, worker safety and well-being, community involvement, diversity, and professionalism. Instead of just presenting a trophy to the top salesperson, consider creating an Employee of the Month award for community service or recognizing effective value-based mentoring with testimonials. Seek incentives that will point people outward to actions that build trust and community, not just inward toward individual interests.

Role Expectations. Heifetz's adaptive leadership approach is especially informative here. Build ownership of values into everyone's job description. Then train employees to manage conflict when values collide, push past avoidance mechanisms, and respect those who raise inconvenient issues of principle.

Systemwide Cultural Forces. The larger cultural forces at work in your organization can be the hardest ones to influence. At the very least, your job as a team leader is to protect the morale of your group from corrupting influences active in other parts of the organization. But to the extent that your leadership creates a value-based center of excellence and your team experiences the benefits of a positive workplace, others in the organization may notice. Your team can become a model for other units to follow, spearheading something rare: a positive cultural transformation.

The Path to Value-Based Leadership

The task of turning these situational forces in the right direction begins with the three leadership attributes I highlighted earlier: character, initiative, and conflict capability. To these I'll add two additional qualities my students have repeatedly highlighted in the behavior of the people they have worked for whom they most admire. The first emphasizes your role as a values mentor, seizing "teaching moments" to show team members the way core principles inform daily work. The second emphasizes role modeling, demonstrating daily consistency between your words and actions, especially when those actions demonstrate the price you are willing to pay to stay true to your values.

First, let's look at a simple example of the art of value-based mentoring, which will be the last of the stories I share about my students. A student, "Benjamin," had a boss and mentor ("Alex") who supervised him in his analyst job at the small hedge fund. Alex was the director of research at the fund. As a first-generation immigrant from an Eastern European country, Alex had earned his professional position the hard way: through work that always went above and beyond expectations and an honest, direct way with people.

Benjamin, an ambitious student from a middle-class home, met Alex by chance at a social event while Benjamin was an undergraduate at a little-known college in South Carolina. But it did not take Alex long to recognize the spark that eventually won Benjamin a place in the dual-degree program where I met him (earning diplomas from both the Wharton School and the University of Pennsylvania's Carey School of Law).

Alex hired Benjamin first as a summer intern and then persuaded the managing director of the fund, Max, to hire him as a full-time employee. Benjamin felt enormous loyalty to Alex for giving him a chance in the finance world, but what impressed him most was Alex's steadfast focus on values. For example, when Benjamin was a summer intern, Alex had emphasized that the best way Benjamin could repay him for the career break he had received was to pay it forward—not pay it back. Benjamin, Alex suggested, did not owe him anything on a personal level, but he did owe a kindness to some talented person he might meet someday who, like Benjamin, needed a break.

Later, as a full-time employee, Alex taught Benjamin one of those vivid workplace lessons about truth telling that can save a career—and that make trust possible on a small, high-performing team. Benjamin had been sitting at his desk when the firm's managing partner, Max, stopped on his way down the aisle. "So how was the Haverford earnings call, Benjamin?" Benjamin had forgotten to listen in on the call but, as he put it, "I panicked and said the first thing that came into my head."

"It was mixed, Max. Can I drop by your office to discuss in an hour? I just need to finish up my work on this model first." That was enough time for Benjamin to review the recording of the call and make his report.

Max nodded and kept going. Less than a minute later, Alex (whose desk was near Benjamin's) was standing next to him. He motioned for Benjamin to join him in a nearby conference room.

"I know that you didn't listen to that earnings call," Alex said. "But I also know that you are very conscientious and that you did not have time to think before you answered Max's question. But listen to me—don't you ever, ever lie like that again. If Max finds out you have lied once, you will never have credibility with him." Alex then said he would keep the moment "between us" because "I know it is the last time it will happen."

Benjamin summed up the lesson (only one of the many that Alex taught him about teamwork): "That was not the last time I wanted to lie at work, but it was the last time I did."

Beyond this example, we need look no further than the way Cynthia Cooper (Rule #9, "Hold Them Accountable") led her internal auditing team through months of high-pressure work uncovering the WorldCom fraud. Nobody on her team worked harder, took more flak from the WorldCom bosses, or stayed the course more courageously when the pressures were on than Cooper. Yet her book, *Extraordinary Circumstances*, launches its introduction with a reference to the group she led: "My team and I were ordinary citizens," she wrote, "who found ourselves facing extraordinary circumstances."

The epilogue of Cooper's book is a value-based leader's manifesto on how to be a good role model and mentor. I have paraphrased her ten rules below.

1. Always make values the top priority, and know which among those values comes first.
2. Treat the team as you yourself want to be treated.
3. Don't forget, you make bad decisions, too.
4. Assume everyone will know about your actions. Will you be proud of them?
5. Be consistent. Commit to ethical decision making on every issue, large and small.
6. "Courage is acting in the face of fear." Practice it every day.
7. Consult the team on all the tough decisions. Don't go it alone.
8. Live a "unified life." Apply the same personal code of conduct at home and at work.
9. Trust your moral intuitions. If it doesn't feel right, it probably isn't.
10. When your principles and your superiors disagree, follow your principles.

A MOMENT FOR PERSONAL REFLECTION: WHAT IS YOUR VALUE-BASED LEADERSHIP STORY?

An important part of being an effective leader is establishing confidence in your leadership abilities. And one proven way to summon your confidence is to have identifiable moments from your past when you confronted a challenge, made the right call, and lived to tell about it. The leadership literature refers to such formative events as "crucible moments." Leadership scholar Warren Bennis and a colleague once interviewed forty top leaders from across the leadership spectrum seeking common factors that had led to their success. As they later reported in the *Harvard Business Review*, "All of them—young and old—were able to point to intense, often traumatic, always unplanned experiences that had transformed them and had become the sources of their distinctive leadership abilities." Coming through these experiences, they wrote, had left these leaders "stronger and surer of themselves and their purpose."

Value-based leadership is no different.

As your final commitment to the Conscience Code, therefore, I ask you to look back on your life and identify a story that will help you renew your confidence in your value-based leadership abilities and, when appropriate, communicate your core values to your team.

As an example of such a narrative, recall a story from Rule #2 ("Commit to Your Values") about Dr. Jeff Thompson, the CEO of the Gundersen Health System in Wisconsin. Thompson himself is a values-based leader and used this story to tell others where his commitment to values was born. As he told it, he had been a young intern only a few months out of medical school when he found himself facing a crisis in an operating room. He was working under a senior attending physician who was having difficulty inserting a breathing tube into the trachea of a nine-month-old baby. After three failed attempts, the senior physician took a break and told the team he would return in half an hour.

With the senior physician on his break, the baby's skin began turning blue from lack of oxygen. The nurses begged Thompson to break hospital protocol and take over for the absent doctor. Thompson was young, but the nurses knew he had the experience needed for this insertion procedure.

He faced a make-or-break career choice: violate the hospital's rules and save the baby or play it safe and let the attending physician take the blame if the baby died. As we saw earlier, Thompson later wrote that, "I didn't have time to ponder the long-term ramifications of doing one thing over another. The baby was dying, and I had to make a choice immediately." He chose to insert the tube, and the baby lived. The medical staff backed Thompson, and this story served him for the rest of his career as the crucible moment when he learned to "lead with values."

Consider the search for your own stories as an investment in your leadership effectiveness. Ask close friends and family members for their memories of times when you went "above and beyond" to do things right or do the right thing. Capture these memories. They will help you summon the motivations that got you through those challenging situations. Learn to tell the stories behind these experiences. They will make you a better, more compelling leader for your values.

CHOOSING TO LEAD:
A LIFETIME COMMITMENT

Near the end of the Responsibility course, I tell my students the fable of the Two Wolves. If you have not heard it before, it goes like this.

The Fable of the Two Wolves

One evening, an elder of the Cherokee tribe was sitting with his grandson at the campfire and spoke of a battle that goes on within us—a battle for our hearts and souls.

"Grandson, there are two wolves inside us who constantly fight for dominance.

"The first wolf is a bad one who is angry, unkind, jealous, greedy, spiteful, and arrogant. This wolf lies, glorifies only his own deeds, and thinks only of himself.

"The other one is good. This wolf is happy, generous, loving, full of hope, kind, and merciful. It tells the truth, praises, helps others, and knows the power of trust and courage to overcome fear."

The grandson thought about this for a few minutes, then asked his grandfather a question.

"Grandfather, which wolf wins?"

"The one you feed," the elder replied.

Value-based actions feed the good wolf. Value-based leadership goes further, clearing the path for others to stand up for principles they care deeply about and opening up space for them to act on their beliefs and values.

My view: Choosing to lead with your values also strengthens your hand against the bad wolf, which is never far away. As the bad wolf arouses your fears and tempts you with facile rationalizations that "everyone does it" and "nobody will notice," you can answer that you are not alone. Your team is relying on your strength of character to help keep them focused, to carry them through.

The payoff for choosing to lead with your values is, I believe, profound. I therefore want to conclude the book with a passage I have reworded from a famous essay by John Gardner called "The Road to Self-Renewal." Gardner was a Marine, cabinet secretary, foundation president, and founder of a political advocacy group for good government called Common Cause, where I worked briefly in my twenties. His original essay appeared in the *Stanford Alumni Magazine* in the March 1994 issue and concerned career self-renewal—reinvigorating your motivation to do useful work as your life progresses. It is well worth reading. I have revised the end of this essay to apply to value-based leadership. I hope you find them appropriate as the final words of the Conscience Code:

> Value-based leadership is not something you casually adopt. It is something you must build into your life. You build it out of your past experiences, talents, loyalties, and understanding. You build it from the things you believe in and, most importantly, out of the values for which you are willing to sacrifice something. You are the only one who can mix these ingredients into the unique pattern that will make this type of leadership a living aspect of your work. When you do, your profession, whatever it may be, will acquire the dignity and meaning of a true vocation.

ACKNOWLEDGMENTS

This book was a family affair from beginning to end.

First, as always, my wife, Robbie, was the prime mover, encouraging me to get this project off the ground, providing a sounding board for ideas, and reading each and every word multiple times for coherence and narrative flow. When the COVID-19 pandemic turned everything at the University of Pennsylvania upside down, she and my son Ned pressed me to stay on task, nudging me to keep writing and make my deadlines. After too many mealtimes spent coming up with (and then rejecting) titles, Robbie was the first to advance the words "Conscience" and "Code"—a title immediately endorsed by Ned. My older son, Ben, his life interrupted by COVID-19 lockdowns, volunteered to read the entire manuscript with fresh eyes. His insightful comments prompted me to change the book's overall organization, and he challenged me to rethink ideas and examples in almost every chapter.

Beyond the family, two people loom large for their support of this project. First, my research assistant, Marie Barnett, dug into the details of the social conformity and deference-to-authority experiments I write about, found great, real-world stories, and provided valuable editing advice. As a PhD student in philosophy with deep expertise in psychology, she helped me stay true to the normative theory, social science, and case studies I used throughout the book.

Second, and no less important, was the help of a former Wharton undergraduate student (now at Bain Consulting), Jin Qi. Jin is one of the smartest, most well-read students I have ever taught at any level of instruction. He read the first drafts of each chapter as I completed them, providing candid "reader responses" that helped me understand what was getting through and what was getting lost in my attempts to bring to life a subject—"doing the right thing"—that proved exceptionally difficult to capture. When Jin said he liked something, it stayed in the book.

Without the honesty and candor of the MBA students in my Responsibility in Business class, this book would never have come into existence. They challenged and inspired me for nearly a decade to develop tools that could help them better respond to the values challenges they face in the workplace. Their stories were the source code for this book. Former students Kristy Wiehe and Yahuda Katz were especially helpful in providing assistance at the conception stage of the project.

Special thanks go to many faculty colleagues, who took the time to brainstorm with me about what a book like this might look like. Within Wharton, Phil Nichols, Tom Donaldson, Mike Useem, Peter Cappelli, Adam Grant, and Nina Strohminger all helped me explore the ethics and management literatures and, in Phil's case, provided expert content on the specific topic of bribery. Nina directed me to the eye-opening "Ashley Madison" study I describe in Rule #4 ("Summon Your Character"), showing that people who break marital vows are more likely to become targets of government investigations for workplace wrongdoing. Adam Grant, Mike Useem, and former Vice Dean for Wharton Executive Education Bob Mittelstaedt provided important, extra assists with the marketing side of the project. Outside Wharton, I benefited especially from conversations with business ethics scholar (and Rutgers Business School professor) Danielle Warren, who pointed me to scholarship on how ethical/ unethical behavior impacts personal identity.

This is my fifth book with the best literary agent in the business, Michael Snell. As always, he and his partner, Pat, were my collaborators every step of the way. My email folder for this project is replete with Mike's advice, ideas, draft proposals, and title concepts. His rock-solid connections in the publishing industry—based on a lifetime of hard-won personal credibility—have paved the way for every one of my books, and *The Conscience Code* is no exception.

Finally, I am grateful to Tim Burgard, my editor at HarperCollins Leadership, for supporting this project and skillfully guiding it from proposal to publication through a global pandemic. To all of the above, plus Cynthia Cooper—the courageous "person of conscience" who led the team that uncovered the fraud at WorldCom, Inc., and went on to publish *Extraordinary Circumstances*, one of the best business ethics stories ever told—my heartfelt thanks.

—G. Richard Shell

NOTES

Introduction: The Conscience Code

vii   **". . . do what you can":** https://en.wikiquote.org/wiki/Talk:Arthur_Ashe. This quote is also sometimes attributed to Theodore Roosevelt. The Roosevelt quote goes, "Do what you can, with what you have, where you are."

ix   **25 percent of employees report pressure:** Zorana Ivcevic, Jochen I. Menges, and Anna Miller, "How Common Is Unethical Behavior in U.S. Organizations?" *Harvard Business Review* (March 20, 2020) (reporting on survey of some 14,500 employees conducted by the Yale Center for Emotional Intelligence), https://hbr .org/2020/03/how-common-is-unethical-behavior-in-u-s-organizations.

ix   **over 40 percent of US workers:** Ethics Resource Center, *National Business Ethics Survey of the U.S. Workforce* (2013), p. 12 (the 41 percent figure quoted in the text was low compared to the 55 percent reported in 2007). Other surveys conducted on a global sample reveal higher levels of unreported wrongdoing. See Ethics and Compliance Initiative at Bentley University, "Global Business Ethics Survey" (2018) (reporting a 47 percent level for 2017), https://d2f5upgbvkx8pz.cloudfront. net/sites/default/files/inline-files/The%20State%20of%20Ethics_0.pdf.

ix   **motivation to do anything about it:** Jaclyn Jeager, "Survey: Weak Leadership Contributes to Employee Pressure to Bend Rules," *Compliance Week* (August 21, 2020), https://www.complianceweek.com/ethics-and-culture/survey-weak -leadership-contributes-to-employee-pressure-to-bend-rules/29346.article.

ix   **"tranquility" that comes from living an honest life:** Adam Smith, *The Theory of Moral Sentiments*, ed. Ryan Patrick Henry (New York: Penguin, 2009), p. 173. For more on the moral philosophy of Adam Smith, see Ryan Patrick Henry, *Our Great Purpose: Adam Smith on Living a Better Life* (Princeton, NJ: Princeton University Press, 2019).

xi   **". . . leave the rest behind":** There is no agreed source for this oft-said bit of wisdom. But martial arts genius Bruce Lee said something very close: "Absorb what is useful. Discard what is not. Add what is uniquely your own." Dumb Little Man, "11 Inspiring Life Lessons from Bruce Lee," *Business Insider* (October 27, 2011), http://assets.businessinsider.com/11-inspiring-life-lessons-from-bruce-lee-2011-12.

Rule #1: Face the Conflict

1   **"... those who look on and do nothing"**: Robert I. Fitzhenry, ed., *The Harper Book of Quotations* (New York: HarperCollins, 1993), p. 356. According to this source, the quote comes from Einstein's tribute to Pablo Casals in 1953.

4   **a set of research-based rules—a Conscience Code:** There is an abundance of research on the utility of rules in reducing the odds that circumstance will swamp your better judgment in the face of fear or temptation. The Ten Commandments is only the most famous example. As philosopher Kwame Anthony Appiah puts it, a rule makes you "disposed to do or feel the right thing" by removing ambiguity in your response to a given cue from your environment. See Kwame Anthony Appiah, *Experiments with Ethics* (Cambridge, MA: Harvard University Press, 2008), pp. 44–56 (where he provides a set of criteria for setting good ethical rules, i.e., that they be clear, simple, within your capability to follow, and worth the harm if the rule misfires).

5   **Serpico ... during a shootout in 1971**: See Peter Maas, *Serpico: The Classic Story of the Cop Who Couldn't Be Bought* (New York: William Morrow, 2005).

5   **"people of conscience"**: Dr. Jeffrey Wigand's suggestion for a new term to describe "whistleblowers" comes in his "Foreword" to Tom Devine and Tarek F. Maassarani, *The Corporate Whistleblower's Survival Guide: A Handbook for Committing the Truth* (San Francisco: Berrett-Koehler, 2011), p. xi.

7   **research-based process that provides the context for the ten rules of the Conscience Code:** Ethics scholars have constructed a number of multi-stage models for the process that takes a person from an initial perception that a value has been violated to the decision to take action. I have borrowed from several to construct the simple, four-stage process I use in the book. For scholarly background on the stage models I draw from, see A.E. Tenbrunsel & K. Smith-Crowe, "Ethical Decision Making: Where We've Been and Where We're Going," *The Academy of Management Annals*, Vol. 2, pp. 545–607 (2008); Eugene Soltes, *Why They Do It: Inside the Mind of the White-Collar Criminal* (New York: PublicAffairs, 2016), p. 89; Max Bazerman & Ann E. Tenbrunsel, *Blind Spots: Why We Fail to Do What's Right and What to Do about It* (Princeton, NJ: Princeton University Press, 2011), p. 29. See also Anna Halmburger, Anna Baumet, and Manfred Schmitt, "Everyday Heroes: Determinants of Moral Courage," in *Handbook of Heroism and Heroic Leadership* (Scott T. Allison, George R. Goethals, and Roderick Kramer, eds) (London: Routledge, 2016), pp. 168–170.

8   **Sherron Watkins ... face-saving rationalization:** Gerald Beenen & Jonathan Pinto, "Resisting Organizational Level Corruption: An Interview with Sherron Watkins," *Academy of Management Learning and Education*, Vol. 8, No. 2 (2008), pp. 5–6. She credits this insight—which she labeled the "fraud triangle"—to a model presented by the Association of Certified Fraud Examiners at an FBI conference.

11 **a lawyer named Matthew Farmer ... hours the firm had spent on their cases:** Nathan Koppel, "Lawyer's Charger Opens Window on Bill-Padding," *Wall Street Journal* (August 30, 2006), https://www.wsj.com/articles/SB1156893257 18248915.

Rule #2: Commit to Your Values

15   **"... 98 percent of the time":** Clay Christensen, James Allworth & Karen
      Dillon. *How Will You Measure Your Life? Finding Fulfillment Using Lessons from
      Some of the World's Greatest Businesses* (New York: HarperBusiness, 2012), p. 191.

15   **Google . . . sexual harassment and misconduct:** See Daisuke Wakabayasi, Erin
      Griffith, Amie Tsang, and Kate Conger, "Google Walkout: Employees Stage Protest
      over Handling of Sexual Harassment" *New York Times* (November 1, 2018), B3. The
      firm's final response to the walkout came nearly two years later, when it announced
      a number of significant changes to its sexual harassment policies and procedures as
      part of a large shareholder lawsuit settlement. See Rob Copeland, "Alphabet Settles
      Harassment Suits," *Wall Street Journal* (September 26, 2020), p. B1.

15   **online retailer Wayfair:** See Kate Taylor, "Wayfair Furniture Employees
      Walked Out Over Sales to Migrant Facilities," *New York Times* (June 25, 2019),
      https://www.nytimes.com/2019/06/25/us/wayfair-walkout.html.

18   **five [CRAFT] values . . . we are treating in this book:** I derived the five-value
      CRAFT framework from research conducted by Rushworth M. Kidder, *Moral
      Courage: Taking Action When Your Values Are Put to the Test* (New York: William
      Morrow, 2005), pp. 37–65 (multiple surveys converging on honesty, respect,
      fairness, responsibility, and compassion as the five key values embraced by
      leaders across many contexts and cultures); Mary C. Gentile, *Giving Voice to
      Values* (New Haven, CT: Yale University Press, 2010), p.10.

19   **Rokeach . . . visualizing such beliefs:** See Milton Rokeach, *Beliefs, Attitudes,
      and Values.* (San Francisco: Jossey-Bass, 1968), pp. 1–10.

20   **Justin Hopson . . . police officer in grade school:** The story in the text is taken
      from Justin Hopson's book. See *Breaking the Blue Wall: One Man's War against
      Police Corruption* (Bloomington, IN: West Bow Press, 2012).

24   **come to the aid of strangers in distress:** J.M. Darley and C.D. Bateson, "From
      Jerusalem to Jericho: A Study of Dispositional and Situational Variables in Helping
      Behavior," *Journal of Personality and Social Psychology*, Vol. 27 (1973), pp. 100–107.

25   **"Inattentional Blindness":** Christopher Chabris and Daniel Simmons, *The
      Invisible Gorilla and Other Ways Our Intuitions Deceive Us* (New York: Broadway
      Books, 2009).

26   **a big deal for the team:** Clay Christensen, James Allworth & Karen Dillon.
      *How Will You Measure Your Life? Finding Fulfillment Using Lessons from Some of
      the World's Greatest Businesses* (New York: HarperBusiness, 2012), pp. 189–91.

26   **Milgram . . . the value to protect innocent life:** For the complete summary of
      the famous Milgram experiments, see Stanley Milgram. *Obedience to Authority:
      The Experiment That Challenged Human Nature* (New York: Harper Perennial,
      2009). These experiments are described in more detail in the chapter on Rule
      #3, "Know Your Enemy."

26   **speak directly to the potential victims, and ask if they needed help:** See
      Matthew M. Hollander, "The Repertoire of Resistance: Non-Compliance with
      Directives in Milgram's 'Obedience' Experiments," *British Journal of Social
      Psychology*, Vol. 54, No. 3 (2015), pp. 425–44. See also Anna Baumert, Anna
      Halmburger, and Manfred Schmitt, "Interventions against Norm Violations:
      Dispositional Determinants of Self-Reported and Real Moral Courage,"
      Personality and Social Psychology Bulletin Vol. 39, No. 8 (2013), pp. 1053–1068

(reporting that acts of moral courage are best predicted by beneficiary sensitivity).

27   **"ethical fading"...as the "slippery slope" problem:** Max H. Bazerman and Ann E. Tenbrunsel. *Blind Spots: Why We Fail to Do What's Right and What to Do about It* (Princeton, NJ: Princeton University Press, 2011), pp. 30–31 & p. 76 (if a person shifts her ethical stance "gradually and incrementally," it is easier for manifestly unethical behavior to become a "new normal"). The same process can make it easier to ignore unethical behavior going on around you. See Bazerman and Tenbrunsel, pp. 77–99.

27   **"...push the ethical envelop little by little each time":** See Dick Carozza, "Fighting a Culture of Fraud: An Interview with Dinesh Thakur, ACFE's Sentinel Award Recipient," *Fraud Magazine* (July/August 2014), p. 34.

27   **Nick Leeson...criminal bank fraud:** Clay Christensen, James Allworth & Karen Dillon. *How Will You Measure Your Life? Finding Fulfillment Using Lessons from Some of the World's Greatest Businesses* (New York: HarperBusiness, 2012), pp. 187–88.

28   **Astros...application called "Codebreaker":** Ken Rosenthal and Evan Drellich, "The Astros Stole Signs Electronically in 2017—Part of a Much Bigger Issue for Major League Baseball," *The Athletic Ink* (November 12, 2019), https://theathletic.com/1363451/2019/11/12/the-astros-stole-signs-electronically-in-2017-part-of-a-much-broader-issue-for-major-league-baseball/; Jared Diamond, "'Dark Arts' and 'Codebreaker': The Origins of the Houston Astros Cheating Scheme," *Wall Street Journal* (February 7, 2020), p. A12; Jared Diamond, "The Astros' Front Office Created Codebreaker. The Players Took It from There," *Wall Street Journal* (February 13, 2020), p. A13.

29   **your emotions...predict your actions:** For excellent, general treatments of the identity and role of moral emotions in our lives, see Kwame Anthony Appiah, *Experiments in Ethics* (Harvard University Press, 2008); Jonathan Haidt, "The Moral Emotions," in R. J. Davidson, K.R. Scherer, & H.H. Goldsmith (eds.) *Handbook of Affective Sciences* (Oxford University Press, 2003), pp. 852–870.

30   **"...if you are going to do nothing—or get angry":** Roxane Gay, "Work Friend: Taking a Stand against an Employer," *New York Times* (June 14, 2020), p. BU4. For a general treatment of the role of anger in organizational participants' moral decisions, see Katherine A. DeCelles, Scott Sonenshein & Brayden G. King, "Examining Anger's Immobilizing Effect on Institutional Insiders' Action Intentions in Social Movements," *Administrative Science Quarterly*, October 2019, pp. 1–40 (surveying anger literature and noting that insiders at firms targeted by social activists let their anger over a social issue be swamped by their fear that activists may hurt their place of work). Philosopher Adam Smith considered anger to be a "constructive emotion" when channeled properly. See Ryan Patrick Hanley, *Our Great Purpose: Adam Smith on Living a Better Life* (Princeton, NJ: Princeton University Press, 2019), p. 58 (noting that Smith labeled this as "sympathetic indignation").

30   **Tim Bray...Amazon Web Services (AWS):** See Mihir Zaveri, "An Amazon Vice President Quits over Firings of Employees Who Protested," *New York Times* (May 4, 2020), https://www.nytimes.com/2020/05/04/business/amazon

-tim-bray-resigns.html. To read Mr. Bray's blog entry about his resignation, quoted in the text, see Tim Bray, "Bye, Amazon," last updated May 4, 2020, https://www.tbray.org/ongoing/When/202x/2020/04/29/Leaving-Amazon.

31 **"Anger is the white sugar of activism. It's a good rush but it does not provide nourishment":** This quote is attributed to 2020 Democratic presidential candidate and New Age guru Marianne Williamson. See Taffy Brodesser -Akner, "The Gospel According to Marianne Williamson," *New York Times Magazine* (September 3, 2019), p. 43.

31 **Wigand . . . developing a "safer" cigarette:** See, e.g., Marie Brenner, "The Man Who Knew Too Much," *Vanity Fair* (April 1, 2004), https://www.vanityfair .com/magazine/1996/05/wigand199605.

32 **Guilt and shame reside just around the corner from anger:** For general treatments of distinctions between guilt and shame, see June Price Tangney, Jeff Stuewig, and Debra J. Mashek, "Moral Emotions and Moral Behavior," *Annual Review of Psychology*, Vol. 58 (2007), pp. 345–372. (noting that guilt tends to spring from a private transgression of a moral standard based on a failure to control behavior versus shame, which involves a public disclosure of a transgression that is experienced as a judgement on the "self"). See also, Scott Wolf, Taya R. Cohen, A. T. Panter, and Chester A. Insko, "Shame Proneness and Guilt Proneness: Toward the Further Understanding of Reactions to Public and Private Transgressions," *Identity and Self*, Vol. 9, No. 4 (2010), pp. 337–362.

33 **look at guilt first:** For more on guilt as an emotion that fosters virtue, see Roy F. Baumeister and Julie Juola Exline, "Virtue, Personality, and Social Relations: Self-Control as the Moral Muscle," *Journal of Personality*, Vol. 67, No. 6 (December 1999), pp. 1165–1193.

33 **Dr. Jeff Thompson . . . Gundersen Health System:** Jeff Thompson. *Lead True: Live Your Values, Build Your People, Inspire Your Community* (Charleston, SC: ForbesBooks, 2017), pp. 12–13.

34 **". . . to live with a murderer—themselves":** Hannah Arendt, *Responsibility and Judgment* (New York: Schocken Books, 2003), p.44.

34 **"guilt prone" . . . violate even minor social norms:** See Tara R. Cohen, Scott Wolf, A.T. Panter & Chester A. Insko, "Introducing the GASP Scale: A New Measure of Guilt and Shame Proneness," *Journal of Personality and Social Psychology*, Vol. 100, No. 5 (2011), pp. 947—966. Scholars argue that guilt proneness is a critical quality for good leadership. See Rebecca L. Schaumberg and Francis J. Flynn, "Uneasy Lies the Head That Wears the Crown: The Link between Guilt Proneness and Leadership," *Journal of Personality and Social Psychology*, Vol. 103, No. 2 (2012), pp. 327–342.

36 **shame . . . "wish we could vanish":** Annette Kämmerer, "The Scientific Underpin-nings and Impacts of Shame," *Scientific American* (August 9, 2019), https://www .scientificamerican.com/article/the-scientific-underpinnings-and-impacts-of -shame/. See also Michael A. Daniels & Sandra L. Robinson, "The Shame of It All: A Review of Shame in Organizational Life," *Journal of Management*, Vol. 45, No. 6, pp. 2448–2473, 2019, https://journals.sagepub.com/doi/10.1177/0149206318817604.

37 **"you will not be imperiled in one hundred battles":** Sun Tzu, *The Art of War*, Chapter 3 ("Attack By Stratagem") paragraph 18 (translation by Lionel Giles), http://classics.mit.edu/Tzu/artwar.html.

Rule #3: Know Your Enemy

38   "Good and evil both increase at compound interest": C.S. Lewis, *Mere Christianity* (New York: HarperCollins, revised edition, 2015), Book 3, Chapter 9 (on "Charity"), p. 111.

39   Betty Vinson and Troy Normand: Cynthia Cooper, *Extraordinary Circumstances* (Hoboken, NJ: John Wiley & Sons, 2008), pp. 1–11.

40   *meaningful* time: Lonnie D. Kliever, "a philosophical riff," *Artella* (2003) ("Cronos is the time of clocks . . . Kairos is numinous time").

41   Michael Center . . . . admission as an athlete: Melissa Korn, "Ex-Tennis Coach Gets Six Months in Scandal," *Wall Street Journal* (February 25, 2020), p. A3.

43   *Ordinary Men* . . . Polish Jews during World War II: Christopher Browning, *Ordinary Men: Reserve Police Battalion 101 and the Final Solution in Poland* (New York: Harper Perennial revised edition, 2017).

44   reviewer Walter Reich . . . into war criminals: Walter Reich, "The Men Who Pulled the Trigger," *New York Times Book Review* (April 12, 1992), at p.1.

44   *The Altruistic Personality* . . . explores these cases: Samuel P. Oliner and Pearl M. Oliner, *The Altruistic Personality: What Led Ordinary Men and Women to Risk Their Lives on Behalf of Others* (New York: Touchstone, 1992). The Oliners' theory that "extensivity" as an aspect of moral imagination plays a key role in prosocial motivation has been confirmed empirically. See Christopher J. Einolf, "Does Extensivity Form Part of the Altruistic Personality? An Empirical Test of Oliner and Oliner's Theory," *Social Science Research*, Vol. 38 (2010), pp. 141–152.

45   Gies . . . rescuers must have experienced: The quotes in the text come from an interview with Miep Gies in May 1997 during which she answered a series of questions posed by students. See http://teacher.scholastic.com/frank/tscripts/miep.htm.

48   Solomon Asch . . . when peer pressure is applied: S.E. Asch, "Effects of Group Pressure Upon the Modification and Distortion of Judgment," in H. Guetzkow (ed.), *Groups, Leadership and Men* (Pittsburgh: Carnegie Press, 1951); S.E. Asch, "Studies of Independence and Conformity: I. A Minority of One Against a Unanimous Majority," *Psychological Monographs: General and Applied*, Vol. 70, No. 9 (1956), pp. 1–70.

49   Stanley Milgram . . . Yale in the 1960s and '70s: Milgram's experiments are detailed in his book. See Stanley Milgram, *Obedience to Authority: The Experiment That Challenged Human Nature* (New York: Harper Perennial, 2009).

51   Maurice Schweitzer . . . documenting this problem: Maurice Schweitzer, Lisa Ordonez & Bambi Douma, "Goal Setting as a Motivator of Unethical Behavior," *Academy of Management Journal*, Vol. 47, No. 3 (2004), pp. 422–432. For an update on this research and extension to educational and other settings, see Lisa D. Ordonez and David T. Welsh, "Immoral Goals: How Goal Setting May Lead To Unethical Behavior," *Current Opinion in Psychology*, Vol. 6 (2015), pp. 93–96. More generally, on the role of incentives in unethical conduct, see Bernd Irlenbusch and Marie Claire Villeval, "Behavioral Ethics: How Psychology Influenced Economics and How Economics Might Inform Psychology, *Current Opinion in Psychology*, Vol. 6 (2015), pp. 87–92; Julien Benistant and Marie Claire Villeval, "Unethical Behavior and Group Identity in Contests," *Journal of Economic Psychology*, Vol. 72 (2019), pp 128–155 (showing how the desire to win in competition drives unethical behavior). A 2007 survey from the Ethics Resource Center revealed that "Protecting the interests of the

organization" and "Meeting performance goals" were among the top reported causes of pressure to compromise ethics after pressures from top management, supervisors, and coworkers. See Figure 10, page 27 at https://www.shrm.org /hr-today/trends-and-forecasting/research-and-surveys/Documents/08%20 Ethics_Landscape_in_American_Business%20FINAL.pdf.

52 **Eric Shinseki . . . Veterans Administration hospitals:** Michael D. Shear and Richard A. Oppel Jr., "V.A. Chief Resigns in Face of Furor on Delayed Care," *New York Times* (May 30, 2014), p. A1.

52 **"role theory" . . . well-established social roles:** Bruce J. Biddle, *Role Theory: Expectations, Identities, and Behaviors* (New York: Academic Press, 1979); Heinrich Popitz, "The Concept of Social Role as an Element of Sociological Theory," in *Role: Sociological Studies 4* (J. A. Jackson editor) (New York: Cambridge University Press, reissue edition, 2010).

53 **Philip Zimbardo . . . otherwise normal group of people:** Zimbardo's experiment is extensively described in his book on the topic. See Philip Zimbardo, *The Lucifer Effect: Understanding How Good People Turn Evil* (New York: Random House, 2007).

53 **experiment has been strongly criticized . . . might otherwise have done:** For a summary of this criticism, including an allegation that the experiment was essentially a "hoax," see Rutger Bregman, *Humankind: A Hopeful History* (New York: Little, Brown & Co., 2019), pp. 148–157.

55 **larger systems that allocate control in a social order:** Zimbardo is careful to link the role that pressures imposed by role expectations embedded in a "situation" to the "systems" that create these situational patterns of pressure play in the first place. See *The Lucifer Effect* at pp. 9–11. These relate to the power structures of society. For a more general and comprehensive review of systemic pressures, which can include cultural forces such as racism and sexism along with political power structures, see Bridget C. Harrison, *Power and Society: An Introduction to the Social Sciences 14th Edition* (Boston: Centrage Learning, 2017).

Rule #4: Summon Your Character

58 **". . . ordinary people who stepped forward":** This quote appeared on the Weibo account of the Shangdong Province's law enforcement body after the death of Dr. Li Wenliang and was widely circulated. See Li Yuan, "Online Revolt in China as Doctor Is Lionized," *New York Times* (February 7, 2020), p. B1.

59 **Keanon Lowe . . . three security guards:** The Keanon Lowe story took place on May 17, 2019. It was widely reported on in August 2019. The story in the text is drawn from a number of these sources, including some of the quotes used. The earlier stories suggested that Lowe had tackled the student and wrestled him to the ground. See Greg Bishop, "'Active Shooter!' How Life Put Keanon Lowe Where He Was Supposed to Be," *Sports Illustrated*, (August 26–September 2019), https://www.si.com/nfl/2019/08/29/keanon-lowe-stopped-school-shooter -oregon-wide-receiver-eagles-49ers-coach-chip-kelly; Adam Rittenberg, "The Story of Keanon Lowe, Former Oregon Receiver Turned Hero," ESPN.com (August 2, 2019), https://www.espn.com/college-football/story/_/id/27297200 /the-story-keanon-lowe-former-oregon-receiver-turned-hero. After these stories were reported, video footage of the incident revealed that Lowe had actually

embraced and comforted the student after disarming him. This led to another set of stories updating the original ones. See Derrick Bryson and Neil Vigdor, "Dramatic Footage Shows Coach Disarming and Then Hugging Student," *New York Times* (October 20, 2019), https://www.nytimes.com/2019/10/20/us/oregon-football -coach-student-shotgun.html (quoting Bruce Alexander as saying that Lowe's compassionate conduct "says a lot about his character").

60   **"it was kind of like you taught us on kickoff, coach":** This quote appears in Adam Rittenberg, "The Story of Keanon Lowe, Former Oregon Receiver Turned Hero," ESPN.com (August 2, 2019), https://www.espn.com/college-football/story/_/id /27297200/the-story-keanon-lowe-former-oregon-receiver-turned-hero.

61   **"Dark Triad" of personality traits:** See Monica A. Koehn, Ceylan Okan, and Peter K. Jonason, "A Primer of the Dark Triad Traits," *Australian Journal of Psychology*, Vol. 71 (2018), pp. 7–15; Peter K. Jonason, Sarah Slomski, & Jamie Partyka, "The Dark Triad at Work: How Toxic Employees Get Their Way," *Personality and Individual Differences*, Vol. 52 (2012), pp. 449–453; Derlroy L. Paulhus and Kevin M. Williams, "The Dark Triad of Personality: Narcissism, Machiavellianism, and Psychopathy," *Journal of Research in Personality*, Vol. 36 (2002), pp. 556–563.

61   **Good character . . . consists of three facets:** See, e.g., Ayelet Fishbach and Kaitlin Woolley, "Avoiding Ethical Temptation," *Current Opinion in Psychology*, Vol. 6 (2015), pp. 36–40; Roy F. Baumeister and Nawal G. Alghamdi, "Role of Self-Control Failure in Immoral and Unethical Actions," *Current Opinion in Psychology*, Vol. 6 (2015), pp. 66–69; Geoffrey P. Goodwin, Jared Piazza, and Paul Rozin, "Moral Character Predominates in Person Perception and Evaluation," *Journal of Personality and Social Psychology*, Vol. 106, No. 1 (2014), pp. 148–168. For an excellent overview of the role of character in ethical decision making, including the point made in the text, see Mark Schwartz, "Ethical Decision-Making Theory: An Integrated Approach," *Journal of Business Ethics*, Vol. 139, No. 4 (2015), pp 755–776.

61   **whether humans have free will:** See, e.g., Cory J. Clark, Jamie Luguri, Peter H. Ditto, Joshua Knobe, Azim F. Shariff, and Roy Baumeister, "Free to Punish: A Motivated Account of Free Will Belief," *Journal of Personality and Social Psychology*, Vol. 106, No. 4 (2014), pp. 501–513.

61   **"personality" or "situation":** For a comprehensive treatment of this debate and a conclusion that comes down on the side of situation, see John M. Doris, *Lack of Character: Personality and Moral Behavior* (New York: Cambridge University Press, 2002). For work that comes down on the side of personality, see Jennifer P. Green, Reeshad S. Dalal, Kristen L. Swigart, Melissa A. Bleiberg, David M. Wallace, and Amber K. Hargrove, "Personality Consistency and Situational Influences on Behavior," *Journal of Management*, Vol. 45, No. 8 (2019), pp. 3204–3234. You can find a spirited defense of personality as the basis for virtue ethics in Miguel Alzola, "Character and Environment: The Status of Virtues in Organizations," *Journal of Business Ethics*, Vol. 78 (2008), pp. 343–357. For research suggesting both personality and situation combine to produce behavior, see Timothy A. Judge, Lauren S. Simon, Charlice Hurst, and Ken Kelley, "What I Experienced Yesterday Is Who I Am Today: Relationship of Work Motivations and Behaviors to Within-Individual Variation in the Five-Factor Model of Personality," *Journal of Applied Psychology*, Vol. 99, No. 2 (2014), pp. 199–221.

62   **you can harness situational forces to your advantage:** Angela L. Duckworth, Katherine L. Milkman, and David Laibson, "Beyond Willpower: Strategies for Reducing Failures of Self-Control," *Psychological Science*, Vol. 19, No. 3 (2018), pp. 102–129.

62   **daily practice as a habit:** William James, "The Laws of Habits" in *Talks to Teachers on Psychology* (Rockville, MD: Manor, 2008), p.42 ("our virtues are habits as much as our vices"); Tara Parker-Pope, "How to Form Healthy Habits," *New York Times* (February 25, 2020), p. D6. There is a rich literature on forming healthy habits, all of which applies to forming character habits. See Charles Duhigg, *The Power of Habit: Why We Do What We Do in Life and Business* (New York: Random House, 2012); James Clear, *Atomic Habits: An Easy & Proven Way to Build Good Habits and Break Bad Ones* (New York: Avery, 2018). For an integration of this habit literature with character ethics, see Ronald A. Howard and Clinton D. Korver, *Ethics (for the Real World): Creating a Personal Code to Guide Decisions in Work and Life* (Boston: Harvard Business Press, 2008) pp. 151–154.

62   **"Excellence [of character] is therefore not an act, but a habit":** Will Durant, *The Story of Philosophy: The Lives and Opinions of the World's Greatest Philosophers* (New York: Pocket Books, Second Edition, 1991) p. 98.

63   **twenty-four character-related personality traits:** Christopher Peterson and Martin Seligman. *Character Strengths and Virtues* (New York: Oxford University Press, 2004). You can find an assessment to measure your own scores on these traits here: https://www.viacharacter.org/survey/account/register.

63   **Honesty-Humility personality scale:** Kibeom Lee and Michael C. Ashton. *The H Factor: Why Some People Are Manipulative, Self-Entitled, Materialistic, and Exploitative—and Why It Matters for Everyone* (Waterloo, Ontario, Canada: Wilfrid Laurier University Press, 2012). You can find an assessment to measure your own scores on these traits here: https://hexaco.org/hexaco-online. See also Tara R. Cohen, A. T. Panter, Nazli Turan, Lily Morse, Yeonjeong Kim, "Moral Character in the Workplace," *Journal of Personality and Social Psychology*, Vol. 107, No. 5 (2014), pp. 943–963 (identifying high scores for Honest-Humility, self-discipline/conscientiousness, and internalization of moral identity as the three most reliable predictors of moral character in a workplace setting).

65   **Keanon Lowe's story . . . dig a little deeper into it:** See Greg Bishop, "'Active Shooter!' How Life Put Keanon Lowe Where He Was Supposed to Be," *Sports Illustrated* (August 26–September 2019), https://www.si.com/nfl/2019/08/29/keanon-lowe-stopped-school-shooter-oregon-wide-receiver-eagles-49ers-coach-chip-kelly; Adam Rittenberg, "The Story of Keanon Lowe, Former Oregon Receiver Turned Hero," ESPN.com (August 2, 2019), https://www.espn.com/college-football/story/_/id/27297200/the-story-keanon-lowe-former-oregon-receiver-turned-hero. Derrick Bryson and Neil Vigdor, "Dramatic Footage Shows Coach Disarming and Then Hugging Student," *New York Times* (October 20, 2019), https://www.nytimes.com/2019/10/20/us/oregon-football-coach-student-shotgun.html.

67   **Bad behavior at home . . . bad behavior at work:** See John M. Griffin, Samuel Kruger, and Gonzalo Maturana, "Personal Infidelity and Professional Conduct in 4 Settings," *Proceedings of the National Academy of Sciences*, Vol. 116 (July 2019), pp. 16268–16273.

68   **Benjamin Franklin . . . felt deep remorse:** Benjamin Franklin, *The Autobiography and Other Writings*, ed. Peter Shaw (New York: Bantam, 1982), p. 31.

69   **". . . average of the five people you spend most of your time with":** I was unable to find the original source for this well-known quote, which is widely attributed to Rohn. See, e.g., https://medium.com/the-polymath-project/you-are-the -average-of-the-five-people-you-spend-the-most-time-with-a2ea32d08c72. Rohn was a motivational speaker, so it is likely something he repeatedly said in his success talks. For his underlying theory supporting the quote, see Jim Rohn, *7 Strategies for Wealth and Happiness* (New York: Three Rivers Press, 1985), pp. 129–138 ("Strategy Six: Surround Yourself with Winners").

70   **anxiety is "unresolved fear":** Joseph LeDoux, *The Emotional Brain: The Mysterious Underpinnings of Emotional Life* (New York: Simon & Schuster, 1996). See also Joseph LeDoux, *The Deeper History of Ourselves: The Four-Billion -Year Story of How We Got Conscious Brains* (New York: Viking, 2019).

71   **". . . my palms were damp with sweat":** Cynthia Cooper, *Extraordinary Circumstances* (Hoboken, NJ: Wiley, 2008), p. 245.

71   **"stress mindset":** A.J. Crum, P. Salovey, and S. Anchor, "Rethinking Stress: The Role of Mindsets in Determining the Stress Response," *Journal of Personality and Social Psychology*, Vol. 104, No. 4 (2013), pp. 716–734.

71   ***Talk Yourself Down:*** For a useful, Buddhist perspective on fear, see Thich Nhat Hanh, *Fear: Essential Wisdom for Getting through the Storm* (New York: HarperOne, 2014).

73   **various forms of self-deception:** For rationalizations people use to justify unethical behavior, see Mary Gentile, *Giving Voice to Values: How to Speak Your Mind When You Know What's Right* (New Haven, CT: Yale University Press, 2010), 179–180; Celia Moore, "Moral Disengagement," *Current Opinion in Psychology*, Vol. 6 (2015), pp. 199–204; Rachel Barkan, Shahar Ayal, and Dan Ariely, "Ethical Dissonance, Justifications, and Moral Behavior," *Current Opinion in Psychology*, Vol. 6 (2015), pp. 157–161.

73   **"a Reason for everything one has a mind to do":** Benjamin Franklin, *The Autobiography and Other Writings*, ed. Peter Shaw (New York: Bantam, 1982), p.56.

74   **publication called *Stars and Stripes*:** Wyatt Olson, "Do Fired Navy Admirals Suffer from the 'Bathsheba Syndrome,'" *Stars and Stripes* (March 14, 2012), https://www.stripes.com/news/navy/do-fired-navy-cos-suffer-from-bathsheba -syndrome-1.171525.

75   **Jonathan Burrows . . . into this mindset:** Jennifer Rankin, "FCA Bans £43,000 Fare Dodger from Working in Financial Services," *Guardian* (December 15, 2018), https://www.theguardian.com/business/2014/dec/15/ca-ban-43000-fare-dodger -financial-services-industry-blackrock-jonathan-burrows.

76   **Doug Hodge . . . in prison for fraud:** Doug Hodge, "I Wish I'd Never Met Rick Singer," *Wall Street Journal* (February 10, 2020), p. A19.

78   **Scott Capps . . . dead and long-inactive customers:** Joseph N. DiStefano, "Former Vanguard Manager Scott Capps: Why I Stole from Fund Giant's Dead Clients," *Philadelphia Inquirer* (September 16, 2019), https://www.inquirer.com /business/vanguard-scott-capps-dead-accounts-steal-prison-20190916.html.

78   **Bradley Birkenfeld . . . in US history:** See Lynn Stout, *Cultivating Conscience: How Good Laws Make Good People* (Princeton, NJ: Princeton University Press,

2011), pp. 233–234; Lynnley Browning, "Ex-UBS Banker Pleads Guilty in Tax Evasion," *New York Times* (July 20, 2008), https://www.nytimes.com/2008/06/20 /business/20tax.html; Laura Saunders and Robin Sidel" "Whistleblower Gets $104 Million," *Wall Street Journal* (September 11, 2012), https://www.wsj.com /articles/SB10000872396390444017504577645412614237708.

Rule #5: Channel Your Personality Strengths

81   "... bake with the flour you have": G. Richard Shell, *Bargaining for Advantage: Negotiation Strategies for Reasonable People* (New York: Penguin, second revised edition, 2018), p. 3.

81   the genetic aspects of our behavior as "temperament": Susan Cain, *Quiet: The Power of Introverts in a World That Can't Stop Talking* (New York: Crown, 2012), p. 101.

82   Renate ... a city in northern Germany: I drew this story from several sources. See Melissa Eddy, "Hundreds of Bodies, One Nurse: German Serial Killer Leaves as Many Questions as Victims," *New York Times* (May 11, 2019), p. A1; Wiebke Ramm, "Neils Hogel: Nurses Noticed That He Was Dangerous," https ://newstesthtt.wordpress.com/2019/02/03/niels-hogel-nurses-noticed-that-he -was-dangerous/ (quoting nurse saying "I am scared I am to blame"). See also https://www.dw.com/en/german-killer-nurse-sentenced-to-life-for-murdering -patients/a-49058531.

86   The First C: Conscientiousness: Conscientiousness is one of the "Big 5" traits of personality traits identified by personality psychologists: Openness, Conscientiousness, Emotional Stability, Agreeableness, and Extroversion /Introversion. Conscientiousness includes facets ranging from industry to orderliness, with self-discipline being a major component. For a general treatment of the Big 5, see Colin G. DeYoung, Lena C. Quilty, and Jordon B. Peterson, "Between Facets and Domains: 10 Aspects of the Big Five," *Journal of Personality and Social Psychology*, Vol. 93, No. 5 (2007), pp. 880–896. For scholarship that makes the connection between conscientiousness and moral courage, see Yeonjeong Kim and Taya R. Cohen, "Moral Character and Workplace Deviance: Recent Research and Current Trends," *Current Opinion in Psychology*, Vol. 6 (2015), pp. 134–138; Laura Parks-Leduc, Leigh Mulligan, and Matthew A. Rutherford, "Can Ethics Be Taught? Examining the Impact of Distributed Ethical Training and Individual Characteristics on Ethical Decision Making," *Academy of Management Learning and Education* (March 26, 2020), https://journals .aom.org/doi/10.5465/amle.2018.0157; Taya R. Cohen and Lily Morse, "Moral Character: What It is and What It Does," in A.P. Brief and B.M. Staw (eds.), *Research in Organizational Behavior* (Amsterdam: Elsevier, 2014).

89   The Second C: Conflict Management Capabilities: I derive this aspect of the personality-based part of the Conscience Code from my own work on negotiation and assertiveness in bargaining. See G. Richard Shell, *Bargaining for Advantage: Negotiation Strategies for Reasonable People* (New York: Penguin, second revised edition, 2018), pp. 3–26. The assessment in the text is derived from the Bargaining Styles Assessment contained in that book. See also, Adam Kay and Daniel P. Skarlicki, "Cultivating a Conflict-Positive Workplace: How Mindfulness Facilitates Constructive Conflict Management," *Organizational and Human Decision Processes* Vol. 159n (April 2020), pp. 8–20.

96   **"Big 5" personality trait inventory . . . deferential behavior:** Agreeableness
      is one of the Big 5 personality traits. See Colin G. DeYoung, Lena C.
      Quilty, and Jordon B. Peterson, "Between Facets and Domains: 10 Aspects
      of the Big Five," *Journal of Personality and Social Psychology*, Vol. 93, No. 5
      (2007), pp. 880–896.

97   ***"or tolerate those who do":*** The West Point honor code is central to its identity
      and mission to educate leaders with moral courage. It can be found here: https
      ://www.westpoint.edu/about/public-affairs/news/fact-sheets.

97   **Best Buy, Inc. . . . his handpicked successor:** See Miguel Bustillo, "Best Buy
      Chairman to Resign after Probe: Report Says Schultz Didn't Tell Board of
      Allegations about Ex-CEO Dunn," *Wall Street Journal* (May 15, 2012), https
      ://www.wsj.com/articles/SB10001424052702304192704577403922338506912.

98   **newly minted prison guards:** Associated Press, "W. Va. Governor Fires 34
      Prison Guards and Instructor Who Gave Nazi Salute 'As a Sign of Respect' for
      Their Teacher Who Was 'A Hardass Like Hitler,'" *Chicago Tribune* (December 31,
      2019), https://www.chicagotribune.com/nation-world/ct-nw-prison-guards
      -sieg-heil-20191231-dohueh3jpfbpjd33spbxkikn4m-story.html. A copy of
      Secretary Sandy's report can be found here: https://governor.wv.gov/Documents
      /DMAPS%20Executive%20Summary%20and%20Memo%20to%20Governor
      .pdf. I spoke to Secretary Sandy by phone on January 16, 2020, and he emailed his
      confirmation of my conversation with him included in the text (and updated his
      account to reveal that the secretary had been terminated along with the cadets and
      several instructors) on September 8, 2020.

101   **Kim Gwang-ho . . . Hyundai Motor Co.:** See Jayup S. Kwaack, "Whistle-
      Blower Prompts a Hyundai Recall in South Korea," *New York Times* (May 17
      2017), B2; Hyunjoo Jin, "Blowing the Whistle in South Korea: Hyundai Man
      Takes on Chaebol Culture," Reuters (May 15, 2017), https://www.reuters.com
      /article/us-hyundai-whistleblower/blowing-the-whistle-in-south-korea-hyundai
      -man-takes-on-chaebol-culture-idUSKCN18B0J5.

103   **The Third C: Confidence (Locus of Control):** Self-confidence is a
      multifaceted construct that is beyond the scope of this book. I am speaking
      about the sense of self-confidence required to affect your social environment
      through your own choices and actions. Locus of Control is a well-researched
      aspect of personality that captures this idea. It is used to investigate a wide
      range of behaviors. See, e.g., Steven Nowicki, *Choice or Chance: Understanding
      Your Locus of Control and Why It Matters* (New York: Prometheus, 2016). See
      also Wang Sheng Lee and Terra McKinnish, "Locus of Control and Marital
      Satisfaction: Couple Perspectives Using Australian Data," *Journal of Economic
      Psychology* Vol. 74 (2019).

103   **"Be proactive" . . . *The 7 Habits of Highly Effective People*:** Stephen R.
      Covey, *The 7 Habits of Highly Effective People* (New York: Simon and Schuster,
      Anniversary Edition, 2020).

104   **Teach for America . . . recruiting teachers:** Adam Bryant, "Corner Office:
      Charisma? To Her, It's Overrated," *New York Times* (July 4, 2009) (Interview
      with Wendy Kopp), https://www.nytimes.com/2009/07/05/business/05
      corner.html.

Rule #6: Leverage the Power of Two

109 **"We must, indeed, all hang together . . . all hang separately":** Benjamin
Franklin gets credit for saying many things he may or may not have said. But
that does not make the quote any less pithy. This quote, attributed to him at the
signing of the Declaration of Independence in 1776, falls into that category. One
contemporary of Franklin's (who had read Franklin's *Autobiography*) put words
very like these in the mouth of a governor of Pennsylvania, Richard Penn, in
1777. But who knows? See the explanation provided under quotes attributed to
Franklin in https://en.wikiquote.org/wiki/Benjamin_Franklin#Misattributed.

112 **The True Partner:** S.E. Asch, "Effects of Group Pressure Upon the Modification
and Distortion of Judgment," in H. Guetzkow (ed.), *Groups, Leadership and Men*
(Pittsburgh: Carnegie Press, 1951); S.E. Asch, "Studies of Independence and
Conformity: I. A Minority of One Against a Unanimous Majority," *Psychological
Monographs: General and Applied, Vol. 70, No. 9 (1956)*, pp. 1–70. Once the true
partner left the room, the subjects' tendency to go along with the group returned
to the observed experimental levels that existed in the standard condition.
Research on minority groups and microaggressions also suggests that having
a trusted partner can help people resist being "gaslighted" by members of a
majority group. See Sharde M. Davis, "When Sistahs Support Sistahs: A Process
of Supportive Communication about Racial Microaggressions Among Black
Women," *Communication Monographs*, Vol. 86, No. 2 (2019).

113 **The Dissenting Peers . . . Milgram's Experiments:** Stanley Milgram, *Obedience
to Authority* (New York: Harper Perennial, 1974), pp. 118–120.

114 **Zimbardo . . . Outside Perspective:** Philip Zimbardo, *The Lucifer Effect: Understanding How Good People Turn Evil* (New York: Random House, 2008), pp. 168–171.

115 **the five people you spend most time with:** As noted earlier, I was unable to find the
source for this well-known quote, which is widely attributed to him. See, e.g., https://
medium.com/the-polymath-project/you-are-the-average-of-the-five-people-you-spend
-the-most-time-with-a2ea32d08c72. Rohn was a motivational speaker, so it is likely
something he said repeatedly said in his success talks. For his underlying theory supporting
the quote, see Jim Rohn, *7 Strategies for Wealth and Happiness* (New York: Three Rivers
Press, 1985), pp. 129–138 ("Strategy Six: Surround Yourself with Winners").

115 **the Close, the Many, and the Powerful:** James Clear, *Atomic Habits: An Easy &
Proven Way to Build Good Hab8ts and Break Bad Ones* (New York: Avery, 2018),
pp. 115–123.

116 **it helps to be "just down the hall":** Henry Kissinger, *White House Years* (New
York: Simon and Schuster, 1979), p. 47.

116 **two studies . . . can rub off:** James Clear, *Atomic Habits: An Easy & Proven Way
to Build Good Habits and Break Bad Ones* (New York: Avery, 2018), pp. 117–118.

117 **Mahatma Gandhi . . . autobiography:** See M. K. Gandhi, *Autobiography: The
Story of My Experiments with Truth* (New York: Dover edition, 1983), p. 16.

120 **"quorum response":** Elizabeth Preston, "The Vote of the Wild," *New York Times*
(March 3, 2020) ("Science Times" section), p D1, D6 (including quote by
Dr. Marta Manser).

120 **Robert Cialdini's *Influence*:** Robert Cialdini, *Influence: The Psychology of
Persuasion* (New York: Harper Business, revised edition, 2006).

121   **"with moral anchors for their personal convictions"**: Naomi Ellemers and Jo-
        janneke Van der Toorn, "Groups as Moral Anchors," *Current Opinion in Psychology*,
        Vol. 6 (2015), pp.189–194 (the quote is found on page 192). See also Katherine S.
        Zee, Niall Bolger, and Troy E. Higgins, "Regulatory Effectiveness of Social Sup-
        port," *Journal of Personality and Social Psychology* (2020), https://psycnet.apa.org
        /doiLanding?doi=10.1037%2Fpspi0000235 (noting that social support helps you
        understand your situation more clearly and provides a better sense of control over it).

121   **swimming in a "dirty pond" carries three dangers**: Eugene Dimant, "Contagion
        of Pro- and Antisocial Behavior Among Peers and the Role of Social Proximity,"
        Journal of Economic Psychology, Vol. 73 (2019), pp. 66–88. See also Lamar Pierce
        and Parasuram Balasubramanian, "Behavior Field Evidence on Psychological
        and Social Factors in Dishonesty and Misconduct," *Current Opinion in
        Psychology*, Vol. 6 (2015), pp. 70–76; Aharon Mohliver, "How Misconduct
        Spreads: Auditors' Role in the diffusion of Stock-Option Backdating,"
        Administrative Science Quarterly, Vol. 64, No. 2 (2018), pp. 310–336.

122   **"struggling with financial issues"**: Jeremy Roebuck, "Praise from Players,
        Coaches Preceded Probationary Sentence for Ex-Penn Basketball Coach Jerome
        Allen in Admissions Scandal," *Philadelphia Inquirer* (July 2, 2019) (quoting Jerome
        Allen's statement to a federal judge at his sentencing hearing), https://www.inquirer.
        com/news/jerome-allen-sentencing-penn-basketball-college-admissions-bribes
        -scandal-fran-dunphy-20190702.html. For more on Allen's family background, see
        Nicholas Hut, "Jerome Allen Born to Lead," *Daily Pennsylvanian* (March 15, 1995),
        https://www.thedp.com/article/1995/03/jerome_allen_born_to_lead.

123   **"and I didn't"**: Jeremy Roebuck, "Praise from Players, Coaches Preceded Probationary
        Sentence for Ex-Penn Basketball Coach Jerome Allen in Admissions Scandal,"
        Philadelphia Inquirer (July 2, 2019) (quoting Allen as saying, "I had an opportunity
        to say no and I didn't"), https://www.inquirer.com/news/jerome-allen-sentencing
        -penn-basketball-college-admissions-bribes-scandal-fran-dunphy-20190702.html.

123   **medical device company called Theranos, Inc.:** I gathered the facts and
        quotes for the story of Tyler Shultz and Erika Cheung told in the text from a
        number of sources. The principle source is John Carreyrou, *Bad Blood: Secrets and
        Lies in a Silicon Valley Startup* (New York: Knopf, 2019). The early parts of the
        story regarding Tyler Shultz and Erika Cheung can be found in *Bad Blood* at pp.
        184–200; the middle parts when they were employed at the firm at pp. 231–257,
        and the late parts of the story involving the downfall of the firm at pp. 281–287.
        Additional sources are interviews with the two heroes. See Brian Gallagher, "A
        Theranos Whistleblower's Mission to Make Tech Ethical," Ethical Systems.org
        (September 12, 2019), https://www.ethicalsystems.org/a-theranos-whistleblowers
        -mission-to-make-tech-ethical/; Alina Tugend, "'It Kept Failing': Whistleblower
        Erika Cheung on Working at Theranos," *California Magazine* (March 16, 2019),
        https://alumni.berkeley.edu/california-magazine/just-in/2019-03-16/whistleblower
        -erika-cheung-on-working-at-theranos.

132   **"I never even thought of the word 'whistleblower'"**: Hagerman Lecture as
        reported in the *Lehigh News*, https://www2.lehigh.edu/news/tyler-shultz-i
        -didnt-plan-on-being-a-whistleblower.

132   **". . . ashamed of myself for not filing the complaint sooner"**: Taylor Dunn,
        Victoria Thompson, and Rebecca Jarvis, "Theranos whistleblowers filed

complaints out of fear of patients' health: 'It started to eat me up inside,'"
Episode 4 of *The Dropout*, ABC News podcast (March 13, 2019), https://abc
news.go.com/Business/theranos-whistleblowers-filed-complaints-fear-patients
-health-started/story?id=61030212 (quoting Erika Cheung).

133   **"... speaking to me to right that wrong":** John Carreyrou, *Bad Blood: Secrets and Lies in a Silicon Valley Startup* (New York: Knopf, 2019), p. 238.

133   **No regrets:** Alicia Lutes, "In 2019, Theranos Whistleblower Tyler Shultz Has 'No Regrets,'" Refinery29 (March 18, 2019), https://www.refinery29.com/en-us/2019/03/227173/tyler-schultz-now-2019-theranos-whistleblower-interview.

133   **"... congratulate Tyler for his great moral character":** Taylor Dunn, Victoria Thompson, Rebecca Jarvis and Ashley Louszko, "Ex-Theranos CEO Elizabeth Holmes Says 'I Don't Know' 600-Plus Times in Never-Before-Broadcast Deposition Tapes," ABC News, https://abcnews.go.com/Business/theranos-ceo-elizabeth-holmes-600-times-broadcast-deposition/story?id=60576630 (quoting George Shultz statement made to *Nightline*).

Rule #7: Ask Four Questions

135   **"Nothing pains some people more than having to think":** See Hannah Hutyra, "Martin Luther King Jr. Quotes: In His Own Words," *Birmingham Times* (January 15, 2018), https://www.birminghamtimes.com/2018/01/some-of-dr-martin-luther-king-jr-s-profound-quotes/.

136   **Joe Darby ... abused by their American guards:** The story of Joe Darby and his quotes in the text come from two sources. First, his 2005 acceptance speech at the Kennedy Library upon his being given a Profiles in Courage award. See https://www.jfklibrary.org/events-and-awards/profile-in-courage-award/award-recipients/joseph-darby-2005 ("my comrades, my brothers in arms"). Second, an interview he gave to the magazine *GQ* in 2006. See Wil Hylton, "Prisoner of Conscience," *GQ* (August 1, 2006), https://www.gq.com/story/joe-darby-abu-ghraib ("not the kind of guy to rate someone out" and "I couldn't have it both ways").

137   **William James ... "to behave wrongly":** William James, "Psychology and the Art of Teaching," in *Talks to Teachers on Psychology* (Rockville, MD: Manor, 2008), p. 13.

138   **profoundly complex field:** This vastly understates the situation. All of moral philosophy is contained in this sentence. See, e.g., Jonathan Wolff, *An Introduction to Moral Philosophy* (New York: W.W. Norton, 2017). For an excellent text on the application of moral philosophy to business, see the text cowritten by one of my Wharton School colleagues, Tom Donaldson. Thomas Donaldson and Patricia Werhane, *Ethical Issues in Business: A Philosophical Approach*, 8th edition (Upper Saddle River, NJ: Prentice Hall, 2007). An alternate approach to ethical decision making focusing on five factors—duties, rights, utility, virtue, and relationships—can be found in James A. Anderson and Elaine E. Englehardt, *The Organizational Self and Ethical Conduct* (Fort Worth, TX: Harcourt College, 2001), p. 43.

138   **feels too much like murder:** There is a mini academic industry on the so-called "trolley problem." For a brief summary of it, see Max H. Bazerman and Ann E. Tenbrunsel, *Blind Spots: Why We Fail to Do What's Right and What to Do about It* (Princeton, NJ: Princeton University Press, 2011), pp. 24–26.

139   **Consequences:** Consequentialism measures "the good" by a utilitarian calculus that seeks the outcome that yields the greatest good for the greatest number of

people. Bazerman and Tenbrunsel, p. 25. There is psychological evidence that all ethical theories basically boil down to consequentialism when it comes to applying them in specific circumstances, with everything else being an elaborate form of rationalization. See Max Hennig and Many Hutter, "Revisiting the Divide Between Deontology and Utilitarianism in Moral Dilemma Judgment: A Multinomial Modeling Approach," *Journal of Personality and Social Psychology*, Vol 118, No. 1 (2019), pp 22–56.

139 **Loyalties:** See "Loyalty," *Stanford Encyclopedia of Philosophy*, https://plato.stanford.edu /entries/loyalty/. Psychologists often characterize whistleblowing decisions as trade-offs between loyalties and principles such as fairness and justice. See James Dungan, Adam Waytz, and Liane Young, "The Psychology of Whistleblowing," *Current Opinions in Psychology*, Vol. 6 (2015), pp. 129–133; James A. Dungan, Liane Young, and Adam Waytz, "The Power of Moral Concerns in Predicting Whistleblowing Decisions," *Journal of Experimental Social Psychology*, Vol. 85 (2019), p. 103848.

139 **Identity:** See John Dewey, *Human Nature and Conduct* (New York: Dover Publications, 2002) ("The thing actually at stake in any serious deliberation is . . . what kind of person one is to become, what sort of self is in the making.") p. 216–217. The "identity" approach to ethics is most closely associated with Aristotle's concept of personal virtue. See, e.g., Alasdair MacIntrye, *After Virtue: A Study in Moral Theory* (Notre Dame, IN: University of Notre Dame Press, 2007). For an application to the business context, see Joseph L. Badaracco, *Defining Moments: When Managers Must Choose between Right and Right* (Boston: Harvard Business School Press, 1997). For an application of the identity theory to politics, see Kristen Monroe, "How Identity and Perspective Constrain Moral Choice," *International Political Science Review*, Vol. 24, No. 4 (2003), pp. 405–425.

139 **Principles:** This element of moral decision making is the one most associated with the philosophy of Immanuel Kant and is referred to as "deontology." Bazerman and Tenbrunsel, p. 25. The shortness of this note in no way implies it is not important. Rather, it implies that no note can begin to gesture toward the subject.

142 **Professor Phil Nichols . . . facing this kind of dilemma:** For an example of Professor Nichols's work, see his article, "The Good Bribe," *University of California at Davis Law Review*, Vol. 49, No. 2 (2015), pp 647–683.

144 **Harriet Tubman . . . prior to the Civil War.** Professor Nichols discusses the limits of this example in "The Good Bribe," *University of California at Davis Law Review*, Vol. 49, No. 2 (2015), pp 647–683.

145 **Oskar Schlindler . . . a large number of bribes:** Professor Nichols also discusses the limits of this example in "The Good Bribe," *University of California at Davis Law Review*, Vol. 49, No. 2 (2015), pp 647–683.

146 **Kwame Anthony Appiah . . . "itself a moral task":** Kwame Anthony Appiah, *Experiments in Ethics* (Cambridge, MA: Harvard University Press, 2008) p. 196.

148 **Kathe Swanson . . . surprise of her life:** Dick Carozza, "Dixon's Quiet Hero," *Fraud Magazine* (November/December 2018) (cover story), https://www.fraud -magazine.com/cover-article.aspx?id=4295003585.

150 **Mike Saklar . . . in the Midwest:** This story is found in Rushworth M. Kidder, *Moral Courage: Taking Action When Your Values Are Put to the Test* (New York: William Morrow, 2005), p. 87.

Rule #8: Engage the Decision Maker

156   **"... to say something, to do something"**: Congressman John Lewis made these remarks in the hours leading up to the US House of Representatives vote to impeach President Donald J. Trump. See Jeffrey A. Sonnenfeld, "John Lewis's Last Lesson for Leaders," *Yale Insights* (July 20, 2020), https://insights.som.yale.edu/insights/john-lewis-s-last-lesson-for-leaders. See also Kelsey Snell, "Rep. John Lewis, A Force in the Civil Rights Movement, Dead at 80," WGBH News, *Weekend Edition Saturday* (July 17, 2020), https://www.npr.org/2020/07/17/792579944/rep-john-lewis-a-force-in-the-civil-rights-movement-dead-at-80.

159   **Seven Steps to Influence:** I have constructed these seven steps from a number of sources, including Kerry Patterson, Joseph Grenny, Ron McMillan, and Al Switzer, *Crucial Conversations: Tools for Talking When the Stakes Are High* (New York: McGraw-Hill, 2002); Kerry Paterson, Joseph Grenny, Ron McMillan, and Al Switzer, *Crucial Confrontations: Tools for Resolving Broken Promises, Violated Expectations, and Bad Behavior* (New York: McGraw-Hill, 2005); and G. Richard Shell and Mario Moussa, *The Art of Woo: Using Strategic Persuasion to Sell Your Ideas* (New York: Penguin, 2007).

164   **Assess Your Credibility:** Shell and Moussa, pp. 85–110.

165   **Consider Their Interests and Beliefs:** Shell and Moussa, pp. 111–36 (Beliefs); Shell and Moussa, pp. 137–158 (Interests).

165   **use your meeting to ask them:** Nicholas Epley, *Mindwise: Why We Misunderstand What Others Think, Believe, Feel, and Want* (New York: Vintage Books, 2014) (surveying the literature on how easy it is to misread people and concluding that the best way to figure out what is going on in someone else's mind or heart is to ask them).

166   **J.P. Morgan ... "the real reason":** This quote can be found in Ron Chernow, *The House of Morgan* (New York: Simon & Schuster, 1990), p. 114.

167   **a misleading client report:** Mary Gentile, *Giving Voice to Values: How to Speak Your Mind When You Know What's Right* (New Haven, CT: Yale University Press, 2010), pp. 144–145.

170   **avoid the ethical conflict altogether:** Anjier Chen, Linda Klebe Trevino, and Stephen E. Humphrey, "Ethical Champions, Emotions, Framing, and Team Ethical Decision Making," *Journal of Applied Psychology*, Vol. 105 No. 3 (2019), pp. 245–273. For a study that shows how using value-based arguments reduces trade-offs that can lead to win-win outcomes, see Carolin Schuster, Johann M. Majer, and Roman Tritschel, "Whatever We Negotiate is Not What I Like: How Value-Driven Conflicts Impact Negotiation Behaviors, Outcomes, and Subjective Evaluations," *Journal of Experimental Social Psychology* Vol. 90 (2020), p 103993, https://www.sciencedirect.com/science/article/abs/pii/S002210311930464 0?via%3Dihub.

170   **Use Dialogue, Then Seek Commitments:** The section on dialogue draws from the insights provided in Kerry Patterson, Joseph Grenny, Ron McMillan, and Al Switzer, *Crucial Conversations: Tools for Talking When the Stakes Are High* (New York: McGraw-Hill, 2002), and Patrick Lencioni, *The Five Dysfunctions of the Team* (San Francisco: Jossey-Bass, 2002).

175   **A Word on Commitments:** Shell and Moussa, pp. 207–234.

175   **Overcoming Objections:** For an excellent discussion of why discussions and disputes over rights and values are relatively difficult and give rise to multiple objections, see Richard M. Perloff, *The Dynamics of Persuasion: Communication and Attitudes in the 21st Century, 2nd edition* (Mahwah, NJ: Lawrence Erlbaum, 2003), pp. 260–266.

177   **Dealing with Bullies and Tyrants:** See Lynn Curry, *Beating the Workplace Bully, A Tactical Guide to Taking Charge* (New York: AMACOM, 2016).

179   *Flip the Script:* Lizzy Goodman, "Just Ask: The Ex-Dominatrix Teaching Women To Demand Respect Has a Very Simple Secret," *The Cut* (January 2018) (profiling Kasia Urbaniak) https://www.thecut.com/2018/01/profile-kasia-urbaniak-founder-of-the-academy.html.

Rule #9: Hold Them Accountable

182   "**. . . for which we are accountable**": "Thoughts on the Business of Life," *Forbes Quotes*, https://www.forbes.com/quotes/6902/.

188   **Filing an Internal Complaint:** Using human resources complaint systems to flag employee misconduct can be a difficult experience. See Chip Cutter, "Going to HR is a Tough Decision," *Wall Street Journal* (October 18, 2019), p. B6.

192   **Whistleblowing:** The book provides a Topical Bibliography with a number of excellent books on whistleblowing. For example, see Tom Devine and Tarek F. Maassarani, *The Corporate Whistleblower's Survival Guide* (San Francisco: Berrett-Koehler, 2011); Stephen Martin Kohn, *The New Whistleblower's Handbook: A Step-by-Step Guide to Doing What's Right and Protecting Yourself* (Guilford, CT: Lyons Press, 2017).

193   **Erin Brockovich . . . :** For more about this famous whistleblower, see her own book: Erin Brockovich, *Superman's Not Coming: Our National Water Crisis and What We the People Can Do about It,* (New York: Pantheon, 2020).

193   **Dinesh Thakur . . . research and development department:** For the in-depth story about Mr. Thakur and Ranbaxy, see Katherine Eban, *Bottle of Lies: The Inside Story of the Generic Drug Boom* (New York: Ecco, 2019). Thakur's quotes in the text are taken from an interview he gave to *Fraud Magazine*. See Dick Carozza, "Fighting a Culture of Fraud," *Fraud Magazine* (July/August 2014), https://www.fraud-magazine.com/article.aspx?id=4294983341.

194   **CEO of Japanese company Olympus . . . misconduct to the press:** See Michael Woodford, *Exposure: Inside the Olympus Scandal; How I Went From CEO to Whistleblower* (New York: Portfolio, 2014); Jake Edelstein, "What Michael Woodford Saw at Olympus," *Atlantic* (December 21, 2012); Teri Pengilley, Christopher Thomond, Murdo McLeod, Sarah Lee, and words by Caitlin Disken, "I Had a Moral Duty: Whistleblowers on Why They Spoke Up," *Guardian* (October 9, 2018), https://www.theguardian.com/world/2018/oct/09/i-had-a-moral-duty-whistleblowers-on-why-they-spoke-up.

195   **four thousand tips from whistleblowers . . . frauds:** Mengqi Sun, "Tips to SEC Surge as Working from Home Emboldens Whistleblowers," *Wall Street Journal,* "Risk and Compliance Journal" (June 1, 2020), https://www.wsj.com/articles/tips-to-sec-surge-as-working-from-home-emboldens-whistleblowers-11591003800.

195   **$64 million . . . whistleblower tips:** Dave Michaels, "SEC Accelerates Whistleblower Payouts," *Wall Street Journal* (May 5, 2020), p. B10.

195   **Cynthia Cooper and WorldCom:** The story in the text is taken in large part
       from Cynthia Cooper's own account of the scandal and, to a lesser extent, a
       Wall Street Journal story that broke after the fraud was uncovered. See Cynthia
       Cooper, *Extraordinary Circumstances* (Hoboken, NJ: John Wiley & Sons, 2008);
       Susan Pulliam and Deborah Solomon, "How Three Unlikely Sleuths Exposed
       Fraud at WorldCom," *Wall Street Journal* (October 30, 2002), p. A1.

203   **Ebbers . . . passed away a few months later:** For an interesting obituary of
       Bernie Ebbers, see Sarah Krouse, "CEO Was Imprisoned for One of Biggest
       U.S. Frauds," *Wall Street Journal* (February 4, 2020), p. B5.

203   **"Persons of the Year" . . . ethics education:** See "The Whistleblowers," *Time*
       (2002), http://content.time.com/time/specials/packages/article/0,28804,2019712
       _2019710_2019677,00.html.

Rule #10: Choose to Lead

205   **"Fight for the things that you care about":** Quoted in Alanna Vagianos, "Ruth
       Bader Ginsberg Tells Young Women, 'Fight for the Things You Care About,'"
       Huffington Post (June 2, 2015) (Justice Ginsberg made these remarks on the
       occasion of being presented with the Radcliffe Medal at Harvard University),
       https://www.huffpost.com/entry/ruth-bader-ginsburg-fight-for-the-things-you
       -care-about_n_7492630.

207   **Beth's Story:** There is abundant research on the ethical problems of nurse
       leaders. See, e.g., Maasoumeh Barkhordari-Sharifabad, Tahereh Ashktorab,
       and Foroozan Atashzadeh-Shoorideh, "Obstacles and Problems of Ethical
       Leadership from the Perspective of Nursing Leaders: A Qualitative Analysis,"
       Journal of Medical Ethics and History of Medicine, Vol. 10, No. 1 (2017).

211   **character as "the foundation of leadership":** John Maxwell, *Developing the
       Leader Within You 2.0* (Nashville: HarperCollins Leadership, 2019), p. 49.

211   **character as one of the two "preconditions" . . .:** Stephen R. Covey, *Principle-
       Centered Leadership* (New York: Simon and Schuster, 1990), p.196.

211   **"set the example:** James M. Kouzes and Barry Posner, *The Leadership Challenge:
       How to Make Extraordinary Things Happen in Organizations, Sixth Edition*
       (Hoboken, NJ: Wiley, 2017), p. 71 ("Set the Example: Live Shared Values").

212   **"Coach Keanon Lowe Day of Recognition":** Vivienne Walt, Madeleine
       Carlisle, and Melissa Chan, "These Heroes Went Above and Beyond in 2019,"
       Time (December 12, 2019), https://time.com/5748873/2019-heroes/.

214   **roughly twelve times over the course of their working life:** See Bureau of Labor
       Statistics FAQ's "Number of Jobs Held in a Lifetime," https://www.bls.gov/nls
       /questions-and-answers.htm#anch4. See also Allison Doyle, "How Often Do
       People Change Jobs in a Lifetime?" *The Balance Careers* (June 15, 2020), https
       ://www.thebalancecareers.com/how-often-do-people-change-jobs-2060467.

215   **". . . lose their soul":** The Gospel of Mark, Chapter 8, Verse 36. See "https
       ://biblehub.com/mark/8-36.htm.

215   **"constructive confrontation":** Oliver Staley, "Silicon Valley's Confrontational
       management Style Started with Andy Grove," *Quartz* (March 22, 2016),
       https://qz.com/645327/silicon-valleys-confrontational-management-style
       -started-with-andy-grove/.

215 **"radical candor"**: Kim Scott, *Radical Candor: Be a Kick-Ass Boss without Losing Your Humanity* (New York: St. Martin's Press, revised edition, 2019).

215 **"radical transparency"**: Gene Hammett, "Three Steps Ray Dalio Uses Radical Transparency to Build a Billion-Dollar Company," *Inc.* (May 23, 2018), https ://www.inc.com/gene-hammett/3-steps-ray-dalio-uses-radical-transparency-to -build-a-billion-dollar-company.html.

215 **conflict at the very center of the leader's job:** Ronald Heifetz, *Leadership without Easy Answers* (Cambridge, MA: Belknap Press, 1998).

216 **Haidt . . . moral conduct of a business executive:** Jonathan Haidt, "Can You Teach Businessmen to Be Ethical?" *Washington Post* (January 13, 2014), https ://www.washingtonpost.com/news/on-leadership/wp/2014/01/13/can-you -teach-businessmen-to-be-ethical/?arc404=true.

217 **that make ethical behavior the norm:** Legendary educational innovator Maria Montessori summed up the point made in the text as follows: "Control the environment, not the child." See E. M. Standing, *Maria Montessori: Her Life and Work* (New York: Plume, 1984), p. xiv. See also Nicholas Epley and Amit Kumar, "How to Design an Ethical Organization," *Harvard Business Review* (May/June 2019), pp. 144–150; David M. Meyer Smir Nurmohamed, Linda Klebe Trevino, Debra L. Shapiro, and Marshall Schminke, "Encouraging Employees to Report Unethical Conduct Internally: It Takes a Village," *Organizational Behavior and Human Decision Processes,* Vol. 121 No. 1 (May 2013), pp. 89–103.

217 **". . . calls forth your best"**: Elyse Gorman, "6 Quotes from Ancient Philosophers That Can Help You Live Better Today," Thought Catalog (February 15, 2014), https://thoughtcatalog.com/elyse-gorman/2014/02/6-quotes-from-ancient -philosophers-that-can-help-you-livebetter-today/.

220 **paraphrased her ten rules below:** Cynthia Cooper, *Extraordinary Circumstances* (Hoboken, NJ, Wiley, 2008), pp. 365–367.

221 **Warren Bennis . . . led to their success:** Warren Bennis and Robert J. Thomas, "Crucibles of Leadership," *Harvard Business Review* (September 2002).

222 **The Fable of the Two Wolves:** The source of this story is uncertain, but it is thought to come from Native American culture. See https://en.wikipedia.org/wiki/Two _Wolves.

223 **"The Road to Self-Renewal"**: You can find the original essay by Howard Gardner here: John Gardner, "The Road to Self Renewal," *Stanford Alumni Magazine* (March 1994), https://buildinginnovativebrands.stanford.edu/sites /g/files/sbiybj7961/f/johngardner-roadtoself-renewal2.pdf.

TOPICAL BIBLIOGRAPHY

Case Studies in Organizational Corruption
Brockovich, Erin. *Superman's Not Coming: Our National Water Crisis and What We the People Can Do About It.* New York: Pantheon, 2020.
Browning, Christopher R. *Ordinary Men: Reserve Police Battalion 101 and the Final Solution in Poland.* New York: Harper Perennial revised edition, 2017.
Carreyrou, John. *Bad Blood: Secrets and Lies in a Silicon Valley Startup.* New York: Knopf, 2019.
Cooper, Cynthia. *Extraordinary Circumstances.* Hoboken, NJ: John Wiley & Sons, 2008.
Eban, Katherine. *Bottle of Lies: The Inside Story of the Generic Drug Boom.* New York: Ecco, 2019.
Hopson, Justin. *Breaking the Blue Wall: One Man's War against Police Corruption.* Bloomington, IN: West Bow Press, 2012.
Soltes, Eugene. *Why They Do It: Inside the Mind of the White-Collar Criminal.* New York: Public Affairs, 2016.
Woodford, Michael. *Exposure: Inside the Olympus Scandal; How I Went From CEO to Whistleblower.* New York: Portfolio, 2014.

Character-Based Leadership
Arbinger Institute, *Leadership and Self-Deception: Getting Out of the Box.* San Francisco: Berrett-Koehler, 2000.
Brown, Brené. *Dare to Lead: Brave Work. Tough Conversations. Whole Hearts.* New York: Random House, 2018.
Covey, Stephen. *Principle-Centered Leadership.* New York: Fireside, 1990.
Crossan, Mary, Gerard Seijts, and Jeffey Gandz. *Developing Leadership Character.* New York: Routledge, 2016.
Franklin, Benjamin. *The Autobiography and Other Writings.* Peter Shaw, editor. New York: Bantam, 1982).
Gandhi, M.K. *Autobiography: The Story of My Experiments with Truth.* New York: Dover edition, 1983.
George, Bill, and Andrew McClean & Nick Craig. *Finding Your True North: A Personal Guide.* San Francisco: Jossey-Bass, 2008.

Heifetz, Ronald. *Leadership without Easy Answers.* Cambridge, MA: Belknap Press, 1998.

Heifetz, Ronald, and Alexander Grashow & Marty Linsky. *The Practice of Adaptive Leadership: Tools and Tactics for Changing Your Organization and the World.* Boston: Harvard Business School Press, 2009.

Hoyk, Robert, and Paul Hersey. *The Ethical Executive: Becoming Aware of the Root Causes of Unethical Behavior.* Stanford, CA: Stanford University Press, 2008.

Hunter, G. Shawn. *Small Acts of Leadership: 12 Intentional Behaviors That Lead to Big Impact.* New York: Routledge, 2016.

Kouzes, James M., and Barry Posner. *The Leadership Challenge: How to Make Extraordinary Things Happen in Organizations, Sixth Edition.* Hoboken, NJ: Wiley, 2017.

Lee, Gus. *Courage: The Backbone of Leadership.* San Francisco: Jossey-Bass, 2006.

Loehr, Jim. *The Only Way to Win: How Building Character Drives Higher Achievement and Greater Fulfillment in Business and Life.* New York: Hyperion, 2012.

Newman, Ann. *Building Leadership Character.* Los Angeles: Sage, 2019.

Rohn, Jim. *7 Strategies for Wealth and Happiness.* New York: Three Rivers Press, 1985.

Sinek, Simon. *Leaders Eat Last: Why Some Teams Pull Together and Others Don't.* New York: Portfolio, 2014.

Snyder, Steven. *Leadership and the Art of Struggle: How Great Leaders Grow through Challenge and Adversity.* San Francisco: Berrett-Koehler, 2013.

Thompson, Jeff. *Lead True: Live Your Values, Build Your People, Inspire Your Community.* Charleston, SC: ForbesBooks, 2017.

Ethical and Moral Decision Making

Anderson, James A., and Elaine E. Englehardt. *The Organizational Self and Ethical Conduct.* Fort Worth, TX: Harcourt College Publishers, 2001.

Appiah, Kwame Anthony. *Experiments in Ethics.* Cambridge, MA: Harvard University Press, 2008.

Arendt, Hannah. *Responsibility and Judgment.* New York: Schocken Books, 2003.

Badaracco, Joseph L. *Defining Moments: When Managers Must Choose between Right and Right.* Boston: Harvard Business School Press, 1997.

Bazerman, Max H., and Ann E. Tenbrunsel. *Blind Spots: Why We Fail to Do What's Right and What to Do about It.* Princeton, NJ: Princeton University Press, 2011.

Byron, William J. *The Power of Principles: Ethics for the New Corporate Culture.* Maryknoll, NY: Orbis Books, 2006.

Care, Norman S. *Decent People.* Latham, MD: Rowman & Littlefield, 2000.

Christensen, Clay, and James Allworth & Karen Dillon. *How Will You Measure Your Life? Finding Fulfillment Using Lessons from Some of the World's Greatest Businesses.* New York: HarperBusiness, 2012.

Comer, Debra R., and Gina Vega, Editors. *Moral Courage in Organizations: Doing the Right Thing at Work.* New York: Routledge, 2015.

Donaldson, Thomas, and Patricia Werhane. *Ethical Issues in Business: A Philosophical Approach, 8th edition.* Upper Saddle River, NJ: Prentice Hall, 2007.

Gentile, Mary. *Giving Voice to Values: How to Speak Your Mind When You Know What's Right.* New Haven, CT: Yale University Press, 2010.

Haidt, Jonahan. *The Righteous Mind: Why Good People Are Divided by Politics and Religion.* New York: Vintage, 2012.

Howard, Ronald A., and Clinton D. Korver. *Ethics for the Real World: Creating a Personal Code to Guide Decisions in Work and Life*. Boston: Harvard Business School Press, 2008.

Kidder, Rushworth M. *How Good People Make Tough Choices: Resolving the Dilemmas of Ethical Living*. New York: Harper, 2003.

Kidder, Rushworth M. *Moral Courage: Taking Action When Your Values Are Put to the Test*. New York: William Morrow, 2005.

MacIntyre, Alasdair. *After Virtue (Third Edition)*. Notre Dame, IN: University of Notre Dame Press, 2007.

March, James G. *A Primer on Decision Making: How Decisions Happen*. New York: Free Press, 1994.

March, James G. *The Ambiguities of Experience*. Ithaca, NY: Cornell University Press, 2010.

O'Connor, Malachi, and Barry Dornfeld. *The Moment You Can't Ignore: When Big Trouble Leads to a Great Future*. New York: PublicAffairs, 2014.

Oliner, Samuel P., and Pearl M. Oliner, *The Altruistic Personality: What Led Ordinary Men and Women to Risk Their Lives on Behalf of Others*. New York: Touchstone, 1992.

Sinnott-Armstrong, Walter, Editor. *Moral Psychology: Volume 2, The Cognitive Science of Morality: Intuition and Diversity*. Cambridge, MA: MIT Press, 2008.

Tavris, Carol, and Elliott Aronson. *Mistakes Were Made (But Not by Me): Why We Justify Foolish Beliefs, Bad Decisions, and Hurtful Acts*. Boston, MA: Mariner Books, 2007.

Wilson, James Q. *The Moral Sense*. New York: Free Press, 1997.

Wolff, Jonathan. *An Introduction to Moral Philosophy*. New York: W.W. Norton, 2017.

Identity and Life Stories

Appiah, Kwame Anthony. *The Ethics of Identity*. Princeton, NJ: Princeton University Press, 2005.

Dewey, John. *Human Nature and Conduct*. Mineola, NY: Dover Publications, 2002.

Hanley, Ryan Patrick. *Our Great Purpose: Adam Smith on Living a Better Life*. Princeton, NJ: Princeton University Press, 2019.

Loy, David R. *The World is Made of Stories*. Boston: Wisdom Publications, 2010.

McAdams, Dan P. *Power, Intimacy, and the Life Story: Personological Inquires into Identity*. New York: The Gilford Pres, 1988.

McAdams, Dan P. *The Stories We Live By: Personal Myths and the Making of the Self*. New York: Guilford Press, 1997.

Shell, G. Richard. *Springboard: Launching Your Personal Search for Success*. New York: Portfolio, 2014.

Persuasion, Influence, and Organizational Politics

Cialdini, Robert. *Influence: The Psychology of Persuasion*. New York: Harper Business, Revised Edition, 2006.

Cialdini, Robert. *Pre-suasion: A Revolutionary Way to Influence and Persuade*. New York: Simon & Schuster, 2016.

Coyle, Daniel. *The Culture Code: The Secrets of Highly Successful Groups*. New York: Bantam Books, 2018.

Curry, Lynn. *Beating the Workplace Bully: A Tactical Guide to Taking Charge*. New York: AMACOM, 2016.

Daniels, Aubrey. *Bringing Out the Best in People: How to Apply the Astonishing Power of Positive Reinforcement.* New York: McGraw-Hill (3rd Edition), 2016.

Edmondson, Amy C. *The Fearless Organization: Creating Psychological Safety in the Workplace for Learning, Innovation and Growth.* Hoboken, NJ: Wiley, 2018.

Epley, Nicholas. *Mindwise: Why We Misunderstand What Others Think, Believe, Feel, and Want.* New York: Vintage Books, 2014.

Hirschman, Albert. *Exit, Voice, and Loyalty: Responses to Decline in Firms, Organizations, and States.* Cambridge, MA: Harvard University Press, 1970.

Kissinger, Henry. *White House Years.* New York: Simon and Schuster, 1979.

Lencioni, Patrick. *The Five Dysfunctions of a Team: A Leadership Fable.* San Francisco: Jossey-Bass, 2002.

Patterson, Kerry, and Joseph Grenny, Ron McMillan, and Al Switzer. *Crucial Conversations: Tools for Talking When the Stakes Are High.* New York: McGraw-Hill, 2002.

Patterson, Kerry, and Joseph Grenny, Ron McMillan, and Al Switzer. *Crucial Confrontations: Tools for Resolving Broken Promises, Violated Expectations, and Bad Behavior.* New York: McGraw-Hill, 2005.

Perloff, Richard M. *The Dynamics of Persuasion: Communication and Attitudes in the 21st Century, 2nd edition.* Mahwah, NJ: Lawrence Erlbaum, 2003.

Schein, Edgar H. *Humble Inquiry: The Gentle Art of Asking Instead of Telling.* San Francisco: Berrett-Koehler (2nd Edition), 2021.

Scott, Kim. *Radical Candor: Be a Kick-Ass Boss without Losing Your Humanity.* New York: St. Martin's Press, revised edition, 2019.

Shell, G. Richard. *Bargaining for Advantage: Negotiation Strategies for Reasonable People, Third Edition.* New York: Penguin, 2006.

Shell, G. Richard & Mario Moussa. *The Art of Woo: Using Strategic Persuasion to Sell Your Ideas.* New York: Penguin, 2007.

Psychology, Personality, and Sociology

Barrett, Lisa Feldman. *How Emotions Are Made: The Secret Life of the Brain.* Boston: Houghton Mifflin Harcourt, 2017.

Biddle, Bruce J. *Role Theory: Expectations, Identities, and Behaviors.* New York: Academic Press, 1979.

Bregman, Rutger. *Humankind: A Hopeful History.* New York: Little, Brown & Co., 2019.

Cain, Susan. *Quiet: The Power of Introverts in a World That Can't Stop Talking.* New York: Crown, 2012.

Chabris, Christopher, and Daniel Simmons. *The Invisible Gorilla and Other Ways Our Intuitions Deceive Us.* New York: Broadway Books, 2009.

Clear, James. *Atomic Habits: An Easy & Proven Way to Build Good Habits and Break Bad Ones.* New York: Avery, 2018.

Cooley, Charles Horton. *Human Nature and the Social Order.* New Brunswick, NJ: Transactional Publishers, 1983.

Davidson, R. J., K.R. Scherer, & H.H. Goldsmith (Eds.). *Handbook of Affective Sciences.* Oxford, UK: Oxford University Press, 2003.

Doris, John M. *Lack of Character: Personality and Moral Behavior.* New York: Cambridge University Press, 2002.

Duhigg, Charles. *The Power of Habit: Why We Do What We Do in Life and Business.* New York: Random House, 2012.

Guetzkow, H. (editor). *Groups, Leadership and Men*. Pittsburgh: Carnegie Press, 1951.

Hanh, Thach Nhat. *Fear: Essential Wisdom for Getting through the Storm*. New York: HarperOne, 2014.

Harrison, Bridget C. *Power and Society: An Introduction to the Social Sciences, 14th Edition*. Boston: Centage Learning, 2017.

Jackson, J. A. (editor). *Role: Sociological Studies 4*. New York: Cambridge University Press, reissue edition, 2010.

LeDoux, Joseph. *The Deep History of Ourselves: The Four-Billion-Year Story of How We Got Conscious Brains*. New York: Viking, 2019.

LeDoux, Joseph. *The Emotional Brain: The Mysterious Underpinnings of Emotional Life*. New York: Simon & Schuster, 1996.

Lee, Kibeom, and Michael C. Ashton. *The H Factor: Why Some People Are Manipulative, Self-Entitled, Materialistic, and Exploitative—and Why It Matters for Everyone*. Waterloo, Ontario, Canada: Wilfrid Laurier University Press, 2012.

Lewin, Kurt. *Resolving Social Conflicts and Field Theory in Social Science*. Washington, D.C.: American Psychological Association, 1997.

Milgram, Stanley. *Obedience to Authority: The Experiment That Challenged Human Nature*. New York: Harper Perennial, 2009.

Nowicki, Steven. *Choice or Chance: Understanding Your Locus of Control and Why It Matters*. New York: Prometheus, 2016.

Peterson, Christopher, and Martin Seligman. *Character Strengths and Virtues*. Oxford University Press, 2004.

Rokeach, Milton. *Beliefs, Attitudes, and Values*. San Francisco: Jossey-Bass, 1968.

Sternberg, Eliezer J. *Neurologic: The Brain's Hidden Rationale Behind Our Irrational Behavior*. New York: Pantheon, 2015.

Zimbardo, Philip. *The Lucifer Effect: Understanding How Good People Turn Evil*. New York: Random House, 2007.

Virtue Habits

Clear, James. *Atomic Habits: An Easy & Proven Way to Build Good Habits and Break Bad Ones*. New York: Avery, 2018.

Covey, Stephen R. *The 7 Habits of Highly Successful People*. New York: Simon and Schuster, Anniversary Edition, 2020.

Duhigg, Charles, *The Power of Habit: Why We Do What We Do in Life and Business*. New York: Random House, 2012.

Durant, Will. *The Story of Philosophy: The Lives and Opinions of the World's Greatest Philosophers*. New York: Pocket Books, Second Edition, 1991.

Heath, Chip, and Dan Heath. *Switch: How to Change Things When Change Is Hard*. New York: Currency, 2010.

James, William. *Talks to Teachers on Psychology*. Rockville, MD: Manor, 2008.

E. M. Standing. *Maria Montessori: Her Life and Work*. New York: Plume, 1984.

Stout, Lynn. *Cultivating Conscience: How Good Laws Make Good People*. Princeton, NJ: Princeton University Press, 2011.

Whistleblowing

Alford, Fred C. *Whistleblowers: Broken Lives and Organizational Power*. Ithaca, NY: Cornell University Press, 2001.

Devine, Tom, and Tarek F. Maassarani. *The Corporate Whistleblower's Survival Guide.* San Francisco: Berrett-Koehler, 2011.

Glazer, Myron Peretz, and Penina Migdal Glazer. *The Whistleblowers: Exposing Corruption in Government and Industry.* New York: Basic Books, 1989.

Kenny, Kate. *Whistleblowing: Toward a New Theory.* Cambridge, MA: Harvard University Press, 2019.

Kohn, Stephen Martin. *The New Whistleblower's Handbook: A Step-by-Step Guide to Doing What's Right and Protecting Yourself.* Guilford, CT: Lyons Press, 2017.

Mueller, Tom. *Crisis of Conscience: Whistleblowing in an Age of Fraud.* New York: Riverhead Books, 2019.

INDEX

reflection on, 79–80
truths about character, 68–69
Sun Tzu, 37
Swanson, Kathe, 148–49
Switzler, Al, 180
systemic pressure, 54–55, 218

T

targeting decision makers, 163
termination, risk of, 12
Thakur, Dinesh, 27, 193–94, 212
Theranos Inc., 123–33, 183
Thompson, Jeff, 33, 221
Trapp, Wilhelm, 43–44, 47, 48, 50
trusted partners. *see* Leverage the Power
of Two (Rule #6)
truth, in defining values, 19, 22–23
Tubman, Harriet, 144–45
tyrants, 177–80

U

UBS, 78–79
United States Marine Corps, 4, 64
United States Navy, 73–74
Urbaniak, Kasia, 179

V

value-based leadership, 205, 216–20. *see
also* Choose to Lead (Rule #10)
value-based mentoring, 218–19
value conflicts, 38, 211–16. *see also* Know
Your Enemy (Rule #3)
values
committing to, *see* Commit to Your
Values (Rule #2)
compromising, 11
defining, 18–19
distraction from, 24
as goals, 72
leading with, x
in long-term career success, 10–12
in personal and community life, 13
at risk, recognizing, 7–8
situational forces overriding, 47–55
standing up for, vii

values-to-action process. *see* ROAD
values-to-action process
Veterans Administration, 52
Vinson, Betty, 39–41, 75–76, 196, 201,
203
visualizing victims, 26–27

W

Walgreens, 125, 126, 128, 131
Walton family, 125
Watkins, Sherron, 8, 41
Wayfair, 15–16, 18, 29
West Virginia Bureau of Training and
Staff Development, 98–101
Wharton School of Business, vii–viii
"whispering in decision maker's ear,"
186–87
whistleblowing, 5–6, 11, 79, 102, 192–95
Wigand, Jeffrey, 5, 31–32
Woodford, Michael, 194–95
WorldCom, Inc., 39–41, 51–52, 70–71,
75–76, 183, 195–203, 220
wrongdoing, conditions for, 41–43

Y

Yates, Buddy, 39, 40, 201

Z

Zimbardo, Philip, 53–55, 114–15

ABOUT THE AUTHOR

G. Richard Shell is the Thomas Gerrity Professor of Legal Studies, Business Ethics, and Management at the Wharton School of the University of Pennsylvania. He is the author of *Bargaining for Advantage: Negotiation Strategies for Reasonable People, The Art of Woo: Using Strategic Persuasion to Sell Your Ideas* (with Mario Moussa), and the award-winning *Springboard: Launching Your Personal Search for Success.* He led the most recent redesign of the Wharton School's MBA curriculum and helped create its required Responsibility in Business course, which inspired *The Conscience Code.* He has two grown sons and lives with his wife, Robbie, near Philadelphia in Wynnewood, Pennsylvania.